The Sound of Stevie Wonder

THE PRAEGER SINGER-SONGWRITER COLLECTION

The Sound of Stevie Wonder

His Words and Music

James E. Perone

PRAEGER

Westport, Connecticut
London

Library of Congress Cataloging-in-Publication Data

Perone, James E.
  The sound of Stevie Wonder : his words and music / by James E. Perone.
      p.   cm.—(The Praeger singer-songwriter collection, ISSN 1553–3484)
  Includes bibliographical references, discography, and indexes.
  ISBN 0–275–98723–X
  1. Wonder, Stevie—Criticism and interpretation.   I. Title.   II. Series.
ML410.W836P47 2006
782.421644092—dc22   2005034611

British Library Cataloguing in Publication Data is available.

Library of Congress Catalog Card Number: 2005034611
ISBN: 0–275–98723–X
ISSN: 1553–3484

First published in 2006

Praeger Publishers, 88 Post Road West, Westport, CT 06881
An imprint of Greenwood Publishing Group, Inc.
www.praeger.com

Printed in the United States of America

The paper used in this book complies with the
Permanent Paper Standard issued by the National
Information Standards Organization (Z39.48–1984).

10   9   8   7   6   5   4   3   2

Contents

Series Foreword

Although the term, "Singer-songwriters," might most frequently be associated with a cadre of musicians of the early 1970s such as Paul Simon, James Taylor, Carly Simon, Joni Mitchell, and Carole King, the Praeger Singer-Songwriter Collection defines singer-songwriters more broadly, both in terms of style and in terms of time period. The series includes volumes on musicians who have been active from approximately the 1960s through the present. Musicians who write and record in folk, rock, soul, hip-hop, country, and various hybrids of these styles will be represented. Therefore, some of the early 1970s introspective singer-songwriters named above will be included.

What do the individuals included in this series have in common? Some have never collaborated as writers. But, while some have done so, they've all written and recorded commercially successful and/or historically important music and lyrics.

The authors who contribute to the series also exhibit diversity. Some are scholars who are trained primarily as musicians, while others have specialized knowledge in such areas as American studies, history, sociology, popular culture studies, literature, and rhetoric. The authors share a high level of scholarship, accessibility in their writing, and a true insight into the work of the artists they study. The authors are also focused on the output of their subjects and how it relates to their subject's biography and the society around them; however, biography in and of itself will not be a major focus of the books in this series.

Given the diversity of the musicians who are the subjects of books in this series, and given the diversity of viewpoints of the authors, volumes in the series will differ from book to book. All, however, will primarily be organized chronologically around the compositions and recorded performances of their subjects. All of the books in the series should also serve as listeners' guides to the music of their subjects, making them companions to the artists' recorded output.

James E. Perone
Series Editor

Acknowledgments

This book could not have been written without the valuable assistance of a number of people. I wish first to thank Karen Perone for offering moral support throughout this and all of my book projects for Greenwood Press and Praeger Press, and for offering much-needed input at every stage of every project.

Over the course of writing several books, the entire staff of the Greenwood Publishing Group has been most helpful and cooperative. I wish to extend special thanks to acquisitions editor Daniel Harmon, and to Carmel Huestis, copy editor, respectively, for helping me in the fine-tuning of this book. I also wish to thank Eric Levy and Rob Kirkpatrick for their assistance in getting both this book and the Praeger Singer-Songwriter Collection off the ground.

I also wish to thank Ron Mandelbaum and the rest of the helpful staff of Photofest for their assistance in locating and granting the rights to use a number of publicity photographs of Stevie Wonder for this book, as well as photographer Chris Walter of PhotoFeatures for the rights to use six of his photographs of Wonder.

Over the course of several book projects I have found that when I couldn't find the information anywhere else, I was bound to find it at the Music Library and Sound Recordings Archives at Bowling Green State University. I wish to extend thanks to William Schurk, Sound Recordings Archivist, for his assistance in tracking down several difficult-to-find songwriter credits on several of Stevie Wonder's lesser-known releases. I also wish to thank Mount Union College Music Librarian Suzanne Moushey for help in locating several tricky citations.

Despite my own best efforts and the assistance of those named above, there are bound to be errors in this book: they are solely my responsibility.

Introduction

STEVIE WONDER AS A MUSICIAN AND ACTIVIST

Born May 13, 1950, in Saginaw, Michigan, Stevland Hardaway Judkins (later Stevland Morris)[1] became known to the world as Little Stevie Wonder when his debut single, "Fingertips, Part 2," went to No. 1 on the *Billboard* pop charts in 1963.[2] Wonder had become blind as an infant as a result of an accident in his incubator; however, as a child he became proficient as a singer, and on drums, keyboards, and harmonica. He came to the attention of Motown Records, which signed Wonder to its Tamla label in 1961. Because of his unique musical talents, Stevie Wonder—he eventually outgrew the "Little" moniker—became one of the first and only Motown artists who could exercise complete artistic control over the writing, arranging, performance, and production of his studio work.

After his initial success with "Fingertips, Part 2," Wonder released singles that made the *Billboard* pop charts in every year between 1963 and 1988. In total, 64 of his singles made the top 100, with 10 of them reaching No. 1. Most of these recordings were of songs Wonder wrote or co-wrote, including such well-known compositions as "You Are the Sunshine of My Life," "My Cherie Amour," "I Just Called to Say I Love You," "Living for the City," "Higher Ground," "Superstition," "Signed, Sealed, Delivered (I'm Yours)," and "Sir Duke." Wonder's 1982 duet with Paul McCartney, "Ebony and Ivory," held the No. 1 position in the *Billboard* pop charts for seven weeks and was among the 50 top-selling singles of the period 1955–2000. According to Joel Whitburn's book *Top Pop Singles, 1955–1996*, Stevie Wonder was the fourth most successful singles artist of the period, trailing only Elvis Presley, the Beatles, and Elton John.[3] In addition to writing most of his best-known hits, Wonder has also written or co-written songs for other performers, with one of the best remembered of these songs being the Smokey Robinson and the Miracles' No. 1 pop hit "The Tears of a Clown."

Throughout his career Stevie Wonder has also garnered critical success. He received praise in particular as a keyboardist in the first half of the 1970s, in which he virtually defined the new funk synthesizer-clavinet–based style that was in vogue at the time. Wonder was also praised for his compositions and performances on albums such as *Talking Book* (1972), *Innervisions* (1973), *Fulfillingness' First Finale* (1974), and *Songs in the Key of Life* (1976), a period of time in which he dealt with subjects such as racism, ghetto life, and spirituality. As a singer on these albums and on his albums of the 1980s, Stevie Wonder has been compared with some of the great jazz singers of the past in his subtle phrasing. Noted rock critic Robert Christgau wrote of Wonder, "Overlaying track after track in the studio, he's a font of melody, a wellspring of rhythm, a major modern composer."[4]

Wonder's albums of the 1972–1980 period were particularly notable for their displays of political and social consciousness. Songs such as "Living for the City," "Big Brother," "You Haven't Done Nothin'," "Village Ghetto Land," and "Happy Birthday" deal with such topics as the struggle for racial equality, urban poverty, and political corruption. Because of his well-established mainstream appeal as an artist, Wonder brought these issues, as well as the spiritual topics he addressed in his work of the 1970s, to a wider audience than any other musician.

In 1991, Wonder resumed his socially conscious work when he wrote and recorded the soundtrack for Spike Lee's film *Jungle Fever,* a movie about interracial dating. Wonder addressed poverty and genocide (among other, more pleasant topics) in songs on the 1995 album *Conversation Peace.* In addition to addressing social issues through his music, Stevie Wonder lobbied for the creation of a national holiday to honor Dr. Martin Luther King, Jr., during the 1970s and early 1980s. He has also been active in the struggle against apartheid in South Africa, and for AIDS awareness and handgun control in the United States. He has been active in the fight against world hunger.

Stevie Wonder has received numerous awards, including 22 Grammy awards over the years and Grammy's Lifetime Achievement Award in 1996. He was elected to the Rock and Roll Hall of Fame in 1989, and in 1999, received the prestigious Kennedy Center Honors. As a singer, songwriter, record producer, and instrumentalist, Wonder's influence can be heard in the music of Prince, Usher, Michael Jackson, Maxwell, and others. Wonder's compositions and recordings continue to be sampled by hip-hop and contemporary rhythm and blues artists on a regular basis. Stevie Wonder continues to perform at benefit concerts into the twenty-first century and his latest album, *A Time 2 Love,* was released by Motown in October 2005.

THE SCOPE AND ORGANIZATION OF THIS BOOK

The focus of this volume is on the music, lyrics, and recordings of Stevie Wonder; therefore, the book is arranged chronologically and has biographical information woven into the discussion of Wonder's songs and recordings. I have also included a chapter devoted to discussion of other artists' recordings of the works of Stevie Wonder.

With more than 300 copyrighted songs, some written in collaboration with others and some written solo, a detailed analysis of the collected compositions of Stevie Wonder is a daunting task. Because of the nature of the Praeger Singer-Songwriter Collection, I have focused on Wonder compositions that he himself has recorded, and on particularly notable songs from each of his albums. Wonder began acting as his own lyricist more frequently from 1971 on; therefore, I will deal more extensively with the songs on the post-1970 albums than those on the Stevie Wonder recordings of the 1960s.

Given the recent wranglings between Paul McCartney and the estate of John Lennon over the published order of names in songwriting credits, it is worth explaining the apparently inconsistent credits in the discography in this book. I have used, for the most part, the order of names as given on the various albums. Motown and Tamla have not been consistent with these listings for one reason or another. In other words, the same song issued on three albums, for example, might have as many as three different orderings to the writing credits. To further complicate matters, the Web databases maintained by the American Society of Composers, Authors, and Publishers (ASCAP) and Broadcast Music Incorporated (BMI) generally list songwriters' names in alphabetical order. Although Wonder's name sometimes appears at the beginning of some of the published credits and sometimes at the end, generally it does not appear to be related to a particular type of contribution (i.e., lyrics and/or music). In most of his songs of the 1960s, Wonder wrote the music or at least part of the music; Motown staff writers, who often worked around Wonder's music, generally were the contributors of a good part of the lyrics.

In my discussion of Stevie Wonder as a singer, instrumentalist, and songwriter, the reader should be aware of the emphasis I place on the arrangements of the songs. In his recordings from the 1970s to the present, Wonder has most frequently worked as his own arranger, orchestrator, and producer. This has given him an unusually high level of artistic control over the final product. I consider the arrangements and production style of these post-1960s recordings to be part of the overall composition and frequently address them as such.

Whereas the aim of this volume is to provide a guide to the recordings and compositions of Stevie Wonder, I have provided a Discography of Wonder's recordings and a Composition Title Index. The Composition Title Index lists all of the songs mentioned in the text, including those written, co-written and/or recorded by Wonder; songs he recorded but did not write; and songs that Wonder neither wrote nor recorded, but that I have discussed in the text in comparison with Stevie Wonder's compositions. I hope that it will assist the reader in locating discussion of particular songs as well as comparisons of songs across the chapter boundaries.

The Young Virtuoso, 1962–1964

August 16, 1962 was an auspicious day in American music, although the record sales charts of the time failed to register so much as a blip. On that date, Tamla, one of Motown Records' several labels, released Stevie Wonder's first single: "I Call It Pretty Music, But the Old People Call It the Blues" (Tamla 54061). Although Wonder's second single did not fare better, the A-side, "Little Water Boy" (Tamla 54070), a collaborative composition of Wonder and Clarence Paul, showed unrealized potential. No one may have realized it at the time, but the pairing of Wonder and Paul, who was 34 years old then, was most fortunate, for this experienced gospel singer, songwriter, and record producer became a father figure to the young Wonder. And, more than that, Paul introduced Wonder to several musical styles, most notably to gospel, which was one of the essential elements of late 1950s and early 1960s black popular music. This would be an essential ingredient in Wonder's mature vocal and compositional style, but one that was not a part of his early experience on a firsthand basis, as it would be for singers such as Aretha Franklin, James Brown, and Marvin Gaye. In the cases of Franklin and Gaye, it is important to note that at the age at which they were just beginning to hone their musical skills in black churches led by their minister fathers, Stevie Wonder was already becoming part of the secular popular music establishment.

Like his first two singles, Wonder's first two albums, *The Jazz-Soul of Little Stevie* (Tamla 233) and *Tribute to Uncle Ray* (Tamla 232), also failed to break into the charts when they were released in September and October 1962, respectively. Wonder's third single release, on December 26, 1962, "Contract on Love," backed by "Sunset" (Tamla 54074), also failed to make the pop and R&B charts. At this point, Motown's owner, Berry Gordy, Jr., could easily have given up on Stevie Wonder as a solo artist. Gordy, however, stuck with the young virtuoso harmonica player, keyboardist, percussionist, and singer, and included his considerable talents on Motown live revues that played in some of the most significant venues in America in the early 1960s. It was at one of these live shows that the 12-year-old Wonder performed Clarence Paul and Henry Cosby's "Fingertips," a track from his first album, singing and playing harmonica when the tape was rolling. An album, *Recorded Live—The 12 Year Old Genius,* and a single, "Fingertips, Parts 1 and 2,"[1] were issued in 1963. The album hit No. 1 on the *Billboard* pop charts (there was no *Billboard* R&B chart for albums in 1963), and the B-side of the single hit No. 1 on both the *Billboard* pop and R&B charts. This was the real start of the words and music of Stevie Wonder.

THE FIRST THREE ALBUMS

Stevie Wonder's first album, *The Jazz-Soul of Little Stevie,* highlighted the singing and instrumental (on drums and harmonica) talents of a young virtuoso performing primarily songs written by Motown's highly esteemed stable of songwriters, of which he was already a member. While the album contained a version of Clarence Paul and Henry Cosby's "Fingertips," it was not this version that made an impact on the public consciousness. The album's chief distinguishing feature was the pure talent that Wonder exhibited: *The Jazz-Soul of Little Stevie* made few commercial inroads, but it proved how exceptional Wonder was as a performer and suggested that he might be destined for greater achievements as he continued to mature.

If Stevie Wonder's first album provided a hint at the musician's virtuosity, *Tribute to Uncle Ray* was something of a step backward. The second album features Wonder only as a singer, and even then essentially imitating the style of Ray Charles. Ray Charles was still very much a hot artist in October 1962 when Wonder's tribute album appeared. The Wonder album occupies a curious place in his output. On one hand, it can be seen as a corporate exploitation of the fact that Charles and Wonder both happened to be blind soul musicians. And even if the album is not viewed as an exploitation of the two musicians' shared blindness, it can be seen as a Motown exploitation of the popularity of the non-Motown recording artist Ray Charles.[2] On the other hand, it does provide something of a showcase for Wonder's stylistic adaptability, a feature of his work that would be increasingly highlighted by the 1970s. Given the nature of the album, however, *Tribute to Uncle Ray* fails on one serious level: it really does not give Stevie Wonder a full chance to really *be* Stevie Wonder by almost relegating him to the role of a mimic.

In early 1963 Tamla released Wonder's breakthrough album, *Recorded Live— The 12 Year Old Genius.* Although the sales of the album were impressive—it reached No. 1 on the *Billboard* pop charts—chart and sales data alone do not show the importance of this album. For when the success of the live album and the "Fingertips, Part 2" single led to television and film appearances, Wonder suddenly found himself an American popular culture icon.

It is especially interesting to consider Wonder's sudden emergence as a pop culture icon in light of American popular culture of the nineteenth century. Back in 1857, at the age of eight, Thomas Bethune (1849–1908), a blind, black pianist, composer, and slave had created an immediate sensation when he was taken on a concert tour of Georgia by his owner. Under the moniker "Blind Tom," Bethune continued to study music and toured slave states. During the Civil War, his owner, politician James N. Bethune, took the young virtuoso on a tour of the South to raise money for the Confederacy. "Blind Tom" was a sensation and appealed widely to white audiences. Little Stevie Wonder also appealed widely to white audiences, including those that ordinarily would not choose to listen to music by African American performers. Such were the times and the state of American society in the late nineteenth century and early twentieth century that Thomas Bethune had difficulty overcoming being a novelty act (he performed on the vaudeville circuit, never really making it to the concert hall). On the other hand, Stevie Wonder, whose first public exposure would paint him as something of a novelty, would eventually make a powerful transition to the status of a mature, socially and politically relevant artist, and build a career on his own terms, transcending the first impressions the public may have had as a result of "Fingertips."

Because Stevie Wonder, the instrumentalist, has been defined since the very beginning of his career by the harmonica (an instrument that he continued to feature on his recordings into the 1980s and again on his 2005 album *A Time to Love*), it is worth discussing his use of the instrument. First of all, it is important to note that Wonder has focused not on the dime-store-variety harmonica, nor on the blues harp, but on the chromatic harmonica, a more difficult instrument to play, but also one that can be adapted to a far greater range of musical styles because of both its melodic nature and its ability to play pitches that are absent from the simpler types of harmonicas. This is the type of harmonica used by famous soloists such as Larry Adler and Toots Thielmans. It was Thielmans, incidentally, who really established the chromatic harmonica as a legitimate vehicle for jazz improvisation, and as such, was an important influence on Wonder's use of the instrument.

After the initial success of Wonder's live album and single, his career again stagnated, although his singles "Workout Stevie, Workout" and "Hey Harmonica Man" did make the *Billboard* pop top 40. This time, however, the lull was created at least in part by his voice change. Wonder continued to make preparations for a resumption of his career by studying classical piano at the Michigan School for the Blind.

WITH A SONG IN MY HEART AND STEVIE AT THE BEACH

As it would turn out years later, one of the best definitions of the mature Stevie Wonder style, once he had established near-total control over the writing, singing, instrumental performance, arranging, and production of his recordings, was that it resisted narrow definition. Initially, Little Stevie Wonder had been defined as a child prodigy who could sing, write, and play the harmonica, drums, and piano in a soulful, jazz-inspired style. The late 1963 album *With a Song in My Heart* and the 1964 album *Stevie at the Beach* found Motown unsuccessfully trying to reach a broader (and perhaps more white audience) by defining his work far too narrowly and in somewhat scattered and improbable directions.

The collection of standards on *With a Song in My Heart* seems to be calculated to establish the young prodigy as a sort of Sammy Davis, Jr., Las Vegas–style, middle-of-the-road lounge singer. The album did not make the charts, and, needless to say, the material has not found its way into reissues in the compact disc era.

Stevie Wonder himself has described the *With a Song in My Heart* and *Stevie at the Beach* period as "embarrassing."[3] Lest the latter album's title cause confusion, it should be noted that it (fortunately) was not an attempt to cast Wonder as a sort of Motown Beach Boy. Well, not exactly. The album ties in with Stevie Wonder's guest appearances in such movies as *Bikini Beach* and *Muscle Beach Party* alongside the films' stars such as Annette Funicello, Frankie Avalon, and Michael Nadir. Although the album's title does seem to capitalize on the immense popularity of the Beach Boys and other white "surf" groups, musically it is more Motown than surf. The songs revolve around the theme of the beach and the ocean, and include some obvious popular standards such as "Ebb Tide." Like *With a Song in My Heart*, the focus here is too restrictive to allow Wonder to be fully himself: an artist of great range and diversity of expression, at least to the extent that a 13-year-old virtuoso could be. Also, like *With a Song in My Heart*, the songs of *Stevie at the Beach* did not enjoy much in the way of popular success at the time of their release and have not found their way into compact disc reissues of Wonder's early material.

The Soul Shouter, 1965–1967

UPTIGHT

Despite the overwhelming success of "Fingertips, Part 2," by 1965 there were reasons for serious concern at Motown about the commercial viability of Stevie Wonder as a performer. A total of seven singles had been released between September 1963 and August 1965, and none of them came even close to equaling the success of "Fingertips." In fact, the most successful was "Hey Harmonica Man," which topped out at No. 29 on the *Billboard* pop charts. Somehow it seemed that the songs that Motown staff writers were providing for Wonder either did not make a connection with the performer, or Wonder's performance just was not connecting with a wide enough audience. As almost a last resort, songwriter Sylvia Moy turned to an instrumental riff that she had heard Wonder playing and fashioned a song that not only probably saved Stevie Wonder's career, but put him back on top again:[1] "Uptight (Everything's Alright)" hit No. 1 on the *Billboard* R&B charts and No. 3 on the pop charts after its November 1965 release.[2] The song became the centerpiece of the 1966 album *Uptight*. Moy, who had training and performing experience as a classical and jazz musician, continued to collaborate with Wonder, often fleshing out his instrumental riffs to create finished songs, and—like Clarence Paul before her—continued to broaden Stevie Wonder's knowledge of the vast world of musical styles. Sylvia Moy was easily the most highly acclaimed songwriter with whom Wonder worked during the 1960s: she earned a half-dozen Grammy nominations, a score of BMI (Broadcast Music International) awards, and was eventually elected to the National Songwriters Hall of Fame. Although Wonder later studied traditional classical music theory in his 21st year, his real training as a pop/R&B songwriter came from working day after day with Moy, Cosby, and Paul.

It is difficult to determine exactly what lessons Wonder took with him from these Motown regulars from the 1960s into the 1970s and beyond,

as his songwriting style became more and more eclectic and moved gradually farther away from the style of his 1960s collaborations like "Uptight
(Everything's Alright)." Whereas mid-1960s songs like this were musically
more sophisticated than material usually written by teenagers, the craftsman-
ship of Wonder's collaborators certainly seems to have set a high standard for
the young man, just as working with a masterful instrumental ensemble like
the Funk Brothers, Motown's house band, seems to have done. It is probably
this overall standard of excellence—more than anything else—that Wonder
took with him into the not very distant future, when he would write all the
music and all the lyrics, and sing and play all the instruments on his albums.

As suggested by "Uptight (Everything's Alright)," Wonder's contributions to his mid-1960s collaborations generally were more musical, and not
lyrical, in nature. The combination of Wonder's driving Motown soul music
with the lyrics of Henry Cosby, Sylvia Moy, and others (and some of his
own), however, worked well, and certainly much better than the earlier material that did not have Wonder's compositional input. "Uptight (Everything's
Alright)" is a song about a poor boy from "the wrong side of the tracks" who
is in love with a girl who is considerably better off. Although Wonder did not
write the lyrics of this song, he would return to this theme (the attraction
of apparent opposites) time and time again throughout his career when he
was his own lyricist.[3] Musically, "Uptight (Everything's Alright)" features
an easily recognizable and catchy chorus hook. Here, Wonder sings in the
upper part of his range, although the entire chorus section traverses a fairly
wide melodic range. The lyrics of this chorus feature an expansion of the
title of the song—basically just an all-out expression that everything is going
to be alright because of love, despite the inherent difficulties of a relationship between a couple from the proverbial opposite sides of the track. The
verses, in which the story of the opposites is expounded, are musically more
subdued, in a lower part of Wonder's range, and use such a narrow melodic
range as to verge on a monotone.

Of the songs on *Uptight* that were co-written by Wonder, "Uptight (Everything's Alright)" was clearly the most distinguished. Others, though, deserve
at least brief mention. "Music Talk," a collaborative effort with Wonder, Ted
Hull, and Clarence Paul, deals lyrically with the universality of the language
of music. While serious students of music in world cultures would have a bone
to pick with Wonder, Hull, and Paul about cultural universalities in music,
the sentiments have more than a little bit of validity in the context of American pop culture in the 1960s, a time during which the sounds of Hindustani
and African music made it into pop songs. And certainly the music—or love—
conquers-all theme would find its way into other Stevie Wonder recordings
for the rest of his career. "Music Talk" is one of those songs (like the well-
known Sly Stone piece "Dance to the Music" in the late 1960s, or a couple
of different songs by James Brown) in which the singer names several musical
instruments that in turn then play a solo lick. The real kicker here is that the

instruments that play short solo figures, the piano and drums, happen to be instruments associated with Stevie Wonder as an instrumentalist.

Wonder, Sylvia Moy, and Clarence Paul's "Ain't That Asking for Trouble" is catchy and danceable. Although to twenty-first-century ears, it may sound like generic up-tempo soul, it is worth noting that later soul or soul-influenced songs sound as though they could have been inspired by (or at least relate back to) the 1965 Wonder, Moy, and Paul opus, or at least to its style. The 1966 Temptations hit "Ain't Too Proud to Beg" seems to support this possibility, as does (strange as it may sound) the British new wave/pop singer-songwriter Nick Lowe's late 1970s song "When I Write the Book," a song that uses the same type of chromatic, gospel-inspired harmonic motion.

"Hold Me," a collaboration by Wonder, Morris Broadnax, and Clarence Paul, is another song that tends to have something of a generic sound to it. This quality largely comes about because the arrangement sounds very similar to other contemporary Motown products. In particular, the Four Tops' hits "Reach Out I'll Be There" of 1966 and "Bernadette" of 1967 each make use of the same type of orchestration—the flute lines of the No. 1 pop hit "Reach Out I'll Be There" and "Bernadette" are particularly close to what is heard in the arrangement of this Wonder recording. Even the backing vocals resemble the contemporary work of the Four Tops. The problem, however, is that "Hold Me," although a pleasant song, is simply not as catchy or memorable as "Reach Out I'll Be There" or "Bernadette." The teenaged Stevie Wonder was collaborating in writing many songs at the time, but he had not yet developed the consistency and facility he would exhibit in maturity.

Uptight included several songs in which Wonder played no part in the compositional process. As might be expected, Motown's staff songwriters contributed a number of these. The best-known Motown-provided album track was that of Sylvia Moy, Henry Cosby, and William "Mickey" Stevenson, "Nothing's Too Good for My Baby," which was also a successful single. Interestingly, however, the best-known non-Wonder song on the album was Bob Dylan's "Blowin' in the Wind." The single release of "Blowin' in the Wind" made it into both the pop and R&B top 10 in summer 1966. The song, of course, had been around for several years, having reached No. 2 on the *Billboard* pop charts for Peter, Paul, and Mary in 1963.

Of all of Wonder's recordings of the period, "Blowin' in the Wind" stands out as a recording that is effective as much because of who Stevie Wonder was as for how he performed it in the studio. Bob Dylan's rhetorical question about how many years some people will exist before they are permitted to be free, for example, is especially poignant when it is sung by a young black man. In the voices of Peter, Paul, and Mary, or even in the voice of the song's composer, the line was widely interpreted as pertaining to the civil rights movement; however, in the soulful voice of Stevie Wonder backed by the Motown-style swing of the accompanying band, the lyric becomes entirely more personalized. The teenaged Wonder, who as an adult would prove to be one of the strongest and most influential voices in moving forward the creation of a U.S. national holiday to celebrate the birthday of Dr. Martin Luther King, Jr., established a public concern with racism with his recording of the Dylan song. While this time the words and music were not his own, by the 1970s Stevie Wonder was recording some important metaphorical and some very direct songs about racism, for almost all of which he alone would provide words, music, arrangement, and vocal and instrumental performance. Wonder's own compositions dealing with the theme of racism continued into the 1990s, with albums such as *Jungle Fever* and *Conversation Peace*.

The one feature of Stevie Wonder's recording of "Blowin' in the Wind" that is not entirely effective is the arrangement. In Wonder's defense, though, he was not entirely responsible for his own arrangements at this point in his career. The problem stems from the loping swing rhythm, which tends to make the listener want to tap his or her feet. In turning Dylan's song into something of a "toe-tapper," some of the seriousness of the text is lost and the listener tends to focus on the overall effect of the *music,* rather than the message. This effect, however, is tempered by the soulful feeling with which Wonder sings the song and by the sung and spoken lines anonymously performed by Clarence Paul.

Not only was Wonder's recording of "Blowin' in the Wind" important in anticipating his later musical statements about racism, it was also important in defining Wonder's standing at Motown. This was one of the conspicuously few Motown recordings of the era that made any sort of social or political commentary. In fact, it would be several years before Motown staff writers Norman Whitfield and Barrett Strong would pen songs like "Ball of Confusion (That's What the World Is Today)," "War," and "Stop the War" for the Temptations and Edwin Starr, and before Marvin Gaye would produce his famed social activism concept album *What's Going On*. This lack of social and political commentary in the mid-1960s, despite the ever-growing size and vehemence of the antiwar movement and the civil rights movement, was part of the overall corporate strategy at Motown. In fact, historians Kenneth Bindas and Craig Houston attribute both Motown's hands-off approach to social and political protest *and* the company's later embracing of protest in the form of the aforementioned songs "War," "Ball of Confusion," and "Stop the War" to the profit motive. They write, "between 1970 and 1971 a majority [56%] of Americans viewed the war [in Vietnam] as a mistake and sixty-one percent advocated early withdrawal. Motown Records, the General Motors of rock, decided to cash in on the public's new outlook toward war and society."[4] In the mid-1960s Stevie Wonder would turn to more non-Motown-written material than most artists signed to one of the company's labels. That he was able to do so, and that he was able to record a song of social commentary at a time at which the label was still loath to offend any potential customers, suggests the extent to which he stood apart from many of the company's artists.

DOWN TO EARTH

The November 16, 1966 release of *Down to Earth* must have been something of an ironically titled disappointment to executives at Motown Records: the collection only made it to No. 8 on the *Billboard* R&B charts (*Uptight* had hit No. 2) and only No. 72 on the *Billboard* pop charts (*Uptight* had climbed as high as No. 33). *Down to Earth* was also about the only Wonder album after *Uptight* not to include a major hit single, for although the Ron Miller and Bryan Wells composition "A Place in the Sun" did make it to No. 3 on the *Billboard* R&B charts, it just barely entered the top 10 on the magazine's pop singles charts.

Given the relative lack of commercial success of *Down to Earth,* especially among pop music fans, many of the songs have failed to reappear on various compact disc compilations in the 1990s and early twenty-first century. One such song is the Stevie Wonder, Henry Cosby, and Sylvia Moy composition "Thank You Love." The most interesting feature of this song is how it points the way to some of Wonder's more memorable hits of the late 1960s and early 1970s. Beginning with the instrumental introduction, Clarence Paul and Henry Cosby's arrangement and record production anticipates the 1968 hit "For Once in My Life"—the rhythmic feel of the two recordings is remarkably similar. So pervasive is the use of the sunshine metaphor in describing the way in which his love and lover make the singer feel that Wonder, Cosby, and Moy's lyrics also anticipate Wonder's 1972 composition "You Are the Sunshine of My Life." Harmonically, the piece wanders a bit, but it does include the subtle chord changes based on common-tone connections that Wonder would develop in the early 1970s, as well as jazz-oriented, added-note chords (providing yet another direct connection with "You Are the Sunshine of My Life"). Melodically, too, the piece is not as strong as the Wonder compositions of even the near future—it lacks an easily recognizable chorus hook—but it does anticipate Wonder's late 1960s and early 1970s pop hits to a greater extent than some of the nearly monothematic soul songs that were soon to become his trademark. Interestingly, and unfortunately, composers and arrangers try to make up for the lack of a memorable chorus hook by using abrupt upward modulations and ever-increasing brass in the instrumentation as the song progresses. Within a few years, Motown arrangers who worked with Wonder—not to mention Wonder himself when he took over producing and arranging duties in the 1970s—would be able to use instrumentation and key changes to enhance the structure and substance of songs rather than using them, in a sense, to cover up what a song lacked.

The best-known of the *Down to Earth* songs in which Wonder had a hand in the compositional process was "Hey Love." The song was the B-side of the single release of "Travelin' Man," but also appeared on the *Billboard* singles charts on its own merits, reaching No. 9 in the R&B category but only No. 90 in the pop category. "Hey Love," a collaboration of Wonder, Clarence Paul, and Morris Broadnax, is a soulful ballad. The lyrics find Wonder expressing his love to a girl-woman who doesn't know of his feelings—he has been in love with her from a distance. He also does not know if she feels the same way about him. The lyrics present nothing too dramatic or noteworthy. What is notable is Wonder's developing melodic sense over what is a fairly simple harmonic scheme that involves just the tonic, subdominant, and dominant chords. These are the most basic chords in tonal music and are based on the first, fourth, and fifth notes of the scale, respectively. Even the apparent simplicity of the harmony is somewhat deceptive: the use of added sixths and sevenths in the piano part and in the vocal lines gives the piece a touch of jazz feel. This is not the mature jazz ballad style of Stevie Wonder—for one thing, his voice still has not developed its full resonance—but "Hey Love" presents a hint of what was to come in his compositions and performances in the 1970s. The recording also underscores the extent to which Wonder, even as a teenager, was less indebted to the black gospel influence in his brand of soul (as opposed, say, to the Ray Charles, Aretha Franklin, or James Brown soul styles) than he was indebted to jazz. It should also be noted that "Hey Love" is one of the earliest Stevie Wonder compositions to be covered by other artists: R&B singer, producer, keyboardist R. Kelly would record the song in 1992.

I WAS MADE TO LOVE HER

Released in 1967, the album *I Was Made to Love Her* is a mix of originals, Motown staff-composed songs, and covers of what already were or were in the process of becoming soul standards. In all of these there seemed to be an almost conscious move to avoid duplicating the style of the *Down to Earth* album of the previous year.

The album's title track was a highly successful single, reaching No. 1 on the *Billboard* R&B charts and No. 2 on the magazine's pop charts. In sharp contrast to the 1965 song "Uptight (Everything's Alright)" in which there was quite a lot of contrast between the melodic contours and range of verses and chorus, "I Was Made to Love Her" tends to be nearly monothematic and, from a production viewpoint, monolithic, using large blocks of sound. In fact, in this regard the song stands in sharp contrast to most of Wonder's co-written works of the mid- and late 1960s.

Wonder's harmonica solo in "I Was Made to Love Her" shows how pop music was developing a harder edge by 1967: it is more bluesy in nature than earlier Wonder solos tended to be. The recording also presents Stevie Wonder as a maturing young man: the move toward funk in the accompaniment, the bluesy nature of the harmonica solo, and the passion with which Wonder sings his tale of yet another relationship between two lovers from the proverbial opposite sides of the tracks make the story sound entirely believable—he just doesn't sound like "Little" Stevie Wonder anymore. The basic story line resembles that of "Uptight (Everything's Alright)," but the monothematic nature of the music, the rhythmic and stylistic edge, as well as the increasingly mature sound of Wonder's voice, seem more appropriate than in the earlier song. What "I Was Made to Love Her" lacks in relationship to its predecessor is a short, strong, memorable melodic and lyrical hook for a chorus. Despite this, the single release of the song reached No. 1 on the *Billboard* R&B charts and No. 2 on the *Billboard* pop charts.

A good deal of the credit for the musical drive of the song "I Was Made to Love Her," as well as the other up-tempo recordings of the mid-1960s Stevie Wonder, should be given to the so-called Funk Brothers, that "brilliant but anonymous studio band responsible for the instrumental backing on countless Motown records from 1959 up to the company's move to Los Angeles in 1972."[5] In this group of contract musicians, Wonder had the opportunity to record and perform live with some of the top musicians of the day. Perhaps just as important, he had an excellent example of a solidly cohesive band sound to emulate on his later recordings, on which he would perform all or nearly all of the instruments.

"Every Time I See You I Go Wild," a collaborative composition of Stevie Wonder and the seemingly ever-present Sylvia Moy, and Henry Cosby, makes heavy use of a descending accompaniment line in the verses, a structural trait that Wonder would turn to in numerous later compositions. He does the same sort of thing in "You Are the Sunshine of My Life," for example, when he drops one of the voices from the root of a minor chord down a half-step to the major seventh, and then down another half-step to the minor seventh. Wonder's harmonic scheme and the accompaniment instruments and background vocals are essentially riff-oriented in the song. It causes considerable surprise, then, when in the chorus section he writes an unexpected chromatic harmonic shift (a move to a chord outside of the traditional harmonies associated with a simple major or minor scale). Like the descending inner-voice motion, this too became a defining feature of later Wonder compositions, both in up-tempo pieces and in ballads.

I Was Made to Love Her contained a fair number of cover songs. One of the Motown covers, Smokey Robinson and Ronald White's "My Girl," deserves special mention, not so much because of any special merits of Wonder's recording, but because of the relationship between Robinson and Wonder that it symbolizes. Readers may recognize the song as one of the biggest hits by the Temptations. It was back in 1965 when their recording of the song, which was produced by Robinson, went to No. 1 on the pop and R&B charts. Then in 1967, this album features Wonder performing one of Smokey Robinson's best-known compositions—a song with which the writer himself was not associated as performer. This was at the very time that Robinson—with his group, the Miracles—recorded a song on which he collaborated with Stevie Wonder and Henry Cosby, "The Tears of a Clown." Like Wonder's recording of "My Girl," the Miracles' recording of "The Tears of a Clown" was not intended as the A-side of a single. When the Wonder, Cosby, and

Robinson song finally was issued as a single—in 1970—it became Smokey Robinson and the Miracles' biggest hit single.

Although they are not Stevie Wonder compositions, it is worth noting two particular non-Motown cover songs on *I Was Made to Love Her:* "Please, Please, Please" and "Respect." These songs came from writer-performers whose Southern approach to soul was fundamentally different from that of the Great Lakes–area Motown performers—James Brown and Otis Redding, respectively. Although the overall effect of the two recordings does not reach the classic status of the Brown and Redding recordings—not to mention the Aretha Franklin 1967 recording of "Respect," which became far more famous than Redding's own 1965 rendition—the arrangements and performances produce an unusual blending of divergent approaches to soul. Incidentally, Wonder's version of "Respect" does not include one of the most memorable parts of Aretha Franklin's recording: the part in which she spells out the word, "R-E-S-P-E-C-T." The harmonica solo that Wonder plays at that point in the song just cannot compare. The performance of the two non-Motown songs on *I Was Made to Love Her* would be Stevie Wonder's last covers of soul standards—the next phase of his career would find him veering toward the middle of the road. Even before this move toward mainstream pop, however, Stevie Wonder's material was somewhat out of touch with the undercurrents of protest—mostly aimed at the still-growing conflict in Vietnam—and with the hippie subculture that was sweeping young America in 1967. Stevie Wonder, though, was not alone in this regard, as the same thing could be said for all of the artists recording for Berry Gordy's Motown.

SOMEDAY AT CHRISTMAS

Stevie Wonder's move toward the middle was signaled quite suddenly and sharply by his last album release of 1967: *Someday at Christmas.* This album was a collection of Christmas standards, from Franz Schubert's "Ave Maria," to Mel Tormé's "The Christmas Song" and Harry Simeone's "The Little Drummer Boy," as well as Christmas songs by Motown staff songwriters such as Ron Miller, Orlando Murden, and Bryan Wells. The orchestrations and performances are far less soulful than anything Wonder had ever recorded, going so far as to suggest the easy listening style of the day. To his credit as a vocalist, however, the 17-year-old Wonder handles the challenges of the Schubert "Ave Maria" impressively. But *Someday at Christmas,* in trying to appeal to everyone, becomes almost completely generic. Unlike some of Wonder's early albums, *Someday at Christmas* was reissued on compact disc, probably due more to its seasonal sales potential than to its overall strength as an album.

The Middle of the Road
1968–1970

The 1968–1970 period was especially important in terms of defining just who Stevie Wonder would become as a performer as he reached adulthood. Largely defined as a soul shouter in the previous two years, Wonder recorded more mainstream cover material in 1968 and 1969, which led some writers to ask the rhetorical question, "Will Stevie Wonder become another Sammy Davis, Jr.?"[1] To be fair to Wonder and to Motown (which still exercised a great deal of control over what material Wonder recorded, particularly in 1968 and 1969), songs from the albums *For Once in My Life* and *My Cherie Amour* did help Wonder reach a wider, and whiter, audience, helping him to secure a stronger hold on the pop charts. This three-year period ended, however, with Stevie Wonder recording the album *Signed, Sealed & Delivered,* which, although not quite under his total control as writer, performer, arranger, and producer, found Wonder exerting much greater control over his product. The 1970 album steered away from the middle of the road toward jazz ballads on one hand and funk on the other hand, setting the stage for the sometimes wildly eclectic, mature Stevie Wonder productions of the 1970s. Even though Wonder would move musically away from so-called safe material, however, he did not begin writing and recording songs of social and political relevance until the next phase of his career.

EIVETS REDNOW

This period of Wonder's artistic development actually began much as the previous period had ended: with something of a one-off album. In this case, it was the instrumental, harmonica-focused album *Eivets Rednow* (Stevie Wonder spelled in retrograde). Here, Wonder records typical pop songs of the day, as well as older standards. Although *Eivets Rednow* was not particularly successful commercially at the time of its release—save the moderate success of the single "Alfie"—it did showcase Wonder's harmonica playing to a greater extent than the usually short solos on his more typical releases before and after *Eivets Rednow*. Aside from "Alfie," which has appeared on several Stevie Wonder greatest hits collections over the years, this material is among the most difficult Wonder products to find for any music collector today.

FOR ONCE IN MY LIFE

The late 1960s found Wonder co-writing and recording several songs that were in the "I Was Made to Love Her" monothematic, monolithic, block-structured mold. These songs were based on one primary melodic idea and tended to be arranged in such a way as to emphasize massive blocks of sound. Although several of Wonder's recordings from the period ("For Once in My Life," most notably) have remained staples of compact disc compilations and oldies radio into the twenty-first century, the monolithic, monothematic songs, despite their popularity at the time of their initial release, have fared less well. "I Don't Know Why," which was released as a single in addition to appearing on *For Once in My Life,* is perhaps the clearest example of this style. This song, much like "I Was Made to Love Her" from the previous year, is almost entirely monothematic. Here, however, Wonder is backed by a large brass section in addition to the standard Motown house band. The block chord structures played by the brass add significantly to the fanfarelike monolithic feel of the piece. Another difference between the two songs can be traced to Henry Cosby's production style. Cosby places Wonder's lead vocals more forward in the mix on the *For Once in My Life* material than he had in his production work on Wonder's pre-1968 albums. Because of this change and a perceptible use of less studio echo on Wonder's voice, lyrics are much easier to understand in the verses of some of the songs—especially the more pop-oriented ones.

To a large extent, the 1966–1968 riff-based or monothematic compositions of Stevie Wonder rely heavily on rhythmic interest, the soulful vocal stylings of Wonder, and a difficult-to-define "feel" in order to succeed. Melodically, many of Wonder's singles of the period, including "I Was Made to Love Her," "I Don't Know Why," "I'm Wondering," and to a certain extent "Shoo-Be-Doo-Be-Doo-Da-Day," tend to wander somewhat. Harmonically and structurally, they do not have the same level of sophistication as some of Wonder's more mature, jazz-oriented material from the 1970s. In "I Don't Know Why," the listener finds a song that is a series of verses without a chorus—or perhaps an oft-repeated chorus with ever-varying lyrics, but no verses. Whereas this kind of construction was in 1970, and remains today, fairly commonplace in gospel music (a repeated chorus with extemporizing from a soloist), it is not something that one would expect from a pop song. "I Don't Know Why" is saved from being too repetitious by the gradual buildup in the orchestration. As in some other late 1960s Stevie Wonder recordings, though, this use of orchestration tends to cover up some of the song's weaknesses rather than enhancing its strengths.

Although record producer Henry Cosby favored a clearer presentation of Wonder's voice on the pop covers, several of the songs on *For Once in My Life* that Stevie Wonder co-wrote suffer as recordings from the use of old, 1960s Motown-style echo on the lead vocal. This renders the lyrics of the verses of songs such as "You Met Your Match" and "I Wanna Make Her Love Me" almost indecipherable. "Shoo-Be-Doo-Be-Doo-Da-Day" suffers from this as well. But, as mentioned earlier, these are essential "groove" pieces and, with the exception of "Shoo-Be-Doo-Be-Doo-Da-Day," which was also a successful single, most of the Wonder-composed songs are album material that was not the focal point of the package. The other producers with whom Stevie Wonder often worked—Ron Miller and Clarence Paul—also obscured the lead vocal on faster, groove-oriented tracks.

The other effect of Cosby's use of more than a slight touch of reverberation on Wonder's voice and the placement of the voice in the mix is that the gasps, inhalations, and vocables that Wonder performs on his up-tempo, funkier songs are obscured. A song such as Wonder, Don Hunter, and Lula Hardaway's "You Met Your Match," for example, includes some of these effects, but they tend to be deemphasized through Henry Cosby's production. Once Wonder became his own producer on albums such as *Signed, Sealed & Delivered, Where I'm Coming From, Music of My Mind,* and the subsequent megahit albums of 1972–1974, he could actively exploit this vocal technique: he would place the voice front and center, use close microphone placement, and eliminate much of the stereotypical Motown sound echo/reverb. While the use of artificial echo and reverberation simulated the sound of performing in a large auditorium, it obscured the clarity of the vocals. Study of the sound of various Motown recordings of the early 1970s suggests that the new standard at the company was to allow singer-songwriter-producers such as Stevie Wonder to establish their own easily identifiable sound—a sound that could be quite different from that of any other artist on the label. Marvin Gaye's album *What's Going On,* for example, is infused with a clarity in the lead vocal, but has an overall feeling of acoustical spaciousness that is quite different from anything Stevie Wonder or any other Motown producer was doing at the time.

Although Wonder co-wrote most of the songs on *For Once in My Life,* it was the title track—a composition by Ron Miller and Orlando Murden—that quickly became the best-known song on the album. In fact, the single release of the song was No. 2 on the *Billboard* pop charts for two weeks, which equaled the success of the 1967 single "I Was Made to Love Her." The only other Stevie Wonder single that had done as well or better on the pop charts was his 1963 breakthrough "Fingertips, Part 2," which sat atop the charts for three weeks. The next Wonder single that would best "For Once in My Life" with the pop audience would be the 1972 No. 1 hit "Superstition." The important difference between Wonder's earlier No. 1 and No. 2 pop hits, "Superstition," and "For Once in My Life" is that this song was geared to the pop (as opposed to the R&B) audience. It is anything but hard-core soul material because whatever soulfulness can be heard in Wonder's lead vocal and in the piano licks is balanced by a decidedly pop-oriented orchestration. Although the totally pop nature of the song and recording might not find immediate favor with some critics or some members of Wonder's audience, "For Once in My Life" simply is a strong song. In fact, this is probably the strongest song Stevie Wonder has ever recorded in which he did not play a role in the compositional process. Likewise, "Sunny" is strictly pop, with the arrangement veering more toward something that one might have heard in a Las Vegas–style show.

Covers of pop material such as these songs are really what started speculation about the direction Wonder's career would take as he reached maturity. Even the cover of jazz vocal great Billie Holiday's "God Bless the Child" is stylistically closer to lounge music than jazz or soul, not so much because of what Wonder does but because of the orchestration. Wonder's next album added more fuel to the speculation about the direction Wonder would take musically: the Vegas lounge music of an older audience, or the music more closely associated with his own generation, especially the youth counterculture.

My Cherie Amour

Stevie Wonder's 1969 album *My Cherie Amour* occupies a curious place in his output. On one hand, there are some nice jazz-inspired touches on some of the compositions, arrangements, and performances, and some forward motion toward the funk that would start to define more of Wonder's work in the 1970s. On the other hand, some of the covers continued to suggest the kind of material a middle-aged Las Vegas act might include instead of the work of a vital, creative 19-year-old. Stevie Wonder's best-remembered albums of the 1970s, works such as *Songs in the Key of Life, Innervisions,* and *Talking Book,* featured a wide range of styles, but within that diversity there was a greater sense of artistic integrity than on *My Cherie Amour.* Wonder was still under the influence of the Motown corporate structure—although he was at this point getting more artistic freedom than some of the label's artists—and the questions about just where his career would head when he became a voting-age (21 at that time) adult still had not been answered.

The song "My Cherie Amour" is the best-known track on the album. Curiously, when it was issued on a single, this collaborative effort of Henry Cosby, Sylvia Moy, and Wonder appeared as the B-side to "I Don't Know Why," a song that had appeared on Wonder's previous album. "My Cherie Amour" reflects Wonder's growing maturity as a composer, particularly in terms of the contrast evident within the melody, the development of melodic motives, and the chromaticism (the use of notes outside of the traditional pitches of the major scale) of both the melody and the harmony.

"My Cherie Amour" opens with a simple introductory phrase (a short, self-contained section of the melody) consisting of the pitches A-flat, B-flat,

F, E-flat, and D-flat, which then returns to B-flat, the key center. The answer phrase uses the same collection of notes, from the B-flat minor pentatonic scale, but settles on the pitch F. This note, the dominant, leads naturally back to the B-flat. Henry Cosby's scoring of these parallel phrases (phrases that begin with the same melody) at first for guitar and flute—Wonder joins in with his voice on the repeat—provides a vivid, unusual tone color: an orchestrational hook, as it were. Wonder's use of the minor pentatonic scale (a five-note scale sounds like a blues scale missing one note) was nothing new, and he would turn to it again in several other compositions. Of his uses of the scale, incidentally, probably the most memorable is the clavinet riff of "Superstition." The real melodic genius of "My Cherie Amour" lies in the way in which the melody of the verses almost immediately enriches the gamut of pitches to include the notes B-natural and C. Later in the melody, Wonder enriches the gamut further while using chromatically shifting harmonies that stand in sharp contrast to the introductory figure. Also, he moves to a cadence in the key of D-flat major at the end of each of the first two verses. Because that famous introduction occurs later in the piece, the two contrasting forces—the folklike minor pentatonic of the introductory hook and the rich, Tin Pan Alley–like, slightly chromatic, major-key nature of the principal melodic material—provide a high level of interest throughout the song. Adding to the pitch saturation of "My Cherie Amour" is the fact that it modulates up a half-step for the last stanza. Musicians often criticize this type of upward modulation (heard to great effect in Wonder's "I Just Called to Say I Love You," in which he changes key several times) as being a somewhat cheap way to maintain or increase intensity, but it works fairly well for Stevie Wonder, probably because he has used the technique so sparingly throughout his career. "My Cherie Amour," "You Are the Sunshine of My Life," and "I Just Called to Say I Love You," all of which are among his most commercially oriented pop compositions, are the most notable examples of Wonder's upward half-step shifts.

The other notable collaboration between Sylvia Moy, Henry Cosby, and Wonder on the *My Cherie Amour* album, "Angie Girl," is another simple expression of romantic love. On this song the Motown house band and supplementary brass and strings back Wonder. Although the soaring violins steer far too much in the direction of what one might expect from late 1960s, middle-aged pop singers, the song does have a few notable—and redeeming—features. In particular, Wonder's melody is pleasant and it and the harmony contain a nice touch of the unexpected chromatic shifts that define some of his best compositional work. One particular orchestrational touch is also worth noting: "Angie Girl" is one of the few Stevie Wonder songs that is guitar-based as opposed to keyboard-based. Because the accompaniment is largely string-based—with the electric guitar and orchestral strings—it is natural that the piece is written in a "sharp" key, the key of G major (considered a sharp key because of the presence of F-sharp in the scale). This is, however, unusual for a Stevie Wonder composition. Probably due in part to Wonder's voice and his keyboard work, a large number of his songs are in flat keys, such as E-flat minor, A-flat major, and D-flat major.

Johnny Mandel and Paul Francis Webster's "The Shadow of Your Smile," featured in the film *The Sandpiper,* was covered by virtually every pop and easy listening performer of the era, including Perry Como, Frank Sinatra, and the Boston Pops Orchestra, as well as by jazz instrumentalists as diverse as Ron Carter, Pete Fountain, and Dizzy Gillespie. The song found its way onto *My Cherie Amour,* as did other improbable covers such as the Doors' "Light My Fire" and the Broadway song "Hello Young Lovers." The presence of these songs, as well as the definitely poppish "My Cherie Amour," conflicted with Motown's earlier presentation of Stevie Wonder as a forceful soul singer.

Wonder's two end-of-the-1960s albums, *For Once in My Life* and *My Cherie Amour,* established him more securely as a pop culture icon than his less commercially successful material of the earlier 1960s had. He had become a very visible performer—one who had achieved a great deal despite the odds. To acknowledge Wonder's achievements, U.S. President Richard Nixon presented him with a Distinguished Service Award from the President's Committee on Employment of Handicapped People in 1969. Despite, or perhaps because of his greater level of fame and public recognition, though, some music critics had reservations about the path Stevie Wonder's career was taking.

Even the title of an April 1969 *Melody Maker* article about the almost-19-year-old prodigy speaks volumes about the great debate that some of Wonder's late 1960s recordings was prompting: "Will Stevie Wonder Become Another Sammy Davis?"[2] Davis, who had been a child star as a singer, a drummer, and a dancer, was widely viewed as having long before turned toward mainstream material and performance venues in an attempt to reach the largest (and therefore, the whitest) audience. Some saw Davis as a performer who had given up relevance in the black community in order not to offend whites. One example of Davis's catering to the tastes of white audiences could be seen in his concert performances, in which he tamed down his material and included stereotypical black vaudeville genres such as tap dancing when he performed for whites.[3] In his filmed and televised performances, which were geared largely toward a white audience, Davis naturally did his "white" show rather than his "black" show. It was this style of performance that became the best-known Sammy Davis style and increasingly defined him as an artist. In a sense, Sammy Davis, Jr., had given up the chance to be a cutting-edge musician in order to be a popular all-around performer. Certainly, Wonder's inclusion of somewhat bland Broadway songs ("Hello Young Lovers") and pop songs that seemed to be aimed at an older white audience ("For Once in My Life," "My Cherie Amour," and "The Shadow of Your Smile," for example) suggested that he was veering in the direction of Sammy Davis, Jr., in the late 1960s.

Ultimately, Stevie Wonder would make a decisive turn as he reached his 21st birthday and took total artistic control of his recordings: instead of following the lead of a Sammy Davis, Jr., Wonder increasingly incorporated stylistic extremes in his compositions and performances, although not necessarily to appeal to two different audiences. Gone would be Broadway show tunes and pop songs written by others. Stevie Wonder would not be a funk musician; he would not be a pop balladeer; he would not be a top-40, middle-of-the-road singer; he would not be a jazz stylist; he would not be a rock musician; he would not be a social/political activist protest singer; he would not be a soul musician. He would incorporate (and indeed, master) all of these disparate styles; he would do so as well as, if not better than, the strict adherents to each of the individual styles, *and* he would do so by composing, writing lyrics, singing, producing, and playing nearly all of the instruments on his post-1970 recordings. And in taking these musical chances, Stevie Wonder would become one of the more socially relevant, eclectic, and popular musicians of the coming decade, far eclipsing his popularity during the 1960s. Interestingly, Wonder's recordings would continue to fare better on the R&B charts than on the pop charts, proving that he did not have to lose relevance among blacks in order to achieve huge sales numbers.

SIGNED, SEALED & DELIVERED

The 1970 album *Signed, Sealed & Delivered* was Wonder's next recording after the British magazine *Melody Maker* raised the question about what direction the singer-songwriter-multi-instrumentalist's career might take. This album was the first to be produced primarily by Wonder, but did not yet find him writing all of the material. As such, it can be seen as an important transitional record—one that would answer *Melody Maker*'s rhetorical question with a resounding, "No." In another sense, the album represents a sort of "senior thesis" for Stevie Wonder. The musician who had literally grown up in the recording studio doing things the Motown way proves on this record just what he has learned and how he intends to move once he "graduates" to total control. *Signed, Sealed & Delivered* is also important as the first collaborative effort between Wonder and lyricist Syreeta Wright, to whom he would be married from 1970–1972.

Signed, Sealed & Delivered begins with the Wonder, Henry Cosby, and Sylvia Moy composition "Never Had a Dream Come True,"[4] which had actually been released as a single a number of months before the song appeared on the album. Although the single was not nearly as successful as "Signed, Sealed, Delivered (I'm Yours)," "Never Had a Dream Come True" has been reissued on various "Greatest Hits" packages from the early 1970s through the early twenty-first century. The piece stands out from other Wonder songs because of the touches of country and gospel that can be heard in the harmonic progressions and in the piano and guitar accompaniment figures.

The lyrical theme of "Never Had a Dream Come True" reflects back to numerous songs in which Wonder plays a lovable loser character that he had recorded in the 1960s. Although this theme could grow old, in 1970 it still had the power to paint Wonder as a fully sympathetic character, much the same way that "Signed, Sealed, Delivered (I'm Yours)" did. And like "Signed, Sealed Delivered (I'm Yours)," it stood in sharp contrast to some of the more lyrically aggressive material that would appear on the 1972 album *Music of My Mind*.

The song "Signed, Sealed, Delivered (I'm Yours)" is credited to Wonder, Lee Garrett, Syreeta Wright, and Wonder's mother, Lula Hardaway. Despite the fact that the compositional credits make it sound as though the song is 2 minutes and 40 seconds worth of music by committee, the piece sounds thoroughly coherent, and it establishes Stevie Wonder as a mature soul artist. Perhaps because he was acting as his own producer on the track and had a vision for how his voice should be presented to its best effect, Wonder the singer sounds very different on this track than he had on earlier high-energy songs. He sings here with a gospel-like feeling—even doing some throaty octave-jumping screams—sounding more like a Philadelphia-style soul singer than a Motown product. Further, every breath and every emotional gasp he takes is audible. He would continue to make heavy use of close-miked vocables in his even more funk-oriented recordings of the next couple of years. This recorded vocal style clearly influenced Michael Jackson in the "Billie Jean" years of the early 1980s when Jackson was the acknowledged "King of Pop." This aspect of Wonder's vocal production and performance style also can be heard in some of Prince's 1980s recordings.

Paul Riser, one of Motown's most talented arrangers and orchestrators, arranged the track. The use of the brass, in particular, greatly enhances the recording. The other interesting feature of the arrangement that instantly makes "Signed, Sealed, Delivered (I'm Yours)" stand out from other records on the radio airwaves of 1970 is the ingenious use of a sitar-guitar in the introduction. No, this is not the pure sitar music of the Indian subcontinent or of George Harrison or other Ravi Shankar devotees—it sounds more like an instrument that was popular in the late 1960s, a guitar-based instrument that played with the timbre of the pure-bred Indian instrument.

The lyrics of "Signed, Sealed, Delivered (I'm Yours)" present Wonder as a more mature character than many of his earlier recordings did. No longer is he the child-man who has been wronged. In this song, he is the one who has rejected his lover and is now back to beg for forgiveness. Although this description might make it sound like a lyrical remake of the Temptations' 1966 hit "Ain't Too Proud to Beg," composed by Brian Holland and Norman Whitfield, it is in theme only. The two Motown songs are so fundamentally different in musical approach that any thematic similarities between the two songs in terms of basic premise probably would not occur to the casual listener. An important feature that the two songs do share with regard to lyrics, however, is worth noting. That is, the utter contriteness of the character who sings the song. Both the Holland-Whitfield song and "Signed, Sealed, Delivered (I'm Yours)" were highly successful commercially and both continue to be heard on oldies radio even today. Contrast this to some of the material Wonder was to write and record within two years—specifically several of the songs on his self-produced album *Music of My Mind*—material that would present the singer's character as anything but contrite. Songs with a simple moral premise—I realize the wrong I've done, and now I'm begging for your forgiveness—such as "Ain't Too Proud to Beg" and "Signed, Sealed, Delivered (I'm Yours)" made a greater connection with audiences (as measured by record sales) than the "superbad" material Wonder was to record for a fortunately very brief period.

"I Gotta Have a Song," a collaboration of Stevie Wonder, Don Hunter, Lula Hardaway, and Paul Riser, finds the singer having lost at love; however, if he has music, he just might get by. The premise of the lyrics certainly is nothing new. Wonder's melody and harmony are pretty but are not particularly memorable. As a matter of fact, the average person would be hard pressed to whistle or sing the tune after having heard the song even a few times. Even though "I Gotta Have a Song" is essentially album-filler material, it is not without merit. For one thing, the music-conquers-all theme is congruent with the public persona of Stevie Wonder, whom the American public had seen growing up for eight years as an icon in the world of popular music. And the song's harmony suggests the later "Golden Lady," which is a far superior song melodically. Although "Golden Lady," a track on the 1973 *Innervisions* album, was written in its entirety by Wonder, the overall flow, harmonic progression, and sunny feel of the lyrics owe more than a small debt to "I Gotta Have a Song."

Signed, Sealed & Delivered featured two notable tracks in which Stevie Wonder did not play a compositional role, but that show just what direction he was taking in pulling away from the mainstream and in establishing themes for some of his later compositions: "We Can Work It Out" and "Heaven Help Us." John Lennon and Paul McCartney's "We Can Work It Out" had been a No. 1 pop hit for the Beatles at the tail end of 1965. Stevie Wonder's 1970 version of the song begins with a distorted keyboard introduction that serves to place the soulful arrangement squarely at the close of the 1960s and the start of a new decade. Arranger and producer Wonder squares out the quadruple-to-triple meter changes of the Beatles' original version of the song. But, this step was necessary to turn "We Can Work It Out" into a soul-Motown song. The amazing thing about Wonder's version of the song is that it is fundamentally different from the original to the extent that it becomes his own. In other words, if a listener did not know that this was not a song composed by Motown staff or Stevie Wonder, the listener's assumption would be that it was written especially for or by Wonder. In the overall progression of Wonder's history of cover material by non-Motown

songwriters, "We Can Work It Out" stands out as being particularly important. The rocking soul of Wonder's arrangement, the extemporization in his
vocal performance, his harmonica solo, and, yes, that keyboard lick, tackle
head on questions about what direction his career would be taking. No, he
was not destined to become another Sammy Davis, Jr.

The other song not composed by Wonder on *Signed, Sealed & Delivered*
that deserves special attention is Ron Miller's "Heaven Help Us." Before
discussing the song and its place in Wonder's ongoing development as an artist, it should be noted that the song's recording for the album was produced
by Ron Miller and Tom Baird and not by Wonder. This is important to note
when listening to the recording because it explains why the production style
differs so much from the Wonder-produced tracks on *Signed, Sealed & Delivered*. For one thing, Miller and Baird chose to use a huge orchestration, but
even more important, they bathe Wonder's lead vocal in studio reverberation. In short, it resembles the 1970 Motown production standards and not
the close-miked, no-studio-reverb vocal presentation preferred by Wonder in
his productions of the same time period. In short, some of the immediacy of
Stevie Wonder's voice is lost. This, however, detracts only a little from the
overall effect of the song. Certainly, the listener can hear Ron Miller's text
that "Heaven help us" if black men continue to be treated unequally, and
"Heaven help" the young man who has been sent off to die in a foreign war
and will never see the age of 19, etc. Miller places the multitudinous social
and political problems of the early 1970s squarely in the hands of God. This
religious theme would guide the work of Stevie Wonder in his own compositions beginning in 1972 with "Evil," a collaboration between Wonder and
lyricist Yvonne Wright, and even more overtly in songs on the *Talking Book,
Innervisions,* and *Fullfillingness' First Finale* albums in late 1972–1974. The
theme, in fact, continues even into Stevie Wonder's work in the twenty-first
century.

Among the other songs on *Signed, Sealed & Delivered*, "You Can't Judge
a Book by It's [*sic*] Cover," a collaborative composition of Henry Cosby,
Sylvia Moy, and Wonder, hints at the turn toward more hard-core funk that
is evident in other 1970 Motown products, like Edwin Starr's recording of
"War," and the Temptations' recording of "Ball of Confusion (That's What
the World Is Today)." Wonder, his mother Lula Hardaway, Paul Riser, and
Don Hunter collaborated on "Something to Say." This song is one of the
more pleasant filler songs on the album, although the descending bass guitar
line sounds uncomfortably similar to that in Creedence Clearwater Revival's
"Have You Ever Seen the Rain," and, as in a couple of other songs on *Signed,
Sealed & Delivered*, tends to sound overproduced in a way that is uncomfortably reminiscent of the "Sammy Davis, Jr.," Stevie Wonder.

Despite the occasional overproduction, sometimes heavy-handed arrangements,[5] and presence of some substandard filler material, *Signed, Sealed &
Delivered* succeeded on several counts: (1) it found Wonder moving away

from "Las Vegas" in the material he recorded, (2) it hinted at the way in which he would more fully develop within a few years as a record producer, and (3) it contained a few truly potent performances ("Signed, Sealed, Delivered [I'm Yours]," "We Can Work It Out," and "Heaven Help Us") that stand with the very best of his pre–*Talking Book* recordings. The album set the stage for Wonder to take complete control of the composition, vocal and instrumental performance, and production of his material in the next phase of his career. What *Signed, Sealed & Delivered* did not accomplish, however, was to place Stevie Wonder into a position of social relevance at a time period in which political activism—and indeed, sometimes political radicalism—ruled the day. The next phase of his recording career would find him increasingly turning toward politically and socially relevant topics, once he took the step of becoming not only a composer, but also a lyricist.

The Independent Artist, 1971–1973

Upon his 21st birthday, at which time his contract with Motown Records expired, Stevie Wonder initially did not renew his attachment to the label, but then again, he did not sign with any other label. Instead, he enrolled in music theory classes at the University of Southern California in 1971. Wonder eventually did sign another contract with Motown, one that lasted until 1974. The new Stevie Wonder—now totally in control of his product—wrote, performed, and produced two albums that heralded his newfound freedom: *Where I'm Coming From* and *Music of My Mind*, both released by Motown's Tamla label. Because of the somewhat experimental nature of these albums and the general lack of material with a focus on immediate commercial appeal, the albums were not as widely accepted as some of his earlier work. Perhaps the biggest boost to Wonder's career, especially in securing a greater place of prominence with white fans of rock music, was his opening for the Rolling Stones on their 1972 U.S. tour. In the wake of tremendous success on the Stones tour, Wonder's most commercially successful album to date, *Talking Book*, appeared and moved Wonder to the level of superstar through its songs of social and political consciousness and broad commercial appeal.

WHERE I'M COMING FROM

He had practically been raised in the recording studio, and now in 1971, he really was out on his own. So, the album *Where I'm Coming From* found Stevie Wonder experimenting with orchestrations, electronic sounds, and even with song forms. Despite this, Wonder was still searching to fully define himself as a mature star on the album. In particular, two tracks, "I Wanna Talk to You" and "Take Up a Course in Happiness," represented stylistic anomalies in that these styles dropped out of the eclectic mix that would represent the mature Stevie Wonder by late 1972 and beyond. But, then the exploration of stylistic extremes has always been one of Wonder's strengths—the mid-1980s album *In Square Circle* is one of his few projects that suffers from too much of a sameness throughout—and even the more "out there" tracks on *Where I'm Coming From* succeed on some level. One of the contributing factors to the overall success of the album is the work of lyricist Syreeta Wright who, for the only time in the Wonder-Wright partnership, contributed to every song on the album.

Where I'm Coming From begins with the sound of an electronically synthesized harpsichord. If there was ever an opening instrumental introduction that screams out, "This is not your father's Motown," then this timbre at the opening of "Look Around" is it. This moderate-tempo piece, which includes some of the most impressionistic lyrics Stevie Wonder would ever set to music and record, sounds completely unlike anything Wonder had ever recorded up to that time.

"Do Yourself a Favor" sounds suspiciously like Stevie Wonder imitating Sly and the Family Stone, with the Hammond organ sound of a Billy Preston thrown in. Musically, it is heavier than even most hard-core Wonder funk to come in his best-known albums of the 1970s, especially with the insistent organ licks. The resemblance to the Sly Stone recordings of the period is clear in the overall feel of the song, and even more specifically, in the childlike melodic figures that appear at the very end of the song—think of Sly Stone's "Everyday People." Syreeta Wright's lyrics once again exude impressionism. The overall theme is that of using education to improve one's life and pull oneself out of the ghetto. This is evident in the chorus, although the verses throw widely scattered images of a sort of hell on earth, all of which easily fit the ghetto metaphorically. Thematically and musically, it could certainly fit right in with the socially conscious non-Motown African American popular music of the day. It is, interestingly, the only truly potent funky workout on *Where I'm Coming From*—the album is the most heavily weighted album toward ballads that Stevie Wonder would ever write and record. One can only speculate how a single release of "Do Yourself a Favor" might have fared; it is easy to imagine that it might have hastened Wonder's breakout as one of the strongest musical forces of the first half of the 1970s, such is the degree of Sly Stone–like social consciousness and funkiness of the track.

"Think of Me as Your Soldier" finds Wonder accompanied by the sounds of guitar, bass, drums, solo English horn, and other woodwinds in the first verse; the orchestration is expanded to include the orchestral strings in the chorus and subsequent verses. The moderately slow, gentle ballad features straightforward lyrics by Syreeta Wright, the basic premise of which is that the woman to whom Wonder is singing should think of himself "as her soldier," whose life is given to present "an endless love" to her.

The next track, "Something Out of the Blue," continues the guitar and woodwind-dominated ballad feel. Wright's lyrics describe the love that Wonder's character has found for the woman to whom he sings as "something out of the blue," while Wonder's music closely resembles that of "Think of Me as Your Soldier," not just in orchestration, but also in melodic shapes and melodic motives. The song's harmonies include more chromatic shifts than do those of the previous song, but so close is the overall resemblance that they seem a minitheme and variation in the middle of *Where I'm Coming From*. The classical chamber music feel of "Something Out of the Blue" is something of a one-off for Stevie Wonder: this type of orchestration would not be heard on his megahit albums of 1972–1976, although more fully integrated but synthesized references to traditional European classical music would be heard on a couple of tracks on *Songs in the Key of Life*. He would return to this type of classically inspired texture, however, more fully in the synthesizer-based orchestrations he would do for his *Journey Through the Secret Life of Plants* soundtrack at the end of the 1970s. The thematic linking of songs and the classically inspired orchestrations show the range of Wonder's musical interests as he reached maturity; however, this was quite unusual in 1971 pop music and probably went well beyond what Wonder's audience was ready to accept, not to mention what they were ready to get behind and fully support. I believe that the incredible width over which he cast his net on *Where I'm Coming From* was, unfortunately, at least partially to blame for the relatively poor sales of the album.

Where I'm Coming From featured two songs that would find their way into the twenty-first century via "Greatest Hits" reissues, despite the fact that the original album had become very difficult to come by (even in its compact disc reissue, which seems to be available in the United States only as a 1993 German import). The first of the two songs, "If You Really Love Me," is one of Stevie Wonder's first great experiments in song form.

"If You Really Love Me" opens with the catchy chorus hook, which is supported by a small horn section and vocal and instrumental harmonies suggesting something midway between the brassy style of the popular jazz-rock of groups of the day such as Blood, Sweat, and Tears and Chicago, to name the two best-remembered such bands, and the thinner jazz-pop sound that Walter Becker and Donald Fagen would popularize with their studio band Steely Dan within a year or so. The verses are based more on the texture of Wonder's solo voice and acoustic piano and are in a slower tempo, in an almost lounge-singer or torch song–influenced style. This stylistic disconnect fits Syreeta Wright's lyrics perfectly. Here is a contrast between the straightforward snappy jazz-rock request that the woman to whom Wonder's character is singing let him know if she really loves him, so that he will know that he "won't have to be playin' around," and the free rubato rhythm (slightly speeding up and slowing down as it suits the mood) of the verses in which Wonder sings about the various mixed signals the object of his affections is sending him.

That a song with the unusual construction and jazzy arrangement and harmony of "If You Really Love Me" made both the pop and the R&B top 10 is testimony to the strength of the song and—especially—the chorus hook. It was a bold move to include a slow, acoustic section in the middle of what was essentially a danceable, upbeat song, but a move that Stevie Wonder, with the new freedom from following the tried-and-true Motown formula, fortunately was willing to make.

"If You Really Love Me" is followed by one of Stevie Wonder's most bizarre songs, "I Wanna Talk to You." This song begins with Wonder playing the role of what sounds to be an aging black, blues piano player/singer; in fact, it sounds like an exaggerated version or parody of Fats Domino. This New Orleans piano professor character sings the blues about how rough his life has been and how he has never found anyone who truly understands him. In between this character's laments, a second character emerges with the leering "I wanna talk to you" refrain. This is Wonder portraying a dirty-old-man sort of fellow. "I Wanna Talk to You" presents such a strange kind of exaggerated humor that it works, in a sense. At least the leering dirty old man can generate a smile here, unlike the leering, smarmy, almost totally unlovable characters Wonder portrayed in the songs "Sweet Little Girl" and "Keep On Running" on *Music of My Mind,* his next album. In a sense, "I Wanna Talk to You" is like the Beatles' "You Know My Name (Look Up the Number)," the bizarre, out there, humor-infused B-side of the popular "Let It Be" single. Unlike "You Know My Name (Look Up the Number)," though, the Wonder song is only funny the first couple of times you hear it—it does not wear particularly well. Strangely enough, as they share so little stylistically, "I Wanna Talk to You" also resembles some of the rather bizarre humorous songs of Frank Zappa and some of the curious experimental work of Brian Wilson in 1967.

"Take Up a Course in Happiness" is an odd sort of combination of the styles of Sammy Davis, Jr. (as has been noted by several commentators),[1] the vocal groups the 5th Dimension and the Mamas and the Papas, and some of the loping, music hall–styled songs sung in the mid-1960s by Davy Jones of the Monkees. In light of what Wonder had recorded before the time of *Where I'm Coming From* and—especially—in light of Wonder's post–*Where I'm Coming From* compositions and arrangements, the musical style of "Take Up a Course in Happiness" is yet another example of a *Where I'm Coming From* anomaly. Although one can feel hints of this when listening to songs like "I Wanna Talk to You," "Think of Me as Your Soldier," and "Something Out of the Blue," the song "Take Up a Course in Happiness" suggests that a major part of the motivation behind *Where I'm Coming From* could have been to highlight the diversity of Wonder's compositional abilities so that his tunes might be covered by a wide variety of other artists. "Take Up a Course in Happiness" could have been a well-placed album track for any one of a number of performers (including those named above), and possibly could have been a commercially viable single for them as well. It is such a stylistic anomaly for a Stevie Wonder performance, however, that is just does not sound "true" in this performance.

"Never Dreamed You'd Leave in Summer" is a lovely ballad and a record-ing that for a reason that completely resists definition sounds more like a Stevie Wonder composition and arrangement meant for Stevie Wonder to sing than most of the other songs on *Where I'm Coming From*. The melodic twists of the song, however, sound as if they presented something of a challenge to Wonder: his intonation is not quite as solid as it is on other songs on the album. It would have been interesting to hear how Wonder would have recorded it again in a couple of years when his ballad interpretation and his vocal tech-nique were even better. The lyrics find Wonder expressing the heartache he feels at having been unexpectedly left by his lover during the summer. Because of the seasonal nature of the lyrics, as well as the ballad musical style, the song bears a superficial resemblance to "Superwoman (Where Were You When I Needed You Most)," which would become the best-remembered song on Wonder's next album, *Music of My Mind*. In fact, *All Music* critic John Bush describes the present song as having been "slightly reworked" in order to pro-duce "Superwoman."[2] The problem with Bush's description is that it fails to acknowledge the very real, basic differences exposed in the psyche of the lead character in each of the songs. "Never Dreamed You'd Leave in Summer" reflects heartache and loss and dismay, while "Superwoman (Where Were You When I Needed You Most)" finds Wonder's character expressing true bitter-ness at the woman who left him, before he expresses his sense of heartache and loss.[3] This bitterness does not go so far as to exhibit signs of misogyny, but it is decidedly patronizing and condescending. The songs simply come from two very different viewpoints. A listener who could sympathize with the character singing "Never Dreamed You'd Leave in Summer" could easily consider the character singing "Superwoman" to be—in the words of the era—something of a male chauvinist pig.

Where I'm Coming From concludes with yet another ballad, "Sunshine in Their Eyes." This song finds Wonder singing that he cannot wait until the day when there is sunshine in the eyes of all the children of the world, espe-cially those who are among the forgotten poor. A children's chorus joins with him. The song includes an up-tempo section that reflects the future when "everything is happy." The quick cuts between the two tempi and the two stylistic feels work nearly as well as the cuts between sections in "If You Really Love Me." And Wonder includes some tasty chromatic harmonic motion—including the use of an augmented tonic chord as a passing harmony between the major tonic and the major subdominant—in each section. The fast, happy section may have sounded very much *au courant* in 1971, but it wears less well more than three decades after the fact: today it sounds like another pos-sible 5th Dimension outtake.

As mentioned earlier, *Where I'm Coming From* has not fared well in the compact disc era. Even at the time of its initial release, it was not one of Stevie Wonder's better-selling albums. In fact, of all of Wonder's studio albums after he made his initial commercial impact with "Fingertips" back in the early

1960s, *Where I'm Coming From* enjoyed the least amount of chart success, despite the fact that it is in some respects superior to his next album, *Music in My Mind*. It was probably because *Where I'm Coming From* was in competition with other 1971 albums of social commentary such as Marvin Gaye's highly acclaimed Tamla Records release *What's Going On* and Sly & the Family Stone's *Greatest Hits* (which preceded the Wonder release) and *There's a Riot Goin' On* (which followed Wonder's *Where I'm Coming From*). And the wild eclecticism, experimentation, and unusual humor of the album make it reminiscent at times of Brian Wilson of the *Smile* and *Smiley Smile* era, or of other more poppish singers, and certainly also helped to make the audience for *Where I'm Coming From*, shall we say, more select than that of any other Stevie Wonder album. This kind of wild eclecticism, however, would emerge in the 1980s and 1990s recordings of Prince. It is difficult to imagine Prince's eclecticism without the early 1970s recordings of Stevie Wonder.

MUSIC OF MY MIND

Released March 3, 1972, Stevie Wonder's album *Music of My Mind* failed to connect in a massive way with both black audiences (No. 6 on the *Billboard* R&B charts) and white audiences (No. 69 on the *Billboard* pop charts), unlike his October 1972 breakthrough album *Talking Book*. *Music of My Mind* largely continues many of the trends of *Where I'm Coming From,* although, interestingly, it did not contain the successful single material of the 1971 album. The lack of commercial success for the album does not necessarily reflect on the quality of the songs overall; it is attributed to the relative lack of commerciality of the songs—few of them approach the instantly recognizable nature of, say, *Talking Book*'s songs. Several of the tracks, in fact, are funky jams that show off Wonder as an instrumentalist, arranger, and producer far more than they highlight his voice, and vocal music is what sells in the record industry. One might even say that *Music of My Mind* represents what Stevie Wonder the musician had always wanted to do in the studio, had he not had to deal with the stylistic and time constraints of 2–1/2 minute, mass market, R&B/Motown pop. As one travels through the tracks on the album, it is worthwhile to consider just what the package's title means: are these songs from Wonder's heart and soul, or literally songs from his mind—his imagination? The answers to this question form both the genius of the album as well as *Music of My Mind*'s fundamental structural problem. I will discuss this theme in connection with several songs in particular.

Music of My Mind begins with one of only two songs on the package that include an instrumentalist other than Stevie Wonder, the Wonder and Syreeta Wright collaborative composition "Love Having You Around." This recording includes a trombone solo by Art Baron. The piece is a funky, clavinet-based jam in which Wright's lyrics present a simple, free expression of love. Wonder's vocals (which include a touch of vocoder—an electronic device, popular at the time, that was used to manipulate sounds to give them a mysterious, computerlike quality—processing in one of the backing vocal tracks) and his work on keyboards and drums exhibit a spontaneity that belie the way the recording of this album was done. Wonder was no longer backed by the Motown house band in 1972; except for Baron's short trombone solo, all of the components of this recording were put together by Wonder through the tedious process of studio overdubbing. It is remarkable, then, that piece sounds for all the world like a studio jam of a band, lead vocalist, and backup singers. The song degenerates at the end—after more than 7 minutes of music—just as a real studio jam might do when the band had not quite worked out a proper ending, or before the record producer had constructed the song's fade out.

Possibly because of its very modest success as a single release, the best-known song on *Music of My Mind* was "Superwoman (Where Were You When I Needed You Most)." The success of this song is surprising, considering what the sociopolitical tone of the United States was at the time of its release. For, "Superwoman" appeared just as the women's movement was gaining steam. In the world of Carole King's *Tapestry* album, not to mention Helen Reddy's song "I Am Woman," and other overtly political popular songs of women's liberation, "Superwoman (Where Were You When I Needed You Most)" seemed out of place. In particular, the differences between the overall lyrical sentiment of the Stevie Wonder song and some of the more radical songs of women's liberation—John Lennon and Yoko Ono's ill-titled "Woman Is the Nigger of the World" is perhaps the most extreme example—is absolutely striking. Although the sentiments of some of the songs of the early 1970s women's movement have not worn well (especially the aforementioned Lennon-Ono song and the often-parodied Helen Reddy song), the plight of women in American society generally has been acknowledged as one of the primary areas in which significant political and social change has been seen in the past several decades. Because of that, "Superwoman" perhaps has fared worse than just about any other Stevie Wonder composition in terms of lasting acceptance.

Basically, "Superwoman (Where Were You When I Needed You Most)" is a juxtaposition of what easily could have been two separate songs. The first section, the one that deals directly with the dreams of the Superwoman character, is what can really make feminists angry. Wonder's lyrics describe the hopes, dreams, and visions for the future of the woman who wants to have it all. The problem lies in the fact that Wonder—or the character he is portraying as he sings the song—downplays these dreams: they are just things that are "really in her mind." He continues by suggesting that these dreams of "what she wants to be" are the things "she needs to leave behind." Because Mary, the Superwoman character, wants "to boss the bull around," and because Wonder's character indicates that he simply is not going to allow this to happen in this relationship, he makes it clear who is boss—at least in his mind. The dismissal of Mary's hopes and dreams and the pointing out of who in this relationship ultimately will win being placed in male *versus* female terms comes off as condescending and patronizing. Mary's hopes and dreams are to take second place to the dreams of Wonder's character, for he is the "bull" not to be bossed around.

The tone of Mary's partner's putdown of her dreams in "Superwoman" causes the listener to deal with a basic rhetorical problem as he or she digests the song: "Are the words and attitudes coming from the heart and soul of Stevland Morris/Stevie Wonder or from a character he has invented for the song?" As I mentioned before, this is the real dilemma of *Music of My Mind*—the listener is not given adequate direction by the liner notes or by the lyrics alone. For example, on one hand, the listener hears the male figure described as the "bull." Stevie Wonder fans might know that his astrological sign is Taurus, the bull, and that his publishing company was called Black Bull Music. However, the kind of self-serving "love" expressed by that character goes against the forms of love espoused by Wonder in virtually every other song he had recorded up to that point. It also contradicts the notions of universal love without hidden agendas and a lifelong purpose of building others up that forms the basis of his post–*Music of My Mind* corpus. So, just who is singing "Superwoman?"

The second part of the song, which features some tasteful jazz-based guitar work by Buzzy Feiten, might provide some clues as to the true identity of the singer of "Superwoman." In this part of the song, which harmonically, melodically, and even tempo-wise, contrasts with the first half, Wonder's character asks his lost lover just where she was when he needed her most, "last winter." It seems as though some time has gone by and Wonder's character is reflecting on how "bitter words" came between the couple and dissolved the relationship. The lyrics imply that Wonder's former lover, however, was really the one to blame, as she tells him that she "has changed." He reiterates that he needs her. So, why don't the two get back together? Pride? The listener never gets an answer.

Why do I suggest that "Superwoman" is even more embarrassing today than when *Music of My Mind* was first released in 1972? Didn't the main male character get what he deserved? To the extent that the song seems to suggest that he lost at love because his attempts to control the heart, mind, and even the very life, of Mary failed, one could argue that he did get what he deserved. The problem with this character and his just reward is that the basis of his question, "Where were you when I needed you, last winter," suggests that he just doesn't get it. He simply does not realize why Mary left him. He also continues to frame literally everything around himself. For example, he even seems to get Mary to admit that she was wrong to have dreams of her own. Despite the beautiful major-seventh chords that suggest the commercial contemporary jazz of the time, and despite the soaring melodic material and how well Stevie Wonder handles it as a vocalist, his character remains

song, except that in this case Wonder's character is actively taking on Evil, acting as a sort of instrument of the Almighty. Religion would play an even greater role on some subsequent Stevie Wonder albums, particularly as he increasingly wrote just about all of the words and music on those albums. Certainly, the tradition of "Heaven Help Us" and "Evil" continued on songs such as "Higher Ground" and "Heaven Is 10 Zillion Light Years Away," just to mention two that were wholly Stevie Wonder products.

Wonder's musical setting of the Yvonne Wright text of "Evil," as one might reasonably assume, was what attracted instrumentalists like Stanley Turrentine to the song. The music, however, fits very well with the text and the complete song package—words and music—is stronger than the sum of the individual components. Melodically, Wonder bases the song on easily identifiable motives. The harmonic progression owes a debt to black gospel music, particularly in some of the chromatic harmonies of the chorus section.[6] Wonder arranged the track, and his arrangement also resembles black gospel music, especially with the use of acoustic piano and a large backing choir.

The piece is one of the most striking of Wonder's compositional career up to that point because of the ending. Wonder leaves Wright's closing line about Evil's work having left "sweet love, all alone, an outcast of the world" unresolved harmonically. In fact, the song ends quite abruptly on that line, almost as though the recording is simply cut off by accident. Of course, it is no accident. The effect is that Evil has silenced the singer just as he reaches the high point—it is the high point pitchwise—of his inquisition of Evil. As Stevie Wonder would move into his next several albums, he would provide the resolution in the form of his love-conquers-all-possible-evils songs. Despite the gospel twinges in the piano and the backing choir, Wonder's synthesizer-based orchestration on "Evil" has not worn well (it smacks of the early days of the use of synthesizers in pop music, with the distinctive timbres of the Moog and Arp synthesizers painting the piece into the proverbial corner as a late 1960s–early 1970s piece). Early 1970s synthesizers aside, the gospel-like nature of Wonder and Yvonne Wright's brave face-off with Evil, not to mention the startling ending and the richness of Wonder's voice, is so strong that it is surprising that the song has not been better represented on Motown's turn-of-the-millennium compilations of the best of Stevie Wonder.

In *Where I'm Coming From* and *Music of My Mind*, Stevie Wonder finally broke free of many of the constraints of Motown hit making. In doing so, he proved himself to be a more talented instrumentalist, producer, arranger, and overall musician than the public at large may have imagined, for he had been cast as a singer and harmonica player for so long. The bittersweet irony of these two albums was that the record-buying public did not latch onto the new, finally-on-his-own musician. *Music of My Mind*, in particular, seemed to suffer from a diffuse theme—just who were these characters, manifestations of the heart and soul of Stevland Morris/Stevie Wonder, or theatrical constructs? The question that remained to be answered was, "What would happen if this 22-year-old newly liberated talent with a decade of experience in American popular music would write, arrange, sing, play, and produce songs that were focused on making a connection with the emotions and social concerns of the record-buying public?" A further question was, "What would happen if that musician would also adopt a more consistent literary voice, one that would allow the public to perceive an album as a collection of statements from the experience of one clearly defined main character?" Those questions would be answered a little more than half a year after the release of *Music of My Mind*.

TALKING BOOK

The 1972 album *Talking Book* was and remains a favorite of music critics.[7] The collection certainly contains striking songs, each of which achieves a clear individual identity. The album suffers in part, though, from too much contrast from song to song, causing a sense of disconnection as a package. In large part, Wonder's arrangements and record production account for this, for no two consecutive songs share a common sound. For example, Wonder's lead vocals are recorded quite differently in each of the songs on side 1: "You Are the Sunshine of My Life," "Maybe Your Baby," "You and I (We Can Conquer the World)," "Tuesday Heartbreak," and "You've Got It Bad Girl." Curiously, the album is more thematically cohesive than it seems, given the arrangements and production. With Wonder writing all of the album's music, Wonder, Syreeta Wright, and Yvonne Wright authored lyrics that dealt with various aspects of love—from exuberance (Wonder's "You Are the Sunshine"), to suspicion and dejection from being trampled in a relationship (Wonder's "Maybe Your Baby") to the hope that a new relationship might take the place of the ended one (Syreeta Wright's "Lookin' for Another Pure Love") to a vision of what the nature of that new relationship might be (Yvonne Wright's "I Believe [When I Fall in Love It Will Be Forever]"). Unlike the views of love expressed on Wonder's previous album, *Music of My Mind*, however, the lyrics of *Talking Book* are considerably more autobiographical, believable, and capable of making emotional connections with a wide audience. And even if the songs are not strictly autobiographical, the characters Wonder, the singer, portray share at least part of Stevie Wonder/Stevland Morris's soul.

The other two songs, "Superstition" and "Big Brother" (both with lyrics by Wonder), deal with social concerns. "Big Brother," in particular, was topical at the time of the album's October 27, 1972, release, less than a month before the November election. In a musical setting that suggests a somewhat twisted take on blues form, Wonder creates a song that predicts doom for an America run by politicians who ignore the poor and disenfranchised, except when they are campaigning for election. Wonder's text is pointed and suggests some of the vehemence of early 1960s protest songs such as Bob Dylan's "Masters of War," themselves based on a folk tradition of "in your face" protest songs that date to the early days of the U.S. labor movement in the nineteenth century. Stevie Wonder's use of a twisted blues form and the basic harmonies of blues music stand in sharp contrast to the jazz-standard chromaticism and lush harmonies and straightforward form of "You Are the Sunshine in My Life" and the album's lyrical ballad, "You and I." Interestingly, it also stands in contrast to most of Wonder's compositions in the 1970s: clear-cut, textbook blues form was largely absent from his compositional palette throughout the decade.

"Superstition," which happened to be *Talking Book*'s first big hit single,[8] stands apart from the rest of the album, both musically and lyrically. Musically, its closest earlier relative in the Stevie Wonder canon is "Keep On Running" from *Music of My Mind*. It was, however, the only overtly funk-fashioned piece on *Talking Book,* and the only song on the album that dealt with religion (in this case the occult and—as the title suggests—superstitions) head on.

Despite the production and stylistic disconnect from song to song, however, there are a few thematic links from song to song in the music of *Talking Book.* The clearest example is an instrumental phrase in "Maybe Your Baby" (side 1, track 2) that is echoed in "Superstition" (side 2, track 1). But, the most important thing that links the songs on *Talking Book* is that here Stevie Wonder was writing from the heart. The compact disc reissue of the album, in fact, includes the following statement from Wonder: "Here is my music. It is all I have to tell you how I feel. Know that your love keeps my love strong."[9] Although this note from Wonder was not included in the notes to the original vinyl version of the album in 1972, *Talking Book* clearly is a "heart," or "belief" album, whereas its immediate predecessors, *Where I'm Coming From* and *Music of My Mind,* had been "head" or "theatrical imagination" albums. The Stevie Wonder who expresses his feelings and beliefs was an infinitely more loveable character than the imaginary characters—some of whom had dubious views and lifestyles—of *Music of My Mind,* in particular.

It would be almost impossible to single out one of Wonder's 1970s albums as an example of the extent to which he transcended even very good pop music as a composer, but *Talking Book* cannot be overlooked in that regard. For one thing, "You Are the Sunshine of My Life" quickly became a bona fide standard, embraced by jazz and pop instrumentalists and vocalists. Harmonically, the song transcends typical early 1970s pop music with the use of added minor ninths, minor triads with added major sevenths, and the striking whole-tone scale material in the introduction, all of which create a rich palette of sounds. "You and I (We Can Conquer the World)" managed to sound current at the time (the combination of Wonder's expressive dynamic shadings on piano, the electronic reverb of the vocals, and the slightly-other-worldly synthesizer melodic phrases) and yet tied to the great American popular song styles of the first half of the twentieth century. Let us now take a detailed look at the words and music of this fascinating album in the order in which they appeared in the original vinyl release.

Talking Book begins with what probably is Stevie Wonder's best-known, most frequently covered song: "You Are the Sunshine of My Life." Several features of the introduction and first stanza of the recording stand out as examples of the bold steps Wonder was taking as a writer, arranger, and producer at the time. The opening electronic keyboard introduction, for example, makes use of whole-tone scale material. Although this particular scale had been used by the French Impressionist composers of the later nineteenth century and early twentieth century—Claude Debussy most notably—it was quite rare in pop songs. Rarer still was the use of the whole-tone scale in R&B and soul music. Wonder the producer also took the unusual step of having backing vocalists Jim Gilstrap and Gloria Barley sing the first verse of the song. At first listening, then, unless the listener knew that "You Are the Sunshine of My Life" was supposed to be a Stevie Wonder recording, he or she would not realize that fact until Wonder took over the lead vocals in the second stanza. For the "owner" of a solo album not to sing the first verse of the first song on the album was unheard of—the effect is to force the listener to pay close attention to the rest of the track, and to the vocal work on the rest of the album.

The lyrics of "You Are the Sunshine of My Life" express the exuberance of a new love. Wonder the lyricist makes use of just about every hackneyed cliché—"the sunshine of my life," "the apple of my eye," "drowning in my own tears"—used by pop songwriters from throughout the Tin Pan Alley–era and beyond.[10] Wonder gets away with it in this case because the simple innocence of the newfound love finds perfect expression in these cliché sentiments: the character that Wonder the performer assumes simply could not express these feelings any other way. In large part, the lyrics can work only in conjunction with the music to which Wonder the composer has set them. As a mood piece, this music is not meant to fit with profound lyrical sentiments.

The music of "You Are the Sunshine of My Life" became a near-instant standard among jazz musicians. In fact, very shortly after the enormous commercial success of *Talking Book* and the single release of the song, "You Are the Sunshine of My Life" began appearing in editions of the infamous fake book known as *The Real Book*.[11] Despite the whole-tone nature of the introduction, the melodic and harmonic material of the rest of the song is fairly conventional; however, not within the world of early 1970s rock and R&B music. Wonder's music incorporates the seventh chords, including the very rare (in pop music) minor chord with an added major seventh, of jazz. The sophisticated harmonic scheme, coupled with an easily identifiable melody, made the song ideal for the jazz musicians of the day: not only could they do a tune at a gig that the audience would instantly recognize as a hit by Stevie Wonder, they also could improvise over chord changes that transcended most of the pop material out there, and indeed that seemed more like the harmonic changes jazz composers wrote than those composed by a pop/R&B musician. In this way, jazz musicians could satisfy the audience and themselves.

"Maybe Your Baby," with words and music by Wonder, immediately follows "You Are the Sunshine of My Life." With Wonder's clavinet-based funk and funk/disco star Ray Parker, Jr.'s bluesy electric guitar playing, the piece begins with riffs that closely resemble "Keep On Running" from *Music of My Mind*. The song also resembles late 1960s and early 1970s work by Sly & the Family Stone. Wonder sings the text with a tortured blues phrasing, which is perfectly in keeping with his lyrics of betrayal and cheating. Wonder's character's "baby" has left him alone, and he becomes increasingly suspicious that she is cheating on him. One of the masterful touches of Wonder's performance and production can be found in his background vocals, which sound just like a female backing chorus due to the tessitura (or predominant range) of Wonder's voice and the way in which his voice is processed in the studio. This treatment adds to the Sly & the Family Stone sound of the track. Ultimately, "Maybe Your Baby" is one of the least substantial songs on *Talking Book*, despite the fact that it is the longest, clocking in at nearly seven minutes—most of it is a funk workout.

"You and I (We Can Conquer the World)" follows "Maybe Your Baby," and therein lies part of the problem with *Talking Book* as what at first appears to be a concept album. The album revolves so fully around love relationships in their various stages—the exuberance of new love, developing plans for a life together, coming to grips with the relationship falling apart, and anticipating that maybe the next relationship will be with "the one." However, the logical progression that one might typically experience in real life is broken by the order of the songs. The illogical progression of "You Are the Sunshine of My Life," "Maybe Your Baby," and then "You and I," which essentially is a song of thanks for a beautiful past and an expression of hope for a beautiful future, exposes the fact that *Talking Book* is not really a concept album at all. Maybe it is in part, but it is more a collection of individual songs, most of which revolve around a common general theme. There really is no other way to explain the sentiments of thanks and an only slightly muted hope immediately following the suspicion of "Maybe Your Baby." In this respect, *Talking Book* contrasts sharply with Wonder's next album, *Innervisions*, which would be the closest collection Stevie Wonder would produce to a fully integrated concept album.

But, let us return to "You and I (We Can Conquer the World)." With both words and music by Wonder, this song exposes him as a student of Tin Pan Alley pop song classics of the jazz era. Wonder's lyrics find him telling his lover that "God has made us fall in love," and that although she "may not be here forever to see" him through, she currently is and has been the source of his strength. Wonder's character also tells his beloved that no matter what the future may hold, he hopes that he has shown her "a brighter day." Perhaps they are not the most profound lyrics ever written, but they are an open expression of pure love, thanks, and hope, tempered by a nod to the fact that people really do not know exactly what the future will hold. Wonder's lyrics are fully in keeping with the American pop songwriting tradition.

Several features of Stevie Wonder's music for "You and I" stand out. The dated synthesizer figures notwithstanding, Wonder's music uses and expands upon short, easily identifiable melodic motives that are supported by lush harmonies and chromatic harmonic shifts suggested both by jazz standards and gospel music. The song starts out with an AABA structure (two verses, chorus, another verse). This is followed by an extended statement of the chorus in which Wonder reaches into the upper part of his vocal range for the lines, "You and I, You and I, In my mind we can conquer the world."

Although the use of what were high-tech synthesizers in 1972 help Wonder make "You and I" a song that, at the time, sounded both contemporary and connected to the past, his use of the instruments makes the song sound dated in the twenty-first century: they sound overly machinelike and relatively void of nuance compared with today's electronic musical instruments. In this regard, it is especially enlightening to compare "You and I" with the slow, standard-styled ballad on *Innervisions,* "All in Love Is Fair." Less than a year after *Talking Book,* Wonder would incorporate synthesizer timbres that more closely resembled acoustic instruments and would, as an arranger and producer, focus on acoustic instruments such as the piano. When all is said and done, however, the composition "You and I" is a very positive one in Wonder's development as a singer-songwriter, especially in the way in which Wonder the singer exhibits his growing maturity as a ballad singer.

"Tuesday Heartbreak," with its David Sanborn saxophone obbligato (solo figures played behind the vocals), chromaticism, and use of major-seventh chords, also suggests a connection to jazz standards. The kind of harmonic sophistication of songs like this and "You Are the Sunshine of My Life" is one of *Talking Book*'s features that distinguished it from just about everything else that was around in the pop and R&B music of 1972. That being said, "Tuesday Heartbreak" is a curious song in the lyrics-musical setting department. Wonder expresses his feeling that "Tuesday heartbreaks" are "unfair" and a "drag," but most of the lyrics deal with how he wants to be with the one who (presumably) caused the Tuesday heartbreak. The quick tempo, the emphasis on major chords, the happy-sounding Sanborn sax obbligato and female background chorus—actually Shirley Brewer and Denise Williams overdubbed—give the listener the impression that the last thing on Wonder's mind is the heartbreak. The overall effect is a suspension of reality because of the lyrical-musical conflict, and it relegates "Tuesday Heartbreak" to the unfortunate category of album filler. It is pleasant enough, but not particularly memorable.

Wonder and Yvonne Wright's "You've Got It Bad Girl" follows "Tuesday Heartbreak." This song espouses the general theme of love. In this case,

Wonder's character tells his lover—or rather, his potential lover—the fact that she is so resistant to him indicates that she has it bad (for him, colloquially). Ultimately, he tells her that when she allows herself to feel his love, then she will have it good. The music continues the jazz connection felt in "You and I," and "Tuesday Heartbreak," and "You Are the Sunshine of My Life," and which will return at the end of the album. Wonder's electric piano and synthesizer here sound more like a big band orchestration. The timbres he uses, as well as the pitch bends he incorporates into the obbligato solo lines, resemble traditional instruments more so than the way in which he used the synthesizers in "You and I." In fact, his "synthestration" could easily be converted to the instrumentation of a jazz band. Although it would seem like a natural fit, the song was not picked up en masse by jazz band arrangers: it simply did not have a strong enough melodic hook to generate much interest in cover versions. In fact, all the other overtly jazz-oriented material on *Talking Book* pales somewhat in comparison to "You Are the Sunshine of My Life."

One of the more interesting features of "You've Got It Bad Girl" can be found in Wonder's drum set work. Although he places the drums somewhat back in the mix, Wonder's playing shows his command of jazz rhythmic vocabulary. His drum playing on both *Talking Book* and *Innervisions,* in general, shows Wonder to be much more than a time keeper. On "You've Got It Bad Girl," the fills show his inventiveness: he never gets caught in the trap of repeating fill patterns, much the way his early 1970s keyboard playing might use riffs, but ever slightly varying riffs.

The second side of *Talking Book* in its original 33–1/3 rpm vinyl form kicks off with the album's other (besides "You Are the Sunshine of My Life") megahit: "Superstition." The song finds Wonder in nearly the ideal musical mix: him playing keyboards, synthesizers, and drums, accompanied by a horn section. Wonder the lyricist deals with the problems that various unsubstantiated superstitions can cause in one's life. In this regard, the song can be considered one of Wonder's early 1970s religious statements; however, unlike songs such as "Higher Ground" and "Jesus Children of America," which would appear within a year, here Wonder does not so much deal with what he believes, as he exposes what he sees as the false beliefs around him. Wonder the composer uses an E-flat minor pentatonic clavinet riff as the basis of the song. The compositional genius of the song, however, lies in the way in which he sets up the chromatic shifts that take place on the line, "When you believe in things that you don't understand, then you suffer," by studiously avoiding chromaticism in the E-flat minor pentatonic material up to that point. It makes that particular line, which sums up the overall theme of the song's text, stand out sharply. And speaking of the E-flat minor pentatonic melodic material and clavinet riff, it is worth noting that Wonder used the same key for his next religious funk piece, "Higher Ground," on *Innervisions.*

"Superstition" is also an important milestone in Stevie Wonder's development as an instrumentalist. Yes, the multitracked clavinet parts are among

the funkiest recorded keyboard parts of the early 1970s, but the real development here is in the total package and in the drum playing. Although Wonder
as record producer placed the drums farther back in the mix than he would
on the forthcoming *Innervisions* album, *Talking Book,* and "Superstition" in
particular, show his inventiveness as a percussionist. Wonder would most fully
expose this talent on *Innervisions*. Even in "Superstition," though, one can
hear the work of an influential percussionist: Stevie Wonder's drumming on
this track hints at some of the double-time rhythms that would later define
hip-hop. Although his synthesizer bass sounds so unlike what a "real" bass
player would perform that Wonder doesn't quite achieve the Wonder-as-
total-band sound he would perfect the following year, he was well on his way
in "Superstition" to creating a convincing ensemble sound. In fact, on *Talking Book,* Wonder already achieved a more realistic sound as a one-man band
than Paul McCartney or John Fogerty—two prominent rock musicians who
tried to do the same thing to varying degrees—ever did.

"Big Brother" is the sole overtly political song on *Talking Book.* It is a curious mix. Wonder the lyricist takes on politicians who come into the 'hood,
promising the world, only to have the people of the 'hood/ghetto disappear
from their minds (and their legislative work) until the next election cycle rolls
around. Wonder the record producer takes the step of using an immediate
segue from "Superstition" into "Big Brother." He is able to accomplish this
because the well-known clavinet riff from the former song very closely resembles the synthesized imitation of a finger-picked electric guitar that forms the
basis of the accompaniment in "Big Brother." By linking the songs in this
way musically, Wonder links the themes of unfounded beliefs in superstitions
with beliefs in politicians who can be counted on just about as much as a
lucky rabbit's foot.

"Big Brother" resembles an updated version of the down-home rural blues
of the early twentieth century, particularly in the faux finger picking and
Wonder's ongoing bluesy harmonica obbligato. In fact, Wonder probably
bends more pitches in this harmonica solo than he did in the rest of his
recorded harmonica output combined. It is completely out of character for
Stevie Wonder, insofar as it is the most rural blues–sounding piece he ever
wrote and recorded, but "Big Brother" is a powerful statement when viewed
as a music-and-lyrics whole. Simply because it is such a stylistic change of
pace, the song stands out dramatically. Even though his later "You Haven't
Done Nothin'" is much better known, "Big Brother" is also a very effective politically motivated song. And this is an important song in the Stevie
Wonder canon in that it takes him out of the strictly defined world of the
apolitical pop musician, and places him into the world of the social and political activist for the first time in his songwriting career. After *Talking Book,*
every subsequent Stevie Wonder album except for *The Woman in Red* would
contain at least one potent song of social and/or political commentary. The
political and social commentary of these songs was enhanced by the fact that

Stevie Wonder was by this point a well-established musician of wide popular appeal: he was not some new, unproven, radical politico with a small core of followers. Because of this, he was able to carry his messages to a wider range of people than most songwriters: this is the real social significance of Wonder's embracing of political and social causes.

The theme of love in its various stages, anticipated, lost, etc., is explored to great effect in the final three songs on *Talking Book*. Significantly, "Blame It On the Sun" and "Lookin' for Another Pure Love" both have lyrics by Syreeta Wright, whose marriage to Wonder was crumbling around this time. In "Blame It On the Sun," Wright deals with the responsibility for lost love, ultimately deciding that instead of blaming the failure of the relationship on one person or the other, or on a particular event, she (as writer)/Wonder (as performer) will "blame it on the sun." She uses the sun as a metaphor for fate. "Lookin' for Another Pure Love" finds Wright (as lyricist)/Wonder (as singer) declaring that after a failed relationship, the singer's character is now looking for another love. Yvonne Wright's lyrics for "I Believe (When I Fall in Love It Will Be Forever)" speaks of hope that the new lover the singer has found will be "the woman I've been waiting for," the one who will be his love forever. Wonder's musical setting of the lyrics reinforces the hopefulness. The three songs form a sort of minisuite to conclude the album. Although none of the individual songs is as memorable as "You Are the Sunshine of My Life," the three work together in thematic harmony much better than the first five songs on *Talking Book*—the entire first side of the vinyl release—which seem to jump around aspects of a love relationship almost randomly. Although "Blame It On the Sun," "Lookin' for Another Pure Love," and "I Believe" work best when listened to as a minisuite, let us examine some of the various aspects of the individual songs.

"Blame It On the Sun" differs fundamentally from the album's earlier ballad "You and I (We Can Conquer the World)" in that it is not really jazz-oriented. There are small hints at black gospel music, especially in the organlike keyboard timbres Wonder uses, as well as in some of the piano fills he plays at the ends of a few of the phrases. All in all, however, it is purely a pop ballad, and it is fairly short and understated—all of which is right in keeping with Syreeta Wright's text of loss of love.

"Blame It On the Sun" makes a direct segue into "Lookin' for Another Pure Love," a song that suggests the moderate tempo, pop jazz of singer-guitarist George Benson and other related artists who enjoyed a run of popularity on Creed Taylor's CTI Records in the 1970s and 1980s. This expression of hope for a new relationship—one that will (hopefully, this time ...) stand the test of time—is enhanced by jazz-based lead guitar parts played by Jeff Beck and Buzzy Feton.[12] Wonder's melody is heavily syncopated, which also plays into the optimistic feel of the song. The tune generally has a consistent rise and fall without a strong hook such as in "You Are the Sunshine of My Life." The shifting harmonies unfold leisurely rather than offer a clear direction toward a cadence, which creates a feeling of meandering. As a mood piece within the minilove suite at the end of the album, it works; however, "Lookin' for Another Pure Love" is not one of Wonder's strongest or most memorable compositions.

Stevie Wonder's music for "I Believe (When I Fall in Love It Will Be Forever)" calls to mind some of the popular, massive, anthem rock ballads of the 1960s through the 1980s: the Beatles' 1968 "Hey Jude," Chicago's 1974 "(I've Been) Searchin' So Long," Prince's famous 1983 live recording of "Purple Rain," and Foreigner's "I Want to Know What Love Is," a huge 1984 hit. The comparison comes naturally because of the enormity of the sound and production in the song's fade out, as well as the song's strong, memorable hook. This chorus hook stands in sharp contrast stylistically to the verses, and in fact, tends to overshadow them. In part, it is because of this imbalance that "I Believe (When I Fall in Love It Will Be Forever)" does not achieve the level of greatness of the aforementioned songs by others, although in some respects it's at least in the same ballpark. And this despite the fact that it was not released as a single. It was an album track, but in no way should it be considered mere filler material.

Talking Book's two best-known songs, "You Are the Sunshine of My Life" and "Superstition," were released as highly successful singles. These songs present a sharp contrast in Wonder's output of the period in terms of what I will call (for want of a better term) *standardness*. Although both songs were highly successful as singles and received significant amounts of radio airplay, "You Are the Sunshine of My Life," with its jazz-oriented harmonies and light, airy arrangement, almost immediately achieved standard status, while the funky "Superstition" did not. The reason for this, in part, may be that "Superstition," the song, was so closely linked with "Superstition," the recording.

Wonder's use of synthesizers, his distinctive jazzy funk drumming,[13] in particular, too fully defined the sound of "Superstition": a different arrangement just would not work, and copying Wonder's arrangement undoubtedly would seem too much like plagiarism. There is support for this view in the 2003 Motown album *Conception: An Interpretation of Stevie Wonder's Songs*. In this collection, which includes contributions from Eric Clapton ("Higher Ground"), Glenn Lewis ("Superstition"), Mary J. Blige ("Overjoyed"), and others, the out-and-out funk numbers such as "Higher Ground" and "Superstition," songs that might most logically lend themselves to more improvisation than the ballads, are presented in arrangements that closely resemble Wonder's original versions. The casual listener might not find anything out of the ordinary in this, but I find it significant. It points out the extent to which a song like "Superstition" is not just a lead sheet-format "song," a collection of melody and chords open to interpretation, but is instead a fully realized studio composition. The arrangement and instrumental performance—not to mention the use of vocables—is simply too distinctive for a remake to

achieve quite the same effect. This stands as a testament to Wonder's significance as a multi-instrumentalist, arranger, and singer as much as it speaks to
his significance as a writer of songs.

Of course, another factor that contributes to the standard nature of "You
Are the Sunshine of My Life" is the fact that the subject matter of the song
is so much brighter (no pun intended)—and therefore has more commercial
appeal—than Wonder's warnings against living one's life based on unsubstantiated superstitions.

The record-buying public loved *Talking Book* and the singles it spawned.
The album itself reached No. 1 on the *Billboard* R&B charts and No. 3
on the magazine's pop charts—the first time Wonder had hit No. 1 on the
R&B album charts, and the first time since 1963 he had reached the top 10
on the pop album charts. "Superstition" hit No. 1 on both the *Billboard*
R&B and pop charts. Because of its style, it is probably no surprise that "You
Are the Sunshine of My Life" was more successful on the pop charts (No. 1)
than on R&B charts (No. 3). The album's success and the singles' success are
interesting in light of the relative quiet with which the record-buying public
had greeted Stevie Wonder's *Music of My Mind* of only half a year before.
Music of My Mind only works lyrically if the listener keeps shifting from Stevie
persona No. 1 to Stevie persona No. 2, etc., while the lyrics of the songs on
Talking Book could all be coming from the same character at different points
along a relationship's timeline. The more commercial nature of the music of
Talking Book, combined with a greater consistency of literary voice, broad-
ened Wonder's appeal on this album.

INNERVISIONS

The 1973 album *Innervisions* was a far more cohesive package than *Talking Book.* The theme of the album, apparent from its title, was that of Stevie
Wonder as a kind of visionary who looks at societal problems in contemporary America and proposes solutions to those problems. Visual metaphors
abound, thereby linking all the songs. Even though there is still stylistic
eclecticism, from the synthesizer-driven funk of "Higher Ground" and "Living for the City" to the acoustically accompanied ballad style of "All in Love
Is Fair," Wonder uses instrumental panning (sometimes in the keyboards
and sometimes in the drums and percussion), with his solo voice front and
center, to achieve a more consistent production style. Also notable is the
fact that, unlike *Talking Book, Innervisions* featured only lyrics by Wonder,
perhaps another reason that the latter package achieves more of a concept-
album level of cohesion. With its unifying themes, which deal with social
problems of the early 1970s, *Innervisions* seems to have been influenced by
Marvin Gaye's *What's Going On.* More than just exhibiting influences from
the 1971 Gaye concept album, however, Wonder's *Innervisions* is a most
worthy successor.

The album begins with "Too High," a jazz-oriented number that tells the story of a woman who eases the pain of having failed to make it big, despite having had the chance to do so "once or twice," through drugs. In the end, she succumbs to the drugs, passing away. Instrumentally, the track highlights Wonder's harmonica playing with a polyphonic pair of independent solos that finally come together in unison at the end of the stanza. Wonder also provides some tasty jazz-inspired drum set. In fact, Wonder's virtuosity as a drummer provides continuity between all of the faster-paced songs on *Innervisions*. Unlike some studio drummers, and certainly in sharp contrast to the drum machines Wonder used in the 1980s, Stevie Wonder the *Innervisions* drummer takes a jazz musician's approach to percussion, avoiding time keeping and focusing on continual development and variation. And if one compares *Innervisions* with its two immediate predecessors, 1972's *Talking Book* and *Music of My Mind,* one can hear that Wonder the record producer places the drums increasingly more prominently in the mix. Among his albums, *Innervisions* was Stevie Wonder's greatest achievement as a drummer.[14] Wonder did record his own drum parts on subsequent albums—although he did use other drummers just as frequently—however, in keeping with later R&B styles, including disco and hip-hop, his drum playing lost some of its jazzy improvisation after *Innervisions*. Wonder would reiterate the antidrug message of "Too High" later in his career from time to time, this becoming one of his social causes.

The album's second song, "Visions," articulates the overarching theme of *Innervisions.* Using a slow tempo and accompanied by Malcolm Cecil's bass, Dean Parks's acoustic guitar, and David "T" Walker's impressionistic and fluttering electric guitar—an exceptionally rare emphasis on traditional pop music stringed instruments in a Stevie Wonder song—Wonder presents a utopian view of the world, asking if a world of universal understanding and love is reality or "just a vision in my mind." Wonder's mental vision of utopia in the song is heartfelt and never comes close to the naïve sappiness some critics have claimed to find in his work from the 1980s.[15] The dreamlike nature of the piece is supported by both the impressionistic soundscape provided by the guest instrumentalists and the understated vocal line. "Visions," in fact, finds Wonder singing in the lower part of his range far more than virtually any other song he has composed for himself and recorded. This is worth noting as Wonder frequently uses melodic extensions into his upper register at points of dramatic tension or for emotional effect. That he does so very little in "Visions," and then only in the chorus, helps to reinforce the dreamlike, mental-vision nature of the text. Wonder also makes use of space in "Visions" in a way rarely used in contemporary pop or R&B music of the day: by incorporating extended silences.

Like other Wonder albums from the first half of the 1970s, *Innervisions* spawned several highly successful singles. "Living for the City," which hit No. 8 on the *Billboard* pop charts and No. 1 on the *Billboard* R&B charts, was one such *Innervision* spin off. The track, more than 7 minutes long in its album version, might at first seem to be a song of limited commercial appeal: it documents the birth and early life of a poor black man from "hard town Mississippi," and the unfortunate events that transpire when he makes his way to New York City after becoming an adult. The themes of economic deprivation, the harshness of urban ghetto life, and personal and institutional racism—the *audio vérité* spoken drama in the middle of the composition finds a white-sounding police officer addressing the main character as "nigger"—as well as the heavy four-beat funk style of the music (as opposed to the typical emphasis on beats two and four of much Motown product), might help to explain the single's relatively greater success on the R&B charts, which emphasized sales among African Americans as opposed to a broader cross section of American record buyers.

Getting into more of the detail of the composition and Wonder's performance of it—he sings all of the vocal lines and plays all the instruments on "Living for the City"—reveals a richness that goes beyond most of the popular hits of 1973. Wonder sets up the protagonist's story in a fairly conventional way: the first stanza places his birth in "hard town Mississippi" and establishes that his parents are trying to bring him up on the straight and narrow path. The second stanza further establishes the themes of poverty and righteous living by describing the low incomes the protagonist's father and mother earn from their respective jobs—he as a laborer who works "some days for fourteen hours," and she as a domestic who "goes to scrub the floors for many."

It is the third stanza that exposes Stevie Wonder the lyricist as a wordsmith who can go beyond the naiveté of which music critics frequently accuse him. Here, Wonder focuses on the protagonist's sister. When Wonder sings that, "Her clothes are old, but never are they dirty," he clearly gets at the sense of pride that survives in the young woman, in spite of her poverty.

Metrically, too, "Living in the City" is actually more complex and sophisticated than it might at first appear. For, even though the verses feature the heavy four-beat feel of funk (and hint at the disco that was to overtake American popular music in a few years), the instrumental, fanfarelike sections in the piece move smoothly into triple meter. Wonder handles the move into the decidedly not funk triple meter of the waltz so seamlessly that it seems entirely right and appropriate in the composition.

Even with the bleak picture of what ultimately has happened to the one who was "born in hard town Mississippi" at the start of the song (he is homeless, unkempt, and spends his time walking the streets of New York City by the fifth stanza), supported by Wonder's gritty, Satchmo-*cum*-Miles Davis voice near the end of the song, "Living for the City" is not ultimately a song of desperation: it is a song of warning. This is in keeping with the visionary theme of the entire album. Wonder concludes the song by singing, "If we don't change the world will soon be over ... stop giving just enough for the city." The text allows that it is still possible to change the situation, in a way suggesting that throughout the song Wonder is playing the role of the Ghosts of Christmas Past, Present, and Future in a late-twentieth-century American musical adaptation of Charles Dickens's *A Christmas Carol*. But, it is not the glimmer of possibility supplied by the text alone that turns "Living for the City" into a song of hope; this feeling is supported by the counterpoint between a multitracked Stevie Wonder choir (he sings all the backing vocals) and fanfarelike synthesizer lines that emerge near the end of the song. Although more than 30 years after Wonder recorded the song, the synthesizer fanfares sound a bit dated and uncomfortably reminiscent of Disney World and Disneyland's "Electric Parade," they manage to retain their effectiveness even though sound-synthesis technology has evolved so much in the intervening years.

Although "Living for the City" might not be as well remembered in the twenty-first century as some of Stevie Wonder's other recordings from the period (despite the song's popularity at the time of its release), Wonder's vocal stylings on the song and his record production style on the recording have been highly influential. In particular, Wonder's close vocal microphone placement and his use of gasps, breaths, and vocables—in short, his use of the voice as a percussion instrument—found its way into Michael Jackson's work of a decade later, especially on the "King of Pop's" 1982 song "Billie Jean." Wonder had hinted at this technique earlier in the song "Signed, Sealed, Delivered (I'm Yours)," which he also produced. Because this close-vocal-microphone recording style is not found nearly to this degree in Wonder's recordings with other producers, the presence of this technique in Wonder's work as a producer, and his exploitation of the close miking in his singing technique, seems to be quite deliberate. It should also be noted that many of Prince's self-produced recordings find him exploiting the same techniques.

"Golden Lady," a fast jazz-influenced love song follows "Living for the City." It is too good a song to relegate to the category of filler, but "Golden Lady" is the closest thing to pop filler on *Innervisions*. The song's one obvious connection to the album's overarching theme is found in the visual references that begin the track. "Golden Lady" was never issued on a single, and it is not necessarily the best-known *Innervisions* album cut to the average listener, but the song has remained a favorite of some Wonder fans and has thus found its way onto some of the turn-of-the-millennium compact disc reissues of Wonder's best twentieth-century recordings. The relatively straightforward theme of love and the pop-flavored melody probably account for the fact that "Golden Lady" has been covered by a number of artists. The fact that Wonder's arrangement of the song could be easily adapted into several other pop and jazz-related styles probably also contributed to the relatively large number of cover versions. Wonder himself has kept this song in his repertoire and performed it at the spring 2005 Tiger Jam, a charity concert that raised money for the Tiger Woods Foundation.

Innervision's middle tracks establish religion as an important secondary theme, which provides something of a carryover from the *Talking Book* track "Superstition." The well-known "Higher Ground," which, when issued as a single, hit No. 4 on the *Billboard* pop charts and No. 1 on the R&B charts, is the first of these religious songs.

Here, we find Wonder evoking the ideas of reincarnation found in Hinduism. Wonder implores a variety of people, including "teachers," "powers," "believers," "sleepers," and others to keep on doing what it is that they do, as he keeps on trying until he reaches the "highest ground," a metaphor for the Nirvana of the eastern religion. His message to others seems to be that they should continue to do all the diverse things that they do because they are called to do so. Besides, Wonder suggests that it "won't be too long" until the next step in the voyage takes place: perhaps one will reach the higher ground, or perhaps one will be reincarnated to take the journey on the path toward spiritual enlightenment once again.

Not only did the religious references of "Superstition" carry over into "Higher Ground," so did the funkiness and the instrumental emphasis on the sound of the clavinet. One of the major sonic differences between the two songs, however, is in the way in which Wonder the record producer places the drums as much up front in the audio mix as the vocals and keyboards. This allows Wonder's inventiveness as a drummer to shine forth in "Higher Ground."

Another interesting similarity between "Superstition" and "Higher Ground" is the shared tonal center of E-flat. Indeed, the keys of E-flat major and minor, and the use of references to the E-flat blues scale, lend themselves to Wonder's voice, particularly when he wants to sing in the high register. Incidentally, other keyboard-based funky pieces of the period find Wonder using other tonal centers. "Jesus Children of America," for example, revolves around A-flat. The song has the same sort of blues-based keyboard licks as "Higher Ground" and the earlier "Superstition," but in "Jesus Children of America," Wonder makes liberal and very calculated use of the lower tessitura of his voice in the lead vocal line—this simply would not be possible with a tonal center like E-flat. Wonder seems to be drawn to flat keys more than most pop songwriters. I believe that this is directly attributable to his work as an instrumentalist, and particularly as a keyboard player. Pop musicians who are primarily guitarists tend to be drawn to the so-called sharp keys because of the regular tuning of the open strings of the guitar—sharp keys sound better in tune and generally are more suitable for guitar technique. As an unsighted keyboard player, Wonder may have found that the black keys of the piano/synthesizer keyboard provide a more reliable tactile reference point than do the white keys. As a result, keys such as A-flat, D-flat, and E-flat logically would be more suitable to Wonder's keyboard technique. Seemingly not coincidentally, they are more highly represented in his keyboard-focused works than sharp keys.

"Higher Ground," which is performed completely by Wonder himself, succeeds instrumentally in several important respects. For one thing, despite the heavy four-on-the-floor bass drum in Wonder's drum set playing, as mentioned earlier, his drum work is thoroughly inventive—a sort of perpetual variation—and as such it is perfectly matched to his keyboard work on the recording. In this respect, "Higher Ground" remains one of his greatest recorded performances as a funk drummer. Likewise, Wonder's several synthesizer lines evoke inventive rhythm guitar, funk keyboard, and improvised-sounding pseudoelectric bass lines. One of the dangers inherent in Wonder's I'm-the-whole-band approach is the potential for the music to sound unintentionally mechanical. Somehow, however, he managed in up-tempo, funky pieces such as "Higher Ground" to avoid any hint of a mechanical sound, due in large part to his use of improvisation in all of the instrumental and vocal parts.

One of the curious things about "Higher Ground" is that the principal riff of the piece (E-flat, G-flat, A-flat, E-flat) closely resembles the riff upon which the late 1960s rock classic "On the Road Again" by the band Canned Heat is based. This riff comes up in other blues-oriented songs as well: it certainly is not unique to Canned Heat and Stevie Wonder. Although its fairly common occurrence in this blues-based type of repertoire could make the figure's presence in "Higher Ground" sound like a cliché, Wonder uses a distinctive enough touch in the pedal-enhanced clavinet parts that his composition transcends blues-lick cliché.

Innervision's specifically religious (as opposed to spiritual) subtheme continues in the album's next track: "Jesus Children of America." The lyrical focus of the song is on the saving power of Jesus of Nazareth, despite some references in the text to Transcendental Meditation, which according to Wonder, "gives you peace of mind." Wonder specifically addresses the need that the junkie has for saving his soul by turning away from the needle and to Jesus. This represents yet another carryover subtheme on *Innervisions:* that of the dangers of drug abuse, which Wonder first explored on "Too High."

Stevie Wonder the singer takes on several different vocal styles in "Jesus Children of America," in particular exploring the lower tessitura of his voice. The musical arrangement includes generally darker timbres and lower-pitched instrumental accompaniment than the other songs on the album. Musically, the composition is in a somewhat gospel-influenced up-tempo groove. It is not a song that would find its way into any black church, however, because of the eclectic range of religious philosophy the song includes: Jesus of Nazareth and the Transcendental Mediation espoused by the Hindu holy man Maharishi Mahesh Yogi would be at doctrinal odds in the traditional black Christian denominations.

Wonder next turns to the style of the great American pop standards in "All in Love Is Fair." This song owes more to the torch songs of the past than to any style that was around in the early 1970s. One could imagine one of the great jazz singers of the 1940s performing this song: the message of the blamelessness of the inevitable breakup of a relationship is timeless, and Wonder's soaring melody and chromatic harmonic motion, which includes rich-sounding seventh and ninth chords, is perfectly in keeping with the very best of Tin Pan Alley. Throughout the 1970s, there were very few examples of such a devotion to recreating the spirit of the great songs of the twentieth century before rock and roll. Sure, there was the odd example, like Elvis Costello's film-noir influenced "Shot with His Own Gun" from the near end of the decade, but Stevie Wonder in "All in Love Is Fair" not only pays tribute to the past, he makes a musical statement that rivals those old torch songs in quality. Such was the jazz-standard character of the song that "All in Love Is Fair" quickly found its way into the most infamous, and widely used, jazz fake book of the 1970s and 1980s, *The Real Book*. Incidentally, the only other Stevie Wonder composition typically found in this sort of lead sheet[16] collection, designed for jazz musicians to use on small group gigs, was his instant classic "You Are the Sunshine of My Life."

Wonder's lyrics in "All in Love Is Fair" recycle cliché lines about the ending of a relationship; however, the song never sounds like just a collection of these clichés, as it is always clear that he is intentionally using them. Wonder weaves his way through the break-up clichés as he demonstrates that when one finds oneself in that situation, all the clichés really do prove true.

Wonder's performance of "All in Love Is Fair" is also notable. The prominent rock music critic Robert Christgau labeled the ballad singing of the Stevie Wonder of 1970 as "immature."[17] Here, Wonder is in 1973 singing a very mature-sounding composition in a voice that is as good as the material. As a pure, autobiographical-sounding vocal showpiece for Stevie Wonder, there is no better example.

The next track on *Innervisions,* "Don't You Worry 'bout a Thing" can easily be interpreted as a friendly farewell to Wonder's former wife Syreeta Wright, with whom he remained a friend and off-and-on again musical collaborator despite the breakup of their marriage. Wonder's lyrics find him "on the sidelines" encouraging his former lover-turned-friend to get on with her love life. The energetic Latin nature of the piece's rhythms, combined with a catchy and easily identifiable hook in the "Don't you worry 'bout at thing, pretty mama" chorus caught the attention of the record-buying public to some extent: the single release of the song went to No. 2 on the *Billboard* R&B charts, but, curiously, only No. 16 on the *Billboard* pop charts. It did, however, capture the attention of jazz musicians, as a number of artists, including big-band legend Woody Herman, issued cover recordings of "Don't You Worry 'bout a Thing." One of the more interesting features of the song is how deeply personal the events were that precipitated the song— the breakup of Wonder and Wright's marriage—yet how unbridled the song is in encouraging the former lover. It succeeds better than its less-than-stellar pop chart activity would suggest.

One of the challenges of an album like *Innervisions,* which tends to focus so heavily on themes that are anything but lightweight—religion, spirituality, drug abuse, politics, and lost love—is to achieve a sense of balance of mood. Wonder's musical eclecticism and funkiness help the album to avoid becoming overly heavy, but the way in which he constructed the introduction to "Don't You Worry 'bout a Thing" plays an important role as well. Over the instrumental introduction Wonder provides a minidrama that finds him delivering pick-up lines to a young woman. Wonder makes a segue into the song proper just as his character's lines are exposed for the jive they truly are. This touch of unexpected humor might seem not to fit the song itself, but it serves to humanize the overall album experience. It also suggests that perhaps one reason that he encourages his former lover in her new love life is because he is also actively seeking a new relationship.

Speaking of jive talking, Stevie Wonder has over the years had more than a word or two to say about what he has perceived as hypocritical politicians, both in public statements and in song lyrics. "He's Misstra Know-It-All" is one of the latter. In sharp contrast to the politician-as-crook-liar-and-hypocrite song of *Talking Book* "Big Brother," the Richard Nixon-focused "He's Misstra Know-It-All" does not include direct mention of politicians at all. Rather, the song's antihero seems on the surface as if he could be a man who is particularly adept at lying to and using women. Critics have, however, universally acknowledged the connection of this character to Nixon,[18] one particular politician of whom Wonder had nothing good to say. Not only do Wonder's lyrics take a softer, more oblique approach to the "man with a plan" than do his lyrics for "You Haven't Done Nothin'," another Nixon song, or "Big Brother," which focuses more on hypocritical local politicians, the music of "He's Misstra Know-It-All" uses the soft sell to an even greater extent. If anything, the song's music resembles that of a medium-tempo ballad. One can almost be lulled into humming along with the tune without thinking about just how shady, if not despicable, the main character is as human being, and in doing so, completely miss the use of "Misstra Know-It-All" as a metaphor for someone who to Stevie Wonder was a particularly despised politician. The harmonic voice-leading of the song is lovely, as is Wonder's arrangement, and the tune truly is catchy, especially on the line, "He's misstra know it all." As a political statement, though, it is not as effective as the funky "You Haven't Done Nothin'": the music is just too pretty sounding, and the lyrics too vague to identify the real subject of Wonder's finger pointing. If the song is understood strictly on the surface level, the prettiness of the music casts the antihero as someone who, although pretty despicable, is also someone for whom the listener can feel sorry. If taken strictly on the surface, the song seems somewhat out of place on *Innervisions.* It is probably best, then, for the listener to try to catch the metaphor and accept it as one of the hazier "visions" on the album.

Each track on *Innervisions* has its own strengths, and several rank among Stevie Wonder's best-ever compositions, productions, and performances as an instrumentalist and as a vocalist. As a thematic whole, and in consistency of production and consistency of poetic voice, however, the album is even stronger than the individual songs. It was not Wonder's most successful album on the charts—his next two albums would do better—but it remains arguably Wonder's best album, and is numbered among the top albums of the rock era by critics.[19]

Wonder's life took a dramatic turn when on August 6, 1973, on the way to a concert, the car in which he was riding was involved in a serious accident with a logging truck. Stevie Wonder sustained head injuries serious enough to cause him to lapse into a coma. Although Wonder's condition was quite serious, he recovered completely, thanks in part to the care given to him by his many friends and business associates. The oft-repeated story of Wonder's emergence from the coma is that his friend and publicist Ira Tucker was singing "Higher Ground" to the comatose Wonder when Tucker noticed that Wonder was moving his fingers in time to the song, fingering the "Higher Ground" keyboard licks on the hospital bed.[20] Some of his most commercially successful work was still to come.

The Mature Superstar, 1974–1980

The period 1974–1980 saw Stevie Wonder return after his near-fatal automobile accident to produce some of his most popular work ever. He produced the 1974 album *Fulfillingness' First Finale,* a collection that pales somewhat in Wonder's 1970s output only because of the albums that preceded and followed it. In the 1976 double album (plus an extended play bonus disc) *Songs in the Key of Life,* Wonder dealt with politics, social causes, and religion in his lyrics, and used elements of big-band jazz, funk, rock, classical music, disco, and ballads. *Songs in the Key of Life* was widely heralded as one of the most important albums of the rock era. In 1979, Wonder produced the soundtrack for a completely obscure documentary film *Journey Through the Secret Life of Plants*—a collection of mostly classically oriented instrumentals that would confound critics and fans. The period ended with the 1980 album *Hotter Than July,* which found Wonder incorporating some of the new rhythms and styles of the time and working for the creation of a national holiday to honor Dr. Martin Luther King, Jr.

FULFILLINGNESS' FIRST FINALE

Fulfillingness' First Finale marked Stevie Wonder's return after his near-fatal automobile accident. The very title of the album suggests the ending of one part of his life and the opening of a new era. The album's cover art, too, paints the collection as a wrap-up to the past: there are pictures of a younger Stevie Wonder, and pictures of his fallen heroes of the past, Rev. Dr. Martin Luther King, Jr., and John F. Kennedy. Generally, though, this is not a somber album—there is perhaps a greater sense of seriousness in some of the songs, but it is balanced by the playfulness of other tracks, such as "Boogie On Reggae Woman."

The album begins with the light Latin-jazz medium-tempo ballad "Smile Please." The lyrics of the verses speak of the smile that love will bring to one's face, while the chorus consists of "nonsense" lines, "Bum bum di ti bum bum." "Smile Please," though, is a mood piece pure and simple. The music itself suggests a nod to the popular *bossa nova* style of the early 1960s by Brazilian composer Antonio Carlos Jobim. In form, however, Wonder's piece is a standard verse, verse, chorus, verse, verse, chorus (repeated) structure, and not the long form peculiar to the true *bossa nova*.

The album's second song, "Heaven Is 10 Zillion Light Years Away," continues the theme of religion that Wonder explored in various ways on his previous albums in songs such as "Higher Ground," "Jesus Children of the World," and others. As with these earlier songs, "Heaven Is 10 Zillion Light Years Away" is one of the strongest album tracks in this collection. The lyrics find Wonder stating that his friends ask him where God is in light of the problems (he mentions racial injustice specifically) in the world. Wonder explains that it has taken God "so long [to fix the problems] because we've got so far to come." In other words, it is humankind's duty to reach to God to effect positive change. Despite the fact that "his color Black" makes him "a lesser man" in the eyes of some, Wonder sees God's spirit alive all around him. The moving gospel-oriented chorus, which features the vocal talents of Paul Anka, Syreeta Wright, Shirley Brewer, and Larry "Nastyee" Latimer, repeats the idea, "Feel it, you can feel His spirit."

Wonder the composer comes to the fore, however, in "Heaven Is 10 Zillion Light Years Away." Considering the restrictions under which he cut his teeth as a composer—2–1/2-minute songs in the Motown mold—works such as this one are important to note. Here, Wonder begins by using a very standard four-bar phrase structure and a simple chord progression in the key of G-flat major, consisting of tonic (a chord built on the first scale degree), submediant (a chord built on the sixth scale degree), supertonic (a chord built on the second scale degree), and dominant (a chord built on the fifth scale degree), which sounds at first listening as though it will simply repeat for each stanza. As Wonder enumerates the criticisms of God and religion that he hears from those around him, he uses some daring harmonic motion while extending the musical phrases. So unexpected is this that it fully pulls the listener into putting his or her full attention on the song. Ultimately, this provides a satisfying sense of completion with the coming of the symmetrically structured chorus with its affirmation that God does provide the answers, provided that humans make the effort to find Him. The first several times I listened to the song with a writer's (as opposed to a fan's) focus, I found the harmonic daring and the phrase extensions to be awkward; however, with subsequent hearings and after the initial shock, I have come to rank the song as among Wonder's finest compositions.

"Heaven Is 10 Zillion Light Years Away" unfolds too slowly, is too spiritually focused, and requires that the listener pay too much attention to ever have made it as a successful single. Therefore, it is not as well known to the general public as it should be. Not only is it among the best of Wonder's spiritual songs, but it is also among the best in his entire output.

The next song on the album, "Too Shy to Say," develops motivically like some of the best compositions of the Tin Pan Alley tradition. Wonder takes short musical motives (easily identifiable melodic fragments) and expands them and repeats them starting on different pitch levels to build the complete melody. Unlike the earlier "All in Love Is Fair," however, it just doesn't have "instant classic" stamped on it. Part of the problem is that Wonder had become increasing self-assured in his lyrics, doing such things as tackling difficult social issues with a voice of increasing authority. "Too Shy to Say" is too much of a stretch as a character piece: no matter how hard Stevie Wonder tried to develop the character singing the song, he did not come across as a man who was "too shy to say I love you" at this point in his career. It is not a bad song by any means. The problem is that Wonder's best ballads have a sense of autobiographical believability, regardless of whether or not they are truly autobiographical. For this reason, in that it is probably better suited to another performer, this is a rare Stevie Wonder composition of this time period.

The album's next track, "Boogie On Reggae Woman," however, is a classic Stevie Wonder composition, performance, and production. Although this one has no inherent autobiographical connection, it succeeds, but then, it is certainly not a ballad either. As the song stylist/aural actor, Wonder has always been more successful at developing non-Stevie characters in his uptempo songs than in his ballads. Despite the song's title, it bears only slight musical resemblance to genuine reggae. Sure, Wonder includes the easily recognizable rhythm guitar–like[1] accentuations on beats two and four, but the tempo is way too fast for Bob Marley–style reggae (and it's even a little quick for the Jimmy Smith style); further, the gospel-inspired piano licks that Wonder plays bring to mind the black church more than a reggae bar somewhere in Jamaica. In fact, these short piano solos are one of the best features of what is an excellent piece. Too often, the full extent of Wonder's keyboard talents is hidden by his use of electronic instruments. The synthesizers he was using in his early 1970s recordings lack the expressive touch of the acoustic piano. His dynamic shadings and sense of phrasing come through more on the short piano solos from "Boogie On Reggae Woman" than on anything he ever recorded on synthesizer.

Wonder's lyrics are a playful nod to some of the sexually suggestive lyrics of reggae masters such as Bob Marley. In the first stanza, Wonder acknowledges that he likes "to do it to" the woman to whom he is singing until she hollers for more. The beginning of the stanza clearly refers to watching the woman dance, but the end of the stanza leaves the meaning of "it" up in the air. The sexual suggestiveness continues in the second stanza. When Wonder repeats the line, "I'd like to see you under the stars above," he inserts the phrase "in the raw" almost under his breath after singing, "I'd like to see you…" In contrast to the sometimes-explicit sexuality of some of Marley's songs, Wonder's line, "I'd like to see you (in the raw) under the stars above," takes on the air of sly mischievousness, almost a schoolboy naughtiness. If anything, it paints Wonder's character as a sort of innocent who is trying to get away with a slightly wicked reference to nudity. He seems very much to be doing a Bob Marley impression, from affecting a Jamaican accent to adopting the slurred style of delivery of some of Marley's recordings.

If "Boogie On Reggae Woman" had not been such a commercial success as a single—in the top five of both the pop and R&B charts—the track could easily be taken as a noncommercially oriented example of Wonder at play in the studio. He seems to be having way too much fun, from imitating the sexual suggestiveness of Bob Marley (as well as the reggae great's accent/idiosyncratic Jamaican pronunciation in the choruses), to the gospel-influenced piano, to the way in which Stevie the harmonica soloist verbally communicates with the Stevie band (he plays all the instruments on the track), asking "Can I play it" as he begins the solo, giving the impression that he's not altogether sure if this is his chorus to play. Even the song's introduction extends the opening riff for more repetitions than usual if one were consciously trying to produce the most commercially viable single possible. Ultimately, "Boogie On Reggae Woman" is perfectly balanced in every way, as a composition, and as an instrumental and vocal performance and record production. The recording shouts—in an intimate, playful way—to anyone who wondered about Stevie Wonder's health after he had been in a coma, "Yeah, I'm back!" But the effect is not that Wonder is deliberately making such a statement. "Boogie On Reggae Woman" sounds more like the listener caught Stevie Wonder at play in the studio with all his musical facilities intact, almost as though he had never had any intention of releasing this as a record. Even though this is not the case, he is absolutely convincing. As a recording in which the lyrics, music, arrangement, performance, and production align so perfectly (and coming at the point in Wonder's life during which it was recorded), it is one of Wonder's greatest achievements.

"Creepin'," a song that has been covered by several jazz artists, including saxophonist Stanley Turrentine, finds Wonder telling a fantasy lover that every night she creeps into his dreams, and wondering if he creeps into hers. The rich harmonies of the piece do not resolve in the expected way, which lends a dreamlike feel to the song, thereby supporting the theme of the lyrics. Although it seems like a minor detail because it takes such a short time, Wonder's use of metric modulation—*a la* twentieth-century American art music composer Elliott Carter—in the brief percussion transition from the introduction to the first stanza is a nice, although unexpected, touch. Minnie Riperton, who had been a member of Wonder's live backing band, joins Wonder on the vocals. Unfortunately, the arrangement does not make full use of the unique qualities of her voice (which are heard to great effect on her 1975 No. 1 hit "Loving You").

"You Haven't Done Nothin'," the one overtly politically motivated song on *Fulfillingness' First Finale*, immediately follows "Creepin'." Wonder enlists the aid of fellow Motown artists the Jackson 5 for backing vocals, as well as electric bass player Reggie McBride for this piece, which is another example of a Stevie Wonder keyboard-based funk piece in the key of E-flat. In sharp contrast to Wonder's fairly anonymous use of Minnie Riperton on "Creepin'," McBride and the brothers Jackson are essential components of "You Haven't Done Nothin'." One of the minor faults of Stevie Wonder's funky recordings of the 1971–1973 period was that his use of a synthesizer to play the bass line often seemed to come up a little bit short on the side of power. This can easily be heard by comparing his funkier recordings ("Super-stition" and "Higher Ground," to name two) with contemporary works by other funk-oriented artists such as James Brown, George Clinton, and Sly Stone. The synthesizer bass tended to be more amorphous on its attacks than an electric bass guitar. Booking a musician such as Reggie McBride solved the problem on "You Haven't Done Nothin'." Michael, Tito, Jermaine, Marlon, and Jackie Jackson sing modified doo-wop vocal harmonies. Wonder had great success on recordings on which he sang all the vocal parts (his work on "Living for the City" near the end of the song is stellar, for example); however, the Jackson 5 provide a greater vocal richness and depth (and lower range) than an overdubbed chorus of Stevie Wonders could. The track is a clear demonstration of the extent to which Wonder had—at the ripe old age of 24—matured as an arranger and producer.

Wonder's lyrics for "You Haven't Done Nothin'" resemble those of the earlier song "Big Brother," except that instead of taking on all politicians who promise the world to the downtrodden of the ghetto and provide noth-ing, here Wonder takes on one politician. Although not named, given the his-torical context, the song seems to be directed squarely at President Richard Nixon. The heavy, moderately slow-paced funk of the instrumental tracks, combined with the vocal depth of the Jackson brothers and the urgent-sounding lead vocal melody with its expressive upward leaps, heightens this indictment of Nixon.

When issued as a single, the song was paired with "Big Brother," creat-ing a doubly powerful political statement. Such was the strength of "You Haven't Done Nothin'" as a composition and recording, and such was the post-Watergate mood of the United States that the single went to No. 1 not only on the *Billboard* R&B charts (where it might have been expected to have hit the top spot, based on its musical style), but it also hit the top spot on the pop charts (where Wonder's funk numbers generally did not fare quite as well). The single also remained on the charts a week or two longer than Wonder's big hits generally had up to that time. It is not a record that one is likely to hear on oldies radio today, because of the topical nature of the lyrics, but it was a bigger hit when it was first released than such long-remembered and still-heard singles as "You Are the Sunshine of My Life" and "Supersti-tion," not to mention all of Wonder's pre-1970s hit singles, save "Fingertips, Part 2."[2]

"It Ain't No Use" finds Stevie Wonder the lyricist addressing a former lover as the two come to grips with the fact that their relationship has ended. Musically, it is a moderate-paced R&B ballad that makes good use of a backing chorus of Minnie Riperton, Lani Groves, and Denise Williams. The tuneful melody, "Bye, bye baby" chorus, and Wonder's backing vocal obbligati all call to mind popular Motown hits of the 1960s. As such, "It Ain't No Use" is an example of an album-construction procedure Wonder had used in his first few albums as a producer and that he would continue to use into his 1990s productions—that of using musical styles of the past, without resorting to mere nostalgia. Not often, though, would these retro pieces reflect back to 1960s Motown.

"They Won't Go When I Go," a product of Wonder and Yvonne Wright, is an entirely different sort of retro composition. The song begins with a lengthy piano introduction by Wonder that suggests the slow movements of piano works by Beethoven and Chopin. Wright's text deals with "lying friends" who end up committing near-emotional torture by their actions. She seems to suggest that through death and rebirth in a better world, these deceivers can be escaped. Wonder's minor key music that brings to mind a funeral march, complete with dramatic downward spiraling chromatic voice leading in his backing vocals (in a multitracked male chorus of Stevie Wonders), is stark, and perfectly matched to Yvonne Wright's tortured poetry. This song has such dramatic power that it is difficult to sit through, much less try to dance to; however, it shows off Wonder's knowledge of the European art music tradition and his still-increasing range as a composer. One could imagine a hushed house listening intently to a performance of "They Won't Go When I Go" in a formal vocal recital, unable to break the dark mood of words and music with applause at the conclusion of the performance until several seconds of silence had elapsed. Wright and Wonder completely break free of the expressive and musical limitations of pop song in this composition.

From the very first sound of guest artist Bobbye Hall playing the *quica,* "Bird of Beauty" establishes a mood of Brazil at Carnival. It is a mood piece and mostly serves to bring the listener back to more pleasant thoughts after the previous song.

"Please Don't Go" finds Wonder the composer and lyricist hearkening back to the pop/R&B blend of such songs as "You Are the Sunshine of My Life" and "For Once in My Life." From the start of the song, however, Wonder displays a more fully soul-oriented vocal approach, and as the track continues, the vocal backgrounds of the Persuasions, Shirley Brewer, and Denise Williams turn the song into a fully realized soul number, with the very obvious influence of gospel music. As Wonder pleads with his lover not to leave him, he highlights his own musical progression from 1968 ("For Once in My Life") to 1974 (now an arguably *bona fide* soul singer). Instrumentally, too, he suggests this musical progression by following his harmonica obbligato with a synthesizer-based obbligato. As the final track on the album that heralded his return from a coma, it is entirely fitting to celebrate the musical changes he had undergone during the previous years.

Fulfillingness' First Finale was a highly successful album, both commercially and artistically. Wonder jumps among so many different lyrical themes and among so many different musical styles and moods that the album does not feel like a cohesive whole quite the way *Innervisions* does. It very clearly, however, proved to the world that Stevie Wonder was back, and it showed that he was continuing to expand his range as a composer, singer, instrumentalist, arranger, and producer.

Such was the strength of Wonder's compositions and performances on *Fulfillingness' First Finale* and its two immediate predecessors, *Innervisions* and *Talking Book,* that one could very easily construct a "Stevie Wonder's Greatest Hits" compact disc from just the three albums. Thus, one might naturally pick the hit singles from the albums, along with favorite album tracks. A 50-minute album consisting of, say, "You Are the Sunshine of My Life," "Superstition," "Visions," "Living for the City," "Higher Ground," "Jesus Children of America," "All in Love Is Fair," "Don't You Worry 'bout a Thing," "Heaven Is 10 Zillion Light Years Away," "Boogie On Reggae Woman," and "You Haven't Done Nothin'" would be quite an impressive representation of a few years' worth of work, especially considering that part of the period was spent recovering from a near-fatal automobile accident.[3]

Although they had split as a couple, Wonder and Syreeta Wright still worked together. In fact, Wonder produced the 1974 album *Stevie Wonder Presents Syreeta,* a package that contained much Wonder-composed material. On *Fulfillingness' First Finale,* Wonder and Wright, who had chronicled their breakup and their feelings of needing to find new soul mates on several songs on *Talking Book,* did not co-write, although Syreeta's sister, Yvonne, did supply the lyrics for "They Won't Go When I Go." Syreeta Wright, however, participated on "Heaven Is 10 Zillion Light Years Away" as one of the background singers.

The title of the Wonder album *Fulfillingness' First Finale* might have been at least a passing reference to Wonder's near-fatal car crash of 1973, but it probably also referred to the album as the fulfillment of Wonder's latest contract with Motown. In 1975, he signed a new $13-million contract with Motown. The year 1975 was also notable for the birth of Stevie Wonder's daughter, Aisha. She inspired one of the most popular tracks on *Songs in the Key of Life,* Wonder's next album.

SONGS IN THE KEY OF LIFE

Curiously, only two Stevie Wonder albums ever made it all the way to No. 1 on both the *Billboard* R&B and pop charts. That *Fulfillingness' First Finale* did so can probably be attributed more to the fact that Wonder had developed a huge fan base with his 1972 and 1973 work and that the album marked his return after many fans feared he would never record again rather than to its necessarily having been his strongest album to date.[4] That *Songs in the Key of Life* was his second album to hit No. 1 on both charts can be attributed directly to the strength of the material: there literally is something for everyone in the massive package. Indeed, this double album—plus a bonus extended play disc—is in many respects Stevie Wonder's greatest achievement as an artist: if *Talking Book, Innervisions,* and *Fulfillingness' First Finale* proved that Wonder was one of the most important singer-songwriter-instrumentalists of the 1970s, then *Songs in the Key of Life* put him in an entirely different class from any of his contemporaries. Even though this Wonder album had none of the structural unity of *Innervisions* and perhaps lacked the kind of instant classics that could compete for airplay decades later in the form of *Talking Book*'s "You Are the Sunshine of My Life" and "Superstition," *Songs in the Key of Life* was by far Stevie Wonder's most exuberant album—his greatest display of keyboard, harmonica, percussion, and vocal performances, as well as possibly his best work as an arranger willing to bring in guest artists with a purpose. But a package like this one can be a double-edged sword. It certainly was for Wonder; for no album he would record into the twenty-first century would ever meet with the broad commercial and critical appeal of *Songs in the Key of Life*. Likewise, this outpouring of creativity, particularly as a performer without peer, would be followed by several years of silence. When that silence was broken in 1979 by Wonder's film soundtrack for *Journey Through the Secret Life of Plants,* it was broken by music that was very different in character and style from *Songs in the Key of Life*. It almost seemed that Stevie Wonder himself knew that he had done the performance of his life as a jazz-based R&B/pop singer and instrumentalist at the ripe old age of 26.

Songs in the Key of Life opens with "Love's in Need of Love Today." Wonder's lyrics speak of the need for love in the turbulent world of the mid-1970s. Wonder performed this song to great effect on the *America: A Tribute to Heroes* telethon shortly after the September 11, 2001, terrorist attacks on the World Trade Center and the Pentagon.[5] This message that love will overcome all evil is one that Wonder has turned to many times since he began writing his own lyrics in the early 1970s. The anthemlike song (more than 7 minutes long) has a sparser accompaniment than many of Wonder's arrangements on *Songs in the Key of Life,* which places the emphasis squarely on the lyrics. Musically, "Love's in Need of Love Today" is in an easygoing R&B ballad style. Wonder's melody incorporates some interesting contrasts from phrase to phrase, involving the use of an upward leap in the first, antecedent phrase of each stanza, a leap that is contrasted with a more consistently downward stepwise motion in the consequent phrases. The harmony of the oft-repeated choruses includes some jazz-oriented added-note chords and some meandering harmonic motion. These harmonic features paint the song as an out-of-the-ordinary example of Wonder's sophistication; however, they also make it a bit difficult for the casual listener to instantly relate to the musical subtleties of the song.

"Love's in Need of Love Today" is followed by the mildly funky, short song "Have a Talk with God," a collaboration of Wonder and Calvin Hardaway. The lyrics suggest that prayer to "the only free psychiatrist that's known throughout the world" can help one through any problem. Although musically "Have a Talk with God" contrasts with the album's first track, lyrically it continues what will become established as one of the primary themes of *Songs in the Key of Life:* the need for love in its many manifestations.

If the first two songs on the album did not establish the fact that Wonder the composer, arranger, and producer would be using extreme stylistic contrasts from song to song in order to hold the listener's attention, then the next couple of tracks certainly would make this attribute of *Songs in the Key of Life* crystal clear. "Village Ghetto Land" finds Wonder and collaborator Gary Byrd exploring the late-eighteenth-century European classical court musical style aligned with graphic lyrics describing the harshness of life in the late-twentieth-century American ghetto. This creates an eerie, haunting mood that is as effective as the well-known "Living for the City," but framed in a musical world that is about as far away from the funk of "Living for the City" as possible. Wonder accompanies his voice solely by orchestral string parts that he plays on the synthesizer. Fortunately, synthesizer technology had advanced enough by 1976 that the sound is very natural. In fact, there is very little difference in arrangement or in timbre between Wonder's *Songs in the Key of Life* recording of "Village Ghetto Land" and the performance of the song on the 1995 *Natural Wonder* album, in which Wonder is accompanied by the strings of the Tokyo Philharmonic Orchestra in an orchestration by conductor Dr. Henry Panion III.

Given Stevie Wonder's excellent credentials as an instrumentalist and his use of jazz harmonic styles and rhythms in his songs, it is unfortunate that he has recorded so little straight-ahead instrumental jazz. "Contusion" is an example of such a work. Filled with metrical changes and tight ensemble work from Wonder, lead guitarist Mike Sembello, and members of Wonderlove (Raymond Pounds, drums; Nathan Watts, bass; Ben Bridges, rhythm guitar; and Gregory Phillinganes, keyboards), "Contusion" is representative of the type of rock/jazz fusion that was quite popular in the mid-1970s. The problem, however, with a piece like this—and quite possibly the reason that Stevie Wonder generally refrained from jazz instrumentals—is that absent Wonder's voice (or his trademark harmonica), it sounds rather generic: good straight-ahead jazz fusion that could have come from any one of several artists of the era.

By the early 1980s, Stevie Wonder had written and recorded a few tribute songs, exemplified especially well by *Hotter Than July*'s Bob Marley tribute "Master Blaster (Jammin')." The first of these songs, however, was "Sir Duke," a tribute to Wonder's musical heroes of the big band swing era, "Basie, Miller, Satchimo [*sic*], and the king of all Sir Duke [Ellington]." Unlike Wonder's 1980 tribute to reggae pioneer Marley, "Sir Duke" does not actually incorporate the style of the subject of the tribute. Sure, there is the superficially big-band sound of a horn section that supplements Wonder's live backing band Wonderlove, but the musical style of "Sir Duke" owes more to R&B, a tinge of funk, reggae, and disco than it does to 1930s and 1940s swing. This is particularly apparent in the overall rhythmic feel and in the unison horn lines. Although it is not as obvious as in some of the other songs on the album, "Sir Duke" carries on the album's theme of spirituality and love conquering all obstacles. The difference is that here it is nostalgic, innocent, rhythmic dance music that effects a positive psychological change on humankind. When Motown issued the song as a single in spring 1977, it hit No. 1 on both the *Billboard* R&B and pop charts.

The next track on *Songs in the Key of Life*, "I Wish," similarly was a No. 1 R&B and pop single. Musically, the song is in a direct continuum from "Sir Duke," although with the funk/disco quotient ratcheted up a couple of notches. It is a thoroughly danceable song, but the real analytical interest lies in its lyrics. Throughout his lyrics-writing career—essentially from the 1970s on—Stevie Wonder has rarely been overtly autobiographical. In fact, it could be argued that by retaining the moniker "Stevie Wonder" instead of his given name, Stevland Morris has maintained a healthy distance from the real world in other ways. The song "I Wish," however, contains much autobiography.

On one level, the song seems to be a simple paean to the composer's childhood—the days before Stevland Morris became Stevie Wonder. Stevie Wonder was, after all, a child star from the age of 12 onward; therefore, he did not have the opportunity to grow up as a normal teenager. Wonder includes one particular turn of phrase, however, that raises questions of a more complex nature. This comes at the start of the song when Wonder sets up the time frame of his reminiscences by singing, "Thinking back to when I was a little nappy-headed boy." At first hearing, the line seems simply meant to place the time as childhood. But why does Wonder define himself as a "nappy-headed boy"? In the 1990s, one noted African American children's author—Carolivia Herron—ran into problems with her audience by using the term *nappy* in the title of her book *Nappy Hair*, because it was viewed as a derogatory term. Although the term did not generate the same level of consternation in the mid-1970s, it was still used to define a particular physical trait of blacks. Could Wonder's use of the term have come from the desire to paint Stevland Morris as just another anonymous black youth facing an uncertain future in a world in which blacks had considerable difficulty surviving, let alone getting ahead? Perhaps. Could Wonder's use of the term have come from his personal experience of texture, as a person without the sense of sight—that is, someone who could relate better to texture through the sense of touch than to color? Perhaps. The point is, no matter what Stevie Wonder's intentions were in using a particular turn of phrase that lends itself to multiple interpretations, he did use it. Opening up his lyrics to a variety of possibilities of understanding—whether by design or by fortunate accident—enriches the overall effect of the song.

One of the notable features of some of Wonder's compositions and recordings is his ability to play roles, much like an actor. Certainly, a song like "Front Line," in which songwriter-singer Wonder portrays a returned Vietnam veteran, relies completely on Wonder's ability to portray convincingly someone his audience knows he never could have been. As mentioned previously, in "I Wish," Wonder takes on an unusual role for him: the mature Stevie Wonder reminiscing about the young Stevland Morris. Wonder's audience might find the picture of Morris to be quite different from what it assumed the early life of a blind boy might be like. By all accounts, however, Stevland Morris really did get in trouble for playing doctor with a neighborhood girl, and he really did climb trees, run and jump, and hang around with the young neighborhood hoodlums writing profanities on the walls of buildings, just as Morris's alter ego, Stevie Wonder, documents in "I Wish."

As Wonder sings that he wishes those days of childhood mischief and innocence had not passed so quickly and, indeed, that they could return again, one cannot help but hear the song as an expression of the plight of the child star. That Wonder speaks so little of his own childhood in his songs and in interviews adds to the importance of "I Wish" as a documentary of his pre-fame days. It is simultaneously one of his funkiest and most touching compositions. "I Wish" gives Wonder fans and would-be biographers a reason to consider just how much childhood the musician had to leave behind when he became a star at such an early age; however, it also causes one to consider just how different Wonder the public adult is from some of the considerably more tragic child stars of the past and some of the idiosyncratic former child stars (including those who at one time recorded for the same record label as Wonder) who came along after Wonder.

Given the thematic focus on spirituality and love on *Songs in the Key of Life*, one can question how a song that essentially praises childhood mischief could possibly fit on the album. The best way to explain what might be behind the song is to quote some lines from the *Northern Exposure* television program of the early 1990s spoken by the character Chris Stevens. When the disc jockey/preacher/biker Stevens is caught stealing radios, he explains his behavior to his discoverer, Ed Chigliak, as follows:

> Wildness, Ed. We're running out of it. Even up here in Alaska. People need to be reminded that the world is unsafe and unpredictable. And at a moment's notice, they could lose everything. Like that.
>
> I do it to remind them that chaos is always out there, lurking beyond the horizon. That plus, sometimes, Ed, sometimes you have to do something bad—just to know you're alive.[6]

I think it is the belief that one needs to participate occasionally in innocent mischief in order to feel alive that drives "I Wish." In the background of Wonder's explorations of love in various forms (romantic, agape, etc.) and spirituality on *Songs in the Key of Life* is the even more overarching theme of healing. What Wonder does in "I Wish" is to place that badness into the mix because of its healing power, its ability to make one feel, as the *Northern Exposure* character Chris Stevens puts it, "alive."

Fortunately, Stevie Wonder the record producer and arranger recognized the need for a real bass player and horn section on "I Wish." One of the minor problems that plagued his otherwise-superb work of late 1972 through 1974 was the fact that the bass sound Wonder achieved on the synthesizer just did not capture the timbre or the spontaneity and power of a real bass player. Part of the problem resulted from the somewhat pedestrian bass lines in some of the funkier early 1970s pieces. Even in the pieces in which Wonder obviously tried to create a feeling of improvisatory spontaneity, like "Jesus Children of America," however, the timbre of the synthesizer sounds today like a dated imitation of the electric bass. In a very real sense, it was not entirely Wonder's fault, but that of the technology of the day. His goal seemed to be to have total control of his product not just as a writer, arranger, singer, and producer, but also as a multi-instrumentalist, so he was forced to rely on a technology in its infancy. But, percussion is another thing altogether—Wonder had recorded as a drummer since he was barely into his teens. One of my personal laments about Wonder's work after *Fulfillingness' First Finale* is his reliance on studio percussionists and drum machines. At times, this would lead to rather pedestrian percussion tracks. On Wonder's recording of "I Wish," however, drummer Raymond Pounds plays with the kind of inventiveness heard in the best of Wonder's own drum playing on the early 1970s albums. Incidentally, "I Wish" figures indirectly into one of Stevie Wonder's more curious achievements as a composer. According to *Billboard* magazine, Wonder achieved "second place among songwriters with the longest span of chart-toppers in the rock era" in 1999 when Will Smith's rap song "Wild Wild West," which was based on Wonder's "I Wish," hit No. 1 on the singles charts. Wonder's first No. 1 single as a composer was Smokey Robinson and the Miracles' 1970 hit "Tears of a Clown."[7]

The album's next track, "Knocks Me Off My Feet," is a gentle moderate tempo love ballad. Wonder, who wrote both music and words for this song—as well as playing all the instruments and providing all the vocal parts—does a nice job recapturing the spirit of the great Motown love songs of the 1960s. A large part of the secret to the song's success lies in Wonder's text painting. He sets the lines "There's sumptin 'bout your love, That makes me weak and Knocks my off my feet" with a deliberate rhythmic stumble during the "Knocks me off my feet" line. As the song progresses, Wonder the drummer also adds a tom-tom roll to capture the spirit of the fall. The melodic hook is also strong in the spirit of earlier Motown hits.

"Pastime Paradise" explores an entirely different subject and an entirely different musical style. Wonder's lyrics speak of the way in which some people waste their lives living in the past, dedicated to the "evils of the world," when they should be living for "the future paradise" of a world of peace. He sets these lyrics to an interesting mixture of Latin dance and Spanish classical sounds. The synthesized, classically oriented strings recall the album's earlier track, "Village Ghetto Land." The text, too, deals with similar issues, especially with a focus on how improving race relations and equality can help to bring about "the peace of the world." Wonder's somewhat stark minor key melody is haunting, and is well supported by the repeated percussion and synthesized string figures. The repetitive nature of the string writing anticipates further steps Stevie Wonder would take in exploring the contemporary classical technique of minimalism at the end of the 1970s in his soundtrack for *Journey Through the Secret Life of Plants*. Although "Pastime Paradise" was not necessarily the best-known song or the best-remembered song from *Songs in the Key of Life*, it was to emerge as a No. 1 hit single in the form of rapper Coolio's version, "Gangsta's Paradise," which hit the top of the charts in 1995.

"Summer Soft" is, as the title suggests, an ode to summer. Here, we find Wonder discovering a kind of spirituality in nature, thereby complementing *Songs in the Key of Life*'s pieces of finding spirituality in God, in music, and in romantic love and agape-type love. Both "Summer Soft," which turns into a kind of rock jam by its end, and "Ordinary Pain" suggest the style of Stevie Wonder's songs just before his career really broke out with the 1972 album *Talking Book*. Musically, the two share a rhythmic feel, the use of chromatic voice leading within jazz-oriented harmonic motion, and the spirit of instrumental jamming that pervaded much of the 1970–1972 albums *Music of My Mind, Where I'm Coming From*, and even a little of *Signed, Sealed & Delivered*. The major difference is that these are more consistent songs: Wonder had by 1976 mastered the art of the melodic hook, and his harmony generally was more goal-focused and less meandering than on some of his songs of a half-decade before. The lyrics, with "Summer Soft" focused on nature and "Ordinary Pain" focused on the emotional pain that comes from struggling and broken relationships, are more populist in nature: presumably nearly anyone can relate to these poems, unlike some of the bizarre humor and unbelievable characterizations in some of Wonder's lyrics from *Music of My Mind* and *Where I'm Coming From*. The end result is that a song like "Ordinary Pain," which is not the most profound lyrical piece Wonder had written, nor the best music he had written, stands as a fully workable and pleasant pop song.

For some strange reason, the song that begins side 3 of *Songs in the Key of Life*, "Isn't She Lovely," was never released as a single. I say "strange" because the song rivaled "Sir Duke" as the best-known track on the album. It still receives airplay today on oldies radio stations. The highlight of the 6–1/2-minute song, which is a tribute to Wonder's young daughter Aisha (who can be heard in the background of the recording), is Wonder's uncharacteristically extended harmonica solo. Throughout the improvisation,

Wonder references the main melody of the song, but remains constantly inventive. In fact, there is a discernable chorus-to-chorus shape and connection and an overall shape to the entire solo. Maybe this is not quite the same sort of overall shaping of an extended improvised jazz solo for which tenor saxophonist Sonny Rollins became famous in the 1950s and 1960s, but Wonder does exhibit attention to motivic shaping beyond the phrase and even beyond the chorus. In doing so, he places himself well above the level of most pop stars as an instrumentalist. The song's relatively simple and goal-oriented harmonic scheme lends itself to the kind of improvisation treatment Wonder gives it. And, although the lyrics of "Isn't She Lovely" consist of three short stanzas of poetry, they serve an important purpose in relation to the focus of *Songs in the Key of Life*. By including this song on the album, Wonder expands the spirituality he finds in love to love of, and love within, a family, especially when it involves the miracle of children. Those who are musicians or aficionados of instrumental improvisations might find the sounds of Aisha and Wonder playing with Aisha, which tend to cover the harmonica solo at times, to be an intrusion, but this documentation of intergenerational interplay fits right in with the overarching theme of the album.

"Isn't She Lovely" is followed by the 6–1/2-minute ballad "Joy Inside My Tears." Unlike the similarly anthemlike "Love's in Need of Love Today," this song unfortunately seems like it might be as long as it is because *Songs in the Key of Life* is a double album and there was time to fill. In other words, it is not one of Wonder's most interesting compositions, nor is it one of his most distinctive vocal performances.

The same criticism cannot be leveled at "Black Man." Here, Stevie Wonder sounds like a man who truly stands committed to everything about which he is singing. His lyrics work through history, providing a chronicle of human achievements and attributing each to the person of a particular race who made the discovery, pioneered the procedure, or created the invention. His point is that *all* of humanity is creative and fully worthy of equal treatment. The one very obvious downside to Wonder and collaborator Gary Byrd's historical choices is that they are not nearly as gender-inclusive as they are racially inclusive: Sacagawea's assistance to Lewis and Clark is the sole example the songwriters cite of a woman, at least until the mention of Harriet Tubman in the song's fade out. Musically, "Black Man" is up-tempo funk, and it features Wonder playing all of the instruments, save the horns.

Wonder maintains the multicultural theme in the album's next song, "Ngiculela—Es Una Historia—I Am Singing." Through these lyrics, Wonder is singing of love, of tomorrow, and from his heart. He sings in English, Spanish, and Zulu, and his musical setting manages to suggest both African and Hispanic pop music styles.

"If It's Magic" presents Wonder in a most unusual texture: voice, harp, and just a touch of harmonica. Although he never actually uses the word love, it seems that the "it" to which he refers is love. Wonder's lyrics ask why we do not act as carefully as we might and "make it everlasting," "if it's special" and "if it's magic." Despite the classical sound of the voice and harp setting, harmonically and melodically, the song resembles the Tin Pan Alley/jazz ballad style of Wonder's earlier "All in Love Is Fair."

Like "Contusion," "As" fits right into the contemporary popular jazz idiom of the mid-1970s. However, unlike the harder-edged jazz-rock fusion style of the earlier *Songs in the Key of Life* track with its tight unison lines and Mahavishnu Orchestra–like metrical changes, "As" represents the lighter CTI jazz of Hubert Laws, George Benson, and others. In fact, the song, with its ostinato groove, would be covered by a number of jazz musicians after the song's appearance on *Songs in the Key of Life,* including trumpeter Blue Mitchell on his 1977 album *African Violet,* and jazz-rock fusion violinist Jean Luc Ponty on his 1982 album *Mystical Adventures.*

Songs in the Key of Life proper concludes with "Another Star," an up-tempo song of unrequited love. As a fast energetic song about Stevie having been wronged in love, it resembles some of the material he was recording back in the mid- and late 1960s. Musically, however, this is a thoroughly contemporary jazz-pop-disco song. In fact, the pop-jazz sound is confirmed by the presence of guest musicians Bobbi Humphrey on flute and George Benson on guitar and background vocals. The 8–1/2-minute song has excellent potential as a disco dance track, but somehow does not fit the overall theme of the album: that love conquers all. In fact, this is part of the problem with *Songs in the Key of Life* as a concept album: there is simply too much material and in too many different styles, for it to hold together as a unified artistic statement in the same way *Innervisions* does.

The songs on the bonus disc originally issued with *Songs in the Key of Life* (they are contained as tracks 8–11 on disc 2 of Motown's 2000 2-compact disc reissue of the album) similarly are not necessarily focused on the album's theme, at least as it was developed fairly clearly over the first three sides. For example, "Saturn," while a musically grand and thoroughly engaging collaboration between Wonder and Mike Sembello—recalling if anything the space-themed anthems of the Canadian studio rock/classical band Klaatu—finds Wonder escaping from the problems of Earth by "going to Saturn where the rings all glow." Throughout the bulk of *Songs in the Key of Life,* Wonder the lyricist deals head on with personal, political, and social issues, so the escapism of "Saturn" seems incongruous. "Ebony Eyes" is a gospel-influenced tribute to "Miss Black Supreme," the "pretty girl with ebony eyes," while "All Day Sucker" with its funkiness, synthesizer effects, and oft-repeated lyrical expression of being a "sucker for your love," recalls *Music of My Mind* and *Where I'm Coming From.* The bonus record concludes with the instrumental track "Easy Goin' Evening (My Mama's Call)." This piece is slow, and features Wonder playing a nostalgic melody on the harmonica. The harmonica tune features short, sequential motives within a fairly narrow range, which suggests Wonder's vocal works. The nostalgic nature of the music and the tune's title recalls the album's funky tribute to the days of Stevland Morris's childhood, "I Wish."

Containing elements of nostalgia, social consciousness, spirituality, and a wide range of musical styles and textures, *Songs in the Key of Life* captured the American public's imagination: it was very successful on the R&B and pop charts, and it spawned highly successful singles ("Sir Duke" and "I Wish"). As a fully developed artistic statement, however, there was just too much material and too much variety in musical style, arrangement, and production to match the cohesiveness of Wonder's work of a few years before. But if viewed as a collection of individual songs, *Songs in the Key of Life* was a formidable achievement, and continues to stand as one of the greatest albums of the rock era. This is not entirely because of the compositional strength of the songs, but also because of the tightness of the instrumental ensemble work, both in the tracks that were recorded entirely by Wonder and in those in which he was accompanied by Wonderlove and other assisting musicians.

JOURNEY THROUGH THE SECRET LIFE OF PLANTS

According to music critic Stephen Holden, "Synthetic instrumentation became an integral textural ingredient of works structured like sweeping murals which bore a humanitarian message in the 1970s work of Wonder."[8] Holden writes that in *Journey Through the Secret Life of Plants,* the use of synthesizers "conjures up a magic garden, in which the notes unfurl like tendrils."[9] Because the film was never released, Wonder's soundtrack must be evaluated entirely as a musical construct, absent any tie-ins with the visuals of the movie. As a double album, featuring mostly instrumental pieces, it is an incredible mix of styles and moods. As I was studying the soundtrack, my thoughts kept coming back to the 2004 release of Brian Wilson's *Smile* album (originally composed in 1966 and 1967). Both Wilson's *Smile* and Wonder's *Journey Through the Secret Life of Plants* contain beautiful music, incredibly naïve music, profundity through simplicity, and some simple, and fully intentional, silliness.

Another noteworthy feature of many of the instrumental pieces on *Journey Through the Secret Life of Plants* is how they demonstrate Wonder's use of what would become in the 1980s a frequently heard sequencing technique: that of additive composition. The basic idea is that the composer begins with one track, often a repetitive ostinato track, and then adds new layers of material over the top. The technical and aesthetic roots of this compositional technique come from the growing prominence of multitrack recording (the technical) and from the birth of the minimalist style of composers such as Terry Riley and Steve Reich, both of which occurred in the 1960s. Once sequencers were built into synthesizers, and with the all-important development of MIDI (Musical Instrument Digital Interface), and the development of sequencing software for computers, this layering, additive composition became more commonplace, especially for pop musicians.[10]

Because of Stevie Wonder's exploration of new compositional techniques, the emphasis on instrumental tracks of an almost classical nature, and the sometimes-obscure references to things that apparently were taking place in a movie that nobody saw, this album confounded his customary audience. Let us examine some of the individual pieces that make up the soundtrack to explore just what Wonder did that, for him at least, was so new, and so perplexing for his fans.

Stevie Wonder's journey begins, appropriately enough, with "Earth's Creation." Here, he uses a mysterious, and somewhat ominous, ostinato of the pitches E, A-sharp, B as the framework for the "verses" of the piece. The slightly ominous sound of the piece comes both from Wonder's emphasis of the tritone (E to A-sharp) in the ostinato, as well as from the heavy use of distortion and synthesized thunder. The "verses"—and I use the terms *verses* and *chorus* in describing the piece because, even though this is an instrumental piece, "Earth's Creation" essentially is in pop song structure—feature reliance on the ostinato that contrasts with the highly chromatic chorus sections. Throughout *Journey Through the Secret Life of Plants,* Wonder segues from one song to the next. Presumably, this suggests the fade outs, fade ins, and dissolves of the motion picture. It does tend to give an overall flow to the double album, although the music strongly suggests a succession of individual pieces, because there is not a great deal of thematic development over the course of the soundtrack as a whole.

Indeed, "Earth's Creation" makes a direct segue into "The First Garden," another instrumental piece. In this composition, synthesized birds, insects, thunder, rain, metal percussion, and strings accompany a simple and somewhat nostalgic harmony and melody. Presumably, this depicts the Garden of Eden before Adam and Eve's fall, or perhaps even before there were an Adam and Eve (or Adam and Lilith, depending upon one's religious background). Wonder uses the synthesized insects (crickets), panning from channel to channel, to create a background rhythmic pulse that continues to the end of the piece, after the other instruments have stopped. In other words, the rhythm of nature establishes the piece, and continues to be heard after the rhythm of humans has ceased. Perhaps this is reading too much into the piece, but Wonder's music could suggest that no matter what humans do—intentionally or unintentionally—to upset God's creation, nature ultimately will win out.

The music that links "The First Garden" and "Voyage to India" proper is the most overtly classical sounding of the opening pieces on the album, due in large part to the nineteenth-century-style chromatic harmony and the counterpoint of the synthesized string parts. The real beginning of the depiction of India, however, is signaled by the appearance of the sitar, played on the recording by Ben Bridges. Although Stevie Wonder evokes the basic sound of Hindustani music by using a traditional Indian scale (*rag*), and by having the music gradually accelerate, there are important distinctions between

"Voyage to India" and authentic Hindustani music. Most important, a piece by a musician like Ravi Shankar, to cite one well-known example, typically would feature melodic improvisation by the sitar player. Bridges's role in the Wonder piece is limited to ostinato-like material (the role that the tambura typically would take in authentic Hindustani music). Another distinction between authentic Hindustani music and Wonder's composition is the way in which the acceleration is handled, as well as the role of the tabla, the traditional Indian drums. Ultimately, this all adds up to the fact that Wonder's "Voyage to India" succeeds as a mood piece because of the way in which it captures the general flavor—one might go so far as to say the stereotype—of Indian music; the subtleties are not there, nor are they necessary to create an atmosphere of India. The casual listener (or documentary filmgoer) might not find this to be a problem, but it highlights one of the complaints classically trained musicians have with pop musicians who branch off into classical music: much of what these composers do is classical on the surface only. This complaint could be leveled not only at *Journey Through the Secret Life of Plants,* but also at works like Paul McCartney's *Liverpool Oratorio,* and the classical instrumental compositions of Billy Joel. Such things as real thematic development, demonstrating the ability to move outside of the traditional pop music tonal system, and, yes, recognizing the subtle differences between writing Indian-sounding music and music that truly owes a debt of gratitude to the whole *gestalt* of Hindustani music theory are examples of this. This is one reason why the classically trained musician might be less than totally receptive to the classical writing of a Stevie Wonder. Wonder's longtime fans, however, probably found this music challenging because a piece like "Voyage to India" has nothing to do with what they had come to expect from—and to love about—the music of Stevie Wonder.

The George Washington Carver tribute song, "Same Old Story," follows "Voyage to India." In a gentle pop ballad, Wonder recounts the achievements of the great botanist and the resistance he encountered from the scientific establishment, both because of his race and because of the novelty of some of his theories. Of Stevie Wonder's tribute songs—"Sir Duke," "Master Blaster (Jammin')," and "Happy Birthday"—"Same Old Story" is the least well known and the weakest. It succeeds in the context of Wonder's *Journey* mostly because of the botanical reference.

The same sense of humor that graced a couple of the quirkier songs on Wonder's 1972 album *Music of My Mind* returns in the *Journey Through the Secret Life of Plants* offering "Venus' Flytrap and the Bug." The smarmy-sounding bug that is stalking the plant, only to be eaten by it, is considerably more successful than Wonder's portrayal of an equally smarmy stalker on the 1972 album, mostly because the humorous context is clear in the present song.

The first side of *Journey Through the Secret Life of Plants* concludes with "Ai No, Sono," a piece in the Japanese Haiku style sung by a children's chorus. As with "Voyage to India," this is not necessarily the best example of World

Music, although Wonder does capture the musical essence of the Asian culture that inspired the song. "Ai No, Sono" is stylistically so different from Wonder's R&B/pop style, though, that it would be most interesting to experience it in the visual context of the *Secret Life of Plants* documentary.

"Seasons," a fairly brief instrumental number that begins with a windswept, frosty sounding introduction, sounds like the backing tracks for a possible vocal number that never was. Aside from the stereotypical portrayal of winter in the introduction, there is nothing about the music itself that suggests any particular season or change of seasons. It is followed on the soundtrack album by "Power Flower," a song that Wonder sings in falsetto, playing the role of the mythical character Pan. Michael Sembello contributed the lyrics to the song that, although pleasant, certainly is not one of Wonder's more substantial works. "Race Babbling," which closes side 2, is a far more interesting composition. Here, Wonder is supported by trumpeter Larry Gittens, saxophonist Hank Redd, and vocalist Josie James, although the bulk of the instrumental and vocal material in the recording comes from Wonder himself. Wonder's lyrics deal with the havoc that humankind's environmental degradation is wreaking on the plant world and with the fact that humans need the plants in order to survive. All of this is presented from the plants' point of view, which is accomplished by electronically manipulating the vocals and through Wonder's use of unusual harmonic progressions. The song has something of a brisk disco/funk sound to it, suggesting at times a very crisp and clean version of Stevie Wonder meets George Clinton meets Sly Stone. As long as the listener can read the lyrics—they are obscured almost beyond recognition by the electronic processing—it works as an effective statement of environmentalism. Presumably in the film, in which viewers obviously would not have the benefit of the gatefold album's printed lyrics, "Race Babbling" would accompany appropriate environmentally related visual images. If it did not, it would not make a whole lot of sense. Compared with anything that Wonder had released commercially up to this time, the song is quite unusual and experimental harmonically and melodically. Although it does not approach the out there nature of the classical avant-garde or experimental jazz musicians of the late 1970s such as Anthony Braxton, it does suggest the extent to which Stevie Wonder's expressive range as a composer went, well beyond what the public generally heard from him.

Easily the best-known song from Wonder's soundtrack album, "Send One Your Love," was also released as a successful single, making it halfway up the top 10 R&B and pop charts. This gentle ballad finds Wonder suggesting a return to the romanticism of the past: a time in which love was expressed both by the giving and receiving of flowers and the metaphorical flowers of the heart. Although "Send One Your Love" works as a romantic love song—undoubtedly there were couples at the time for which it was "our song"—the jaded listener might describe it as too sappy. In fact, this song, with its romantic, commercial pop appeal, was the first such Wonder song that tended to define his musical output of the late 1970s and early 1980s for some critics as lightweight, overly commercial, and overly naïve. It is, however, unfair to characterize Wonder's output of this half-decade this way because of a few songs like "Send One Your Love," "That Girl," and "I Just Called to Say I Love You." There certainly was enough power and social and political commentary in some of the songs on *Hotter Than July* and other early 1980s tracks (such as the superb, but not particularly well known "Front Line") to balance the ballads. The problem might be that Wonder's music of the time period tended to polarize between two stylistic and expressive extremes: the breadth and the depth of the musical and expressive range of his work starting with the vocal compositions from *Journey Through the Secret Life of Plants* became less richly chromatic than what listeners had experienced with the great 1972–1976 albums.

When "Outside My Window" was released as a single, the public did not respond as positively as it had for the "Send One Your Love" single: the recording did not even make the top 40 on any of the *Billboard* charts. "Outside My Window," which immediately follows "Send One Your Love" on the soundtrack album, however, is in many respects a much more interesting song. Certainly, it lacks the overly commercial feel of "Send One Your Love," and it features some very tight, very beautiful vocal harmony by the multitracked Wonder. The guitar-based accompaniment provided by Michael Sembello works beautifully as well, but is so far removed from what Stevie Wonder fans probably expected to hear that this texture might account for at least part of the lack of success for the song in the sales arena. "Outside My Window" is a strong enough song that it probably could have been a commercially successful single in the hands of an artist for whom the style would be a more natural fit. If the listener tosses out any preconceived notions he or she may have of what a Stevie Wonder song should sound like, the listener will realize that this is one of the strongest pop songs of this soundtrack.

Yvonne Wright wrote the lyrics for "Black Orchid." Her collaborations with Wonder earlier in the 1970s had produced some of the best poetic images Wonder would set to music. Here, she writes of the beauty of a rare and delicate flower, the black orchid. The flower can be understood as a metaphor for a beautiful, both inside and out, black woman. The only problem is that the plant side—the literal side—of the double meaning is explored so much that some listeners could miss the deeper subtext. Wonder's setting is in a moderate-tempo ballad style. His chorus features a memorable melodic hook, although the piece mostly succeeds as a mood piece.

"Ecclesiastes" is an altogether different kind of mood piece. This electronic organ-based instrumental number seems to be modeled on the famous "Adagio" of the Italian Baroque composer Tomaso Albinoni. Stevie Wonder had demonstrated his familiarity with the music of the eighteenth-century European court in "Village Ghetto Land" a few years before. Here, music and synthesizer-based orchestration are entirely appropriate for creating the feel of the Italian Baroque.

Without the context of the film, it is somewhat dizzying for the listener to experience the soundtrack sequentially. This is probably most challenging in moving from the contemporary ballad style of "Black Orchid" to "Ecclesiastes" to "Kesse Ye Lola De Ye," a song that reflects African folk song and that incorporates African instruments. Wonder's oft-repeated Bambara text translates to "A Seed's a Star, A Star's a Seed, Peace and More Peace." The song functions as a mood piece, but the English version of the text (which is never actually heard in the recording) anticipates the later song "A Seed's a Star and Tree Medley."

The final track on the third side of Wonder's soundtrack album, "Come Back as a Flower," features the lyrics and lead vocals of Syreeta Wright. Wright sings her text about wanting to be reincarnated as a flower with a childlike innocence and purity that is the perfect fit both for the text and for Wonder's music. And, this just happens to be one of Stevie Wonder's most engaging ballad melodies from the late 1970s and early 1980s, making "Come Back as a Flower" a real gem. In a sense, it is too bad that this song is so tied to the soundtrack for a film that no one saw, as it really should have received more exposure.

"A Seed's a Star and Tree Medley" is a funky disco piece based on the same chromatic bass inner-voice accompaniment line as the instrumental theme music from the old James Bond 007 movies of the 1960s, and in Henry Mancini's "Charade," from the same time period. Wonder's text equates celestial stars with tiny plant seeds as the roots of life. Stylistically, it is the kind of piece that could have had great commercial potential—in fact, it resembles the overall style of Wonder's *Hotter Than July* album of the next year more closely than anything else in the documentary soundtrack. The lyrical theme, especially the electronically manipulated spoken text that is supposed to represent the voice of the Tree, however, places the song squarely into the context of this film, and thereby limits any out-of-context popular accessibility. Still, it is powerful musically and benefits from some tasty electric bass playing by Nathan Watts.

The final three tracks on the *Journey Through the Secret Life of Plants* soundtrack collection are "The Secret Life of Plants," a ballad of environmental awareness, and the instrumental pieces "Tree" and "Finale." "Tree" is a mood piece that not so much resembles contemporary classical music as much as it is an instrumental version of a pop song. "Finale," however, finds Wonder exploring several styles and using a much wider harmonic vocabulary than one would ever find in a pop or R&B song. Although arranged by Wonder to sound orchestral, he produces all the sounds on synthesizers. The tempo and stylistic changes of "Finale" are extreme and probably coordinate with visual images at the conclusion of the film. Out of context, though, the piece is striking in its power and contrast and strangely calls to mind some of the orchestral works of Frank Zappa in which abstract Edgard Varèse–inspired sections might abruptly give way to 1950s style doo-wop.

Wonder's "Finale" shifts from dense, tense, and dramatic classical music to funk. It suggests that, had he pursued the style, Stevie Wonder might have gone well beyond what pop musicians turned classicists Billy Joel and Paul McCartney did in their classical compositions of the 1990s and beginning of the twenty-first century.

Wonder's soundtrack for *The Secret Life of Plants* found him exploring new compositional ground. This is especially evident when one listens to *Journey Through the Secret Life of Plants* and *Hotter Than July* in close proximity— although the albums were products of 1979 and 1980, respectively, they could not be any more different in style. Some of the more atypical Stevie Wonder pieces of the soundtrack album, such as "Ai No, Sono" and "Voyage to India," work fairly well, but would probably be better served by being experienced in the context of the film. The collection might not include a *bona fide* classic, but "Come Back as a Flower" and "Outside My Window" are both songs that deserve to be better known. Ultimately, the reason that this material has slipped into obscurity is that Wonder's work here is so context driven. Unlike the score he would write a little more than a decade later for Spike Lee's film *Jungle Fever*, a movie built around more universally human themes, the songs of *Journey Through the Secret Life of Plants* just cannot make an immediate connection with a wide audience because of the focus of the subject matter.

HOTTER THAN JULY

This period of Stevie Wonder's career was capped off with the 1980 album *Hotter Than July.* With the exception of "All I Do (Is Think about You),"[11] which was nearly a decade old and had originally been written for Tammi Terrell by Wonder and his co-lyricists Morris Broadnax and Clarence Paul, Wonder wrote all the words and music for the album. Because it had been four years since Wonder's huge *Songs in the Key of Life* collection, his most recent non-soundtrack album of new material, *Hotter Than July* makes for some interesting study. Certainly, the second half of the twentieth century was notable for the quick rate at which so-called in musical styles would change. So, then, how did Stevie Wonder change with the fluctuations in popular tastes that had occurred in pop music between 1976 and 1980?

The lyrics and general musical styles of Stevie Wonder actually did not change all that much in the years between *Songs in the Key of Life* and *Hotter Than July.* Unfortunately, what did change was the way in which Wonder adopted some of the trappings of disco and other techno-based dance music on the album. The master drummer of *Innervisions* and even *Songs in the Key of Life* is replaced by studio drummers and even drum machines on some of the tracks. This is not to say that the studio drummers were not fine musicians, they just did not display the kind of jazz-influenced variation style that Wonder used so effectively in the early 1970s. Even Wonder's own approach to percussion and keyboard playing is more predictable. Wonder moved from improvisational-sounding backing keyboard tracks on recordings such as "Living for the City" and "Higher Ground" to a less creative, and certainly more predictable, sounding accompaniment on some of the *Hotter Than July* material. And the material is more fully arranged with guest electric guitarists and horn sections. Yes, it was closer to late 1970s popular aesthetics than early 1970s Stevie Wonder arrangements and performances may have been, but it was also less interesting and a touch less personal sounding. This was not so much Wonder's fault as it was indicative of what had happened in popular music by the end of the decade.

The album kicks off with "Did I Hear You Say You Love Me," which is a funky dance song that bears some resemblance to the work of Ray Parker, Jr., and his group Raydio. Curiously, the phrasing of the verses of Wonder's melody bears at least a passing resemblance to one phrase-ending melodic lick in Richard Berry's recording of his famous R&B song "Louie Louie." With an 11-voice backing chorus and a 4-part horn section, and with Wonder performing only as a lead singer and on keyboards, the recording suggests the sound of Wonder's live band. This aspect of *Hotter Than July* represents a significant change from most of Wonder's albums of the 1970s, works in which he more frequently played all of the instruments and sometimes provided all of the backing vocals. Wonder's lyrics, which find him asking a woman from whom he seems to have been receiving mixed signals, to tell him whether or not she is love with him, are not the focus. The groove and the overall texture and arrangement are. As an example of the 30-year-old Stevie Wonder adapting to the dance styles of 1980, it is a success. As an example of an album track that will endure like some of the album tracks of the 1970s, it is less successful.

There is an immediate cut directly into "All I Do," the 1966 song Wonder, Clarence Paul, and Morris Broadnax had originally written for the late Tammi Terrell. It is another, although slightly slower, danceable love song, and basically matches the late 1970s/early 1980s feel of "Did I Hear You Say You Love Me." The reason that the song does not sound like a product of 1966 can be found in Wonder's arrangement and the rhythmic references to mid-1970s disco in his high-hat cymbal work on the drum set (Wonder plays all the instruments on the track, save the saxophone solo). Wonder is joined on the track by a backing chorus that includes a young Michael Jackson and members of TSOP, a group that represented Philadelphia, as opposed to Motown, soul.

The pace slows down even more for "Rocket Love," a song in which Wonder compares his lover to "symphonies by Bach or Brahms," and "a female Shakespeare of [her] time." The title of the song comes from the chorus, in which Wonder tells her that she took him on a ride on a rocket with her love. Paul Riser provided a technically challenging string arrangement, but the real musical highlights come from Wonder's easy soulful melody and his chromatic harmonies in the introduction and the verses. The chromatic harmonic shifts, incidentally, resemble the opening title theme from the old James Bond spy films. It really doesn't sound derivative, however, because this involves one figure from a melody and harmonic progression that is not at all like the music that Monty Norman composed for the Bond films. Wonder had used this type of harmonic pattern the year before in "A Seed's a Star and Tree Medley" in his soundtrack for *The Secret Life of Plants*.

Over the years, Stevie Wonder has recorded a number of songs in which he has obviously portrayed "non-Stevie" characters. "I Ain't Gonna Stand for It" certainly falls into this category. Not because of the song's theme, which is the statement that Wonder's character "ain't gonna stand for" someone fooling around with his lover, but because of the vocal timbre and Southern-soul-singer pronunciation he affects for the song. In addition, the start of the melodic phrases of the verses is at the very bottom of his vocal range, purposefully causing him to barely croak out the first note. It is as if the song is meant to be a vaguely Al Green parody. There certainly is more than just a little humor in the way in which Wonder phrases his suspicions. A fine example is the line, "someone's been diggin' round in my cake." Yes, it is decidedly vernacular—certainly more so than the vast majority of Wonder's lyrics. The best part of the song is that it proves that Stevie Wonder can and does take himself less than seriously at times—he enjoys and provides a laugh.

One of the problems of cohesion on *Hotter Than July* is caused by the way in which Wonder the producer ordered the love-related songs. For example, the suspicion of "I Ain't Gonna Stand for It" does an abrupt segue into the "let's get high on our love" sentiments of "As If You Read My Mind." The organization of the album sounds as if it was established more for musical reasons (generally on the basis of tempo) than according to any sort of rhetorical scheme as suggested by the lyrics. Contrast this with *Talking Book* and that album's clear progression from establishment of a love relationship, suspicion, betrayal, loss, and finally, the search for a new relationship. The other curious feature of *Hotter Than July* regarding song order is how the first part of the album deals entirely with the love theme, while the end of the album is almost exclusively devoted to politics. Except that "Lately," another love song, is stuck right in the middle of the political material.

Let us return to discussion of "As If You Read My Mind," an up-tempo love song. The melodic range on the verses is quite narrow and limited to the lowest register of Wonder's voice. This sets off the slightly higher tessitura of the chorus. Melodically, however, it is not Wonder's most memorable song. As an example of a pleasant album track, however, it is a nice, entirely appropriate piece. And it finds Stevie Wonder's harmonica making a rare return to the studio; it is allotted a soulful, technically exciting solo.

Wonder's exploration of reggae and ska in "Master Blaster (Jammin')" follows on the heels of various British musicians, including Elvis Costello, the Police, and the Clash, as well as mixed-race bands like the Specials, in bringing these 1960s Jamaican styles into a new (and second- and thirdhand) prominence during the late 1970s. So in a sense Wonder was joining in a current musical craze of sorts. Unlike the work of those mentioned, however, Wonder's composition is a tribute to Bob Marley (who would die of cancer the following year at age 36) and the Pan-African politics expressed in some of Marley's songs. In this respect, "Master Blaster (Jammin')" bears some resemblance to "Sir Duke," Wonder's big band–era tribute song from *Songs in the Key of Life*. Wonder's music and arrangement is appropriately stripped down to the sound of a ska band. The vocal echo Wonder (as the record producer) adds to the lead vocal also reflects the style of Jamaican record making. When "Master Blaster (Jammin')" was issued as a single, it hit No. 5 on the *Billboard* pop charts and No. 1 on the magazine's R&B charts. The song, with Wonder's instrumental and vocal arrangement and his fine vocal performance, proves that he had thoroughly absorbed the Jamaican genre. It ranks as one of the best recordings in which Wonder explores a style that is not usually associated with him.

One of the important themes of the entire *Hotter Than July* album, including the artwork that graces the package, concerns the freedom to live out one's dreams. This is part of the Bob Marley tribute, as well as several of the subsequent songs and Wonder's expressions of his dream to see the United States adopt Rev. Dr. Martin Luther King, Jr.'s birthday as a national holiday. Certainly, the theme is at the center of the song "Do Like You." Here, however, the dream is that of a young boy who wants to become "the baddest dancer" around, and would too, with the help and encouragement of his sister. The problem for the boy, however, is that his parents do not take his dream seriously and refuse to allow him to practice so that he can compete in the school's dance contest. Ah, but he does compete, and he wins, proving that he can boogie better than anyone else. Some might complain that Wonder's premise and the outcome are far too obvious, but the song is highly effective. Partially, this is because of the catchy dance music to which the story is set (it is a perfect match), and partially to the fact that Wonder the performer allows the story (of Wonder the lyricist) to unfold on its own in the listener's ear and mind. He does not do the hard sell, as he does with less successful results in "Cash in Your Face."

The social consciousness that touches "Master Blaster (Jammin')" returns with a vengeance in "Cash in Your Face." Wonder plays the role of three very distinctive characters in the song, and does so convincingly. The first character begins by describing how long he has been trying to move into a particular apartment complex. Now that there is a vacancy, and he has the cash required to rent the apartment, he is turned away because the complex does not allow "his kind." Wonder tells us that this character is black, by mentioning that he holds a degree from Howard University, one of America's historically black colleges.[12] The presumption, then, is that the young man is rejected because of his race. The rejection itself finds Wonder in a rare show of being somewhat over the top, to use the colloquial phrase. He affects an edgy, menacing, "white" voice as he sings the landlord/building superintendent's rejection. Although doing so clearly paints the relationship between the characters in a (pardon the pun) black-and-white manner, it suggests that race-based discrimination might be stated in clear terms: subtle discriminatory wording in rejecting a potential renter would not exist given the way in which Wonder exaggerates the characters.

The third character portrayed by Wonder in "Cash in Your Face" is another potential renter. This person—who is of gender not defined by the lyrics themselves—is rejected because he or she has a baby on the way, and no children are allowed in this particular apartment complex. The presumption is that here Wonder's character is a woman—and possibly an unwed mother (although that may be reading more into the lyrics than Wonder ever intended)—who is being rejected not because of the baby *per se,* but because of who "she" is. Wonder takes on very real social issues in the song. It is less effective than it could be—in my judgment—in particular, because the landlord/superintendent is more a caricature than a true-to-life character. Whether or not the characters as Wonder vocally portrays them are entirely believable, "Cash in Your Face" is a socially relevant song. Discrimination in housing and so-called redlining by financial institutions were very much in the news in the late 1970s.

"Lately" stands alone on the album as a musical look back to the Tin Pan Alley torch song. The texture consists of acoustic piano, synthesized bass, and Wonder's voice, which is treated with some reverb that brings to mind a lounge setting. Although a pleasant enough song, and a reminder of some of the material of this type that he recorded in the first half of the 1970s, it is not of classic nature such as "All in Love Is Fair." The melody and harmony, as well as the lyrics, clearly reflect back to the past like "All in Love Is Fair," but "Lately" is not as immediately memorable, and the sentiments do not ring quite as true, despite the fact that the earlier song was far more filled with clichés than this one. One of the most notable features of the recording, in fact, is Wonder's use of a bass synthesizer. It illustrates just how far sound synthesis had come from the time of Wonder's classic albums of 1972–1974, on which if one could make one consistent criticism of the overall soundscape, it would be that the bass sounded very fake. The synthesizer here matches the quality of an acoustic bass;[13] however, Wonder does not really think like a bass player, so the bass tends to be far more out-front and soloistic than what one would expect from a real acoustic bass player. The lyrics find Wonder's character noticing that his lover has been wearing perfume when she goes out and questioning the strength of their relationship. He receives several other hints that she has been cheating on him, and, therefore, finds that his eyes are crying more and more because, "this time could mean goodbye." It is a very commendable album track, just not a classic composition nor recording.

The fact that "Lately" stands alone stylistically on *Hotter Than July* to the extent that it does highlights a trend in Wonder's writing and recording in the late 1970s and first half of the 1980s: he was turning increasingly to poppish (as opposed to jazz-oriented) ballads on one hand and potent funk on the other. The breadth of musical styles is somewhat thinner in this period than it was in the early 1970s.

Probably the best-known *Hotter Than July* track that was not released as a single, and possibly even better remembered today than the album's relatively successful singles, "Happy Birthday" was notable as part of Stevie Wonder's campaign to establish a national holiday to honor Rev. Dr. Martin Luther King, Jr. As a matter of fact, between the time of the album's release in September 1980 and the eventual congressional vote to establish the holiday, Wonder used every opportunity to campaign for the legislation, both musically and by appearing at rallies and special hearings. Wonder's activities on behalf of the King Holiday generated considerable coverage by the popular African American press, including feature articles in *Sepia, Jet,* and *Ebony.*[14] *Hotter Than July*'s artwork included various photographs from the civil rights movement, as well as a tribute to Dr. King. The album's notes also include the message, "Join me in the observation of January 15, 1981 as a national holiday. Stevland Morris a/k/a Stevie Wonder."[15]

The King tribute song closes *Hotter Than July,* so the album ends with a political and social message and with a musically strong closer. In the song, Wonder praises Dr. King's activities to bring peace to all people's hearts and expresses his dismay that the United States has not yet devoted a holiday to honor the civil rights leader. The song's verses are memorable, largely because of the catchy melodic and harmonic sequence Wonder composed, but the chorus features a truly classic melodic hook that even outshines the verses.

All in all, *Hotter Than July* was a very good album when compared with contemporary pop and R&B product from 1980. Stevie Wonder's lyrics addressed both timeless themes (love, for example) and topical issues (the push for a national holiday to honor Dr. Martin Luther King, Jr., and housing discrimination, for example). His music, too, reflects back to the past a little bit ("Lately"), but mostly sounds like it fits into the late 1970s/early 1980s mainstream. However, because it reflects the musical tastes of the time (and some of the social issues) so well, *Hotter Than July* does not transcend the times in which it was conceived, as do *Innervisions* and *Songs in the Key of Life.*

Early in his career, Stevie Wonder established himself as a
virtuoso harmonica player. He continues to incorporate jazz-
inspired harmonica playing into his recordings and concert
appearances right up to the present. © Chris Walter.

As a teenaged star, Stevie Wonder appeared in *Muscle Beach Party* with Frankie Avalon (left) and Annette Funicello (right). Photofest.

As the 1960s came to close, Wonder turned increasingly to the latest technological innovations in electronic keyboards, including the clavinet, which he plays in this photograph. This instrument was heard in Wonder's funk recordings of the late 1960s and early 1970s. © Chris Walter.

As suggested here, Wonder was one of the more passionate, soulful singers of the 1960s and 1970s. © Chris Walter.

In each phase of his career, Stevie Wonder was an iconic figure, not just musically but also visually. His sunglasses and dreadlocks of the 1970s and 1980s were well known to his audience. © Chris Walter.

This photograph calls to mind Stevie Wonder the composer, pianist, and singer of jazz-influenced ballads. © Chris Walter.

The headphones Wonder wears in this publicity photograph suggest his significant work as a recording artist. Stevie Wonder was one of the first recording artists to write his own material, play all the instruments on his recordings, and control record production. Photofest.

One of the most talented and recognizable R&B and pop keyboard players of the 1970s, Stevie Wonder is in his natural surroundings in this photo. Photofest.

Stevie Wonder, the former child star, has been a champion of children throughout his adult life. Here he is seen with Angela Pollock, the winner of the 1979–1980 Hal Jackson's Talented Teens International Contest. Photofest.

In 1982, the mayor of Wonder's birthplace of Saginaw, Michigan, proclaimed a "Stevie Wonder Day" to mark Wonder's performance at the Michigan State Fair. He is seen here receiving the proclamation from the mayor's special envoy Nate Calhoun. Photofest.

A familiar scene: Stevie Wonder holding a Grammy Award. He has won more than 20 Grammys throughout his career. © Chris Walter.

In this publicity picture, Stevie Wonder is seen doing what he does best: singing and playing the keyboards. Photofest.

From the 1970s onward, Stevie Wonder has championed social causes. One of his main focuses was the establishment of a national holiday to celebrate the birth and work of the Rev. Dr. Martin Luther King, Jr. Photofest.

The Musician with a Cause, 1981–2005

As *All Music Guide* critic Rob Theakston puts it, Stevie Wonder's 1980 album *Hotter Than July* "is the portrait of an artist who still had the Midas touch, but stood at the crossroads of an illustrious career."[1] Wonder had been a major figure in American popular music in the 1960s and even more so in the 1970s, but what would a new decade hold?

STEVIE WONDER'S ORIGINAL MUSIQUARIUM I

Much of Stevie Wonder's work of the 1980s has been dismissed by critics as inferior to the work of 1970–1976, with the critics expressing a particular dislike of the 1984 soundtrack to *The Woman in Red,* and Wonder's hit single from the film, "I Just Called to Say I Love You." But that was to happen in 1984. Although it was more of a greatest hits compilation than a proper follow-up to *Hotter Than July,* Wonder's 1982 album *Original Musiquarium I*—certainly one of his most unusually titled collections—did contain a few significant new tracks. And unlike the work to come, the album met with critical praise.

"That Girl," "Front Line," and "Do I Do" were the new tracks on *Stevie Wonder's Original Musiquarium I,* having not previously appeared on a Stevie Wonder album. "That Girl" was issued as a single at the end of 1981 and reached No. 1 on the *Billboard* R&B charts and No. 4 on the magazine's pop charts. Despite the record's popularity, it sounds tired, with Wonder's harmonica solo not quite capturing the level of excitement or expression of his early work. The solo also sounds out of tune, which is surprising considering Wonder's usually strong sense of intonation as a singer and as a harmonica player. The one feature of the recording that sounds contemporary and alive is the percussion track, which resembles some of the rhythm tracks from younger artists of the times, such as Prince.

"Do I Do" was a somewhat less successful single than "That Girl," reaching No. 2 on the *Billboard* R&B charts but making it to No. 13 on the magazine's pop charts. Although it is a stronger performance than "That Girl," the song sounds less uniquely Stevie Wonder and more like the prevailing pop/light-jazz/R&B dance music of the day. Perhaps the most notable feature of "Do I Do" is the presence of jazz trumpet legend Dizzy Gillespie. It is a delight to hear Wonder on harmonica trading licks with Gillespie, although Gillespie is not featured to the extent that he might have been on this recording, which is more than 10 minutes long. As a matter of fact, Wonder's harmonica licks have more coherence and generate more interest than Gillespie's sparse trumpet playing, which resembles the spare phrases of Miles Davis on his album *You're under Arrest* more than anything else. It is unlikely, however, that this was because Gillespie was aging (he was in his mid-60s at the time), as he was continuing to record and perform, and would even win a Grammy a number of years after his guest appearance with Stevie Wonder. Wonder's inclusion of Dizzy Gillespie was meant as a tribute to the jazz legend and his place in music, and it stands as an entirely appropriate acknowledgment; however, it is too bad that nothing approaching the spark of Gillespie's trumpet on his 1940s recordings of "Shaw 'Nuff" or "Night in Tunisia" is heard. Despite the fact that his appearance is meant as a tribute, the real problem is that Gillespie is not given room to stretch out and play. The piece is melodically and harmonically interesting, but, despite being a so-called song, it is basically instrumental and rhythmic in nature: it is a record that one could dance to, but one would not walk around humming it like "You Are the Sunshine of My Life" or one of Stevie Wonder's other strong vocally oriented pieces. Wonder might have done better to use the approach taken by the Rolling Stones on their 1981 record "Waiting On a Friend." The Rolling Stones' song featured noted jazz tenor saxophonist Sonny Rollins, who was given plenty of space to stretch out and play; indeed, Rollins's contribution to "Waiting On a Friend" is an essential part of the song—Gillespie's contribution to "Do I Do" is far less essential.

Of the newer material on the *Musiquarium I* album, perhaps the most interesting song was "Front Line." After the end of the involvement of U.S. troops in the Vietnam conflict in 1974 and the subsequent fall of Saigon, few pop musicians dealt with the war in recordings until 1982.[2] Between 1982 and 1985, several songs appeared that reflected back on the unpopular war and, in particular, on the war's effect on Vietnam veterans. These included Bruce Springsteen's well-known, but widely misinterpreted, "Born in the U.S.A.," the Charlie Daniels Band's "Still in Saigon," Paul Hardcastle's "19," Billy Joel's "Goodnight Saigon," and Stevie Wonder's "Front Line."

"Front Line" finds Wonder portraying a Vietnam veteran who has returned home a broken man, physically, psychologically, emotionally, and economically. This character, who served on the front line, and had one of his legs shot off in action, now stands "at the back of the line when it comes to gettin' ahead." Wonder's character suffers from posttraumatic stress syndrome, reliving the horrors of Vietnam in flashbacks and nightmares as a result of poisoning by the defoliant Agent Orange. The character also finds that his standing in the community and within his extended family has suffered dramatically because of his participation in the war. He laments that his "nephew's a junkie" and his "niece is a hooker." He finds himself powerless, however, to effect positive change in the lives of his relatives because they view him not as a hero, but as someone with a lesser moral standing for having served in a war to which he (in their minds) never should have gone.

Not only is "Front Line" unyielding in its funkiness, it is also one of Wonder's strongest lyrical statements in a song. Unlike "Living for the City," which offers a ray of hope for positive change, "Front Line" portrays the veteran's plight as one of total desperation and bitterness.

Exactly what makes a singer believable in a characterization is difficult to define in some cases, and in the case of "Front Line," it is especially so. Anyone familiar with Wonder knows that the character has nothing to do directly with the musician's own life experience. The main difference between "Front Line" and, say, "Keep On Running" from Wonder's 1972 *Music of My Mind* album (another song in which Wonder obviously portrays someone other than himself) is that the dismembered, alienated, paranoid veteran of "Front Line" represented real people who Wonder's audience members either knew or at least had heard of. The listener, therefore, feels a connection—in the vernacular, they get where Stevie is coming from. The lover who jumps out of the bushes on "Keep On Running" might represent someone that listeners know or have heard of, but he elicits absolutely no empathy or sympathy.

Wonder also made a guest appearance on Paul McCartney's album *Tug of War*, in a 1982 project entirely separate from *Stevie Wonder's Original Musiquarium I*. The two co-wrote and traded lead vocals on the song "What's That You're Doing," with McCartney playing bass, drums, and electric guitar and Wonder contributing synthesizers.[3] The song, an exercise in funk with a basic and completely nonprofound lyrical message of, "What's that you're doing? Girl I like what you do to me ... Do it some more," sounds more like a Stevie Wonder track from *Hotter Than July* than a Paul McCartney song. The two lead singers obviously have a good time (and McCartney gets in some nice bass and electric guitar lines): it is almost a contest to see who can outfunk the other, though again with McCartney seeming to adopt Wonder's style rather than the other way around.

The best-known collaboration between Paul McCartney and Stevie Wonder, however, is on McCartney's composition "Ebony and Ivory." On the track, Wonder and McCartney provide both lead and backing vocals, with Wonder playing electric piano, synthesizers, drums, and percussion, and McCartney playing bass, guitar, piano, synthesizers, and percussion. Despite the awkward phrasing of some of the lines in the lyrics and the naïveté of the sentiments, the single release of this song of racial harmony stayed at No. 1 on the *Billboard* pop charts for seven weeks; it was easily both McCartney's and Wonder's most commercially successful single. Paul McCartney's *Tug of War* album received mixed reviews, probably because of the overall organization of the collection rather than because of any individual song. The commercial success of "Ebony and Ivory" and the sheer fun these two major figures have on "What's That You're Doing," however, suggests that Paul McCartney and Stevie Wonder could have made a great album as collaborators if they had chosen to work more extensively with each other at the time.

THE WOMAN IN RED

The 1984 release of the soundtrack album for *The Woman in Red* led to some of the harshest reviews of Wonder's career, with critics in particular dismissing "I Just Called to Say I Love You" as "saccharine."[4] Prominent *Rolling Stone* critic Christopher Connelly also gave the soundtrack a less-than-enthusiastic review.[5]

Despite the way in which critics vilified "I Just Called to Say I Love You,"[6] the single release of the song reached No. 1 on both the *Billboard* R&B and pop charts (where it held that coveted position for three weeks). In fact, the record was Stevie Wonder's most commercially successful solo single ever, outsold only by his collaborative singles "Ebony and Ivory" and "That's What Friends Are For." In response to the critical blasts aimed at "I Just Called to Say I Love You," I offer an alternative reading of the song. The recording first and foremost represents a sort of character piece for the film; it serves a cinematic function. Even if one were to separate "I Just Called to Say I Love You" from its context in *The Woman in Red,* I believe that the song and Wonder's recording of it succeed as well on a certain artistic level.

Melodically, "I Just Called to Say I Love You" is almost an exercise in simplicity. The harmony subtly shifts and revolves around common-tone connections and simple voice-leading from chord to chord. In fact, on the surface the music is so basic that the only thing about it that comes as much of a surprise is the abrupt upward key modulations. Behind the foreground simplicity, however, it is worth noting that the slow stepwise voice leading in the chordal keyboard parts mirrors the faster lines in Wonder's vocal melody. It is as if he is using the same basic melodic motive on two different levels of structure—something that happens in highly sophisticated classically oriented compositions, but something that is rare in pop songs.

The lyrics are just as much an exercise in foreground simplicity: the entire premise being that Wonder's character needed no reason to call the person on the other end of the line except to say, "I love you." There is no ulterior motive; there literally is no special reason for this expression of emotion. The verses serve only to enumerate all the holiday-related and other traditionally celebratory reasons that were not behind the telephone call. About the only thing lyricist Wonder leaves out is Groundhog Day.

Wonder's arrangement and production of "I Just Called to Say I Love You" is about the closest he has ever come to composing a totally generic—even artificial sounding—backing track. The master percussionist eschews drums for a simplistic and very obvious drum machine, for example. Even Wonder's backing vocal tracks sound as if they are mildly electronically processed. The sudden, unprepared upward key modulations also sound thoroughly artificial, almost as though someone suddenly flipped the transposer switch on the keyboard. Indeed, the only touch of humanity is in Wonder's lead vocal.

The brilliance of the recording is in the total focus on simplicity and on the solitary humanity of Stevie Wonder's lead vocal: the match of words and music, arrangement and performance is complete. Typically, though, deliberately simplistic songs that observe the realities of day-to-day life have met with severe critical reaction, especially when well-known songwriters who have previously tackled challenging topics write them. Witness, for example, the scathing reactions to Paul McCartney's first post-Beatles solo single, "Another Day," not only by critics but also by McCartney's former band mate John Lennon in the latter's song "How Do You Sleep?"[7] In a way, "I Just Called to Say I Love You," like the McCartney song, presents the same type of critical dilemma as the mid-nineteenth-century sentimental parlor ballads of Stephen Foster. Generally dismissed during and immediately after Foster's lifetime, songs such as "Jeanie with the Light Brown Hair" are now viewed as excellent representations of the popular public taste of the day, and are valued critically as such. "I Just Called to Say I Love You" is hardly a work of lyrical or musical profundity, but then again, it is not supposed to be. As a well-crafted and quite deliberate statement of simple, no-strings-attached love, and as a representative of mid-1980s American public taste, the record succeeds. The extent to which the song defined American pop culture of the time is suggested by Wonder's appearance on the popular daytime drama *All My Children*. He appeared as himself singing "I Just Called to Say I Love You" after being introduced by his "friend," the character Erica Kane. Noted critic Robert Christgau, one of the prominent rock critics to have anything positive to say about the song, wrote at the time of Wonder's 1999 Kennedy Center Award that it was "a broad-spectrum shout-out that spoke to the shared experience of more potential listeners than anything Irving Berlin ever wrote."[8] Yes, the simplicity of the piece and its artificiality in production is out of character for Stevie Wonder, but these traits—the traits that numerous critics have jumped upon—are what make the entire piece work as a composition. And to the extent that it reflects the inner feelings of Stevie Wonder, "I Just Called to Say I Love You" presents him as a considerably more selfless character than his regrettable 1972 composition "Superwoman (Where Were You When I Needed You)."

The public controversy over "I Just Called to Say I Love You" did not end with music critics. Songwriter Lloyd Chiate brought suit against Stevie

Wonder in early 1990, charging that Wonder stole the song from Chiate. When the plagiarism charges were dismissed, Chiate eventually appealed the decision, charging that the earlier trial was biased. In August 1992, the U.S. Ninth Circuit Court of Appeals in San Francisco, California, found that there was no basis to Chiate's charges of bias in the original plagiarism trial and let stand the original verdict of innocence for Wonder. The two trials were closely followed by the black popular press, especially *Jet* magazine, which provided readers with updates (and which, incidentally, has given Wonder's career more than a small amount of coverage).[9]

Naturally, the soundtrack to *The Woman in Red* is not just about one song, although "I Just Called to Say I Love You" certainly received most of the attention in terms of sales, airplay, critical comment, and the Chiate lawsuit. Of the remaining tracks, all of the vocal numbers were composed by Wonder—the other track is Ben Bridges's instrumental composition "It's More Than You." Dionne Warwick sings the Wonder composition "Moments Aren't Moments," Warwick and Wonder duet on "It's You" and "Weakness," and Wonder provides the lead vocals on "The Woman in Red," "Love Light in Flight," and "Don't Drive Drunk."

Let us take a brief look at these songs. "The Woman in Red" is a pop dance number that suggests the dance tracks of Michael Jackson's work at the time. And that really is at the heart of some of the issues that critics have had with the early and mid-1980s recordings of Stevie Wonder: some of them seem to be too anonymous. This particular song establishes the theme of the film, but it also is a good dance track—the problem is that it could be just about anyone's good dance track. "It's You" is a pop love song that, again, is a good, memorable song, but it cannot be considered a classic. Likewise, "Love Light in Flight" fills a cinematic need and is a pleasant love song that returns to the synthesizer-based dance style of "The Woman in Red," although with a more relaxed feel. Overall, the soundtrack project did not offer Wonder a wide enough range of moods and emotions to explore, so, compared with just about every one of his so-called real albums, *The Woman in Red* soundtrack album seems thin. Fortunately, Stevie Wonder's next major soundtrack project, Spike Lee's *Jungle Fever*, would offer him the opportunity to explore a wider range of musical styles and emotions. Unfortunately, *Jungle Fever* would be seven years in the future.

After *The Woman in Red* had pretty much run its course, Wonder began making headlines for his social activism. He was arrested for protesting against apartheid in front of the South African embassy in February 1985. The United Nations Special Committee Against Apartheid honored Wonder later that spring for his work against the South African system of racial inequality. Wonder was also one of the vocal soloists on the USA for Africa recording of the Michael Jackson–Lionel Richie composition "We Are the World." This collaboration of more than 40 top musicians helped to raise money for impoverished people of Africa and the United States.

Throughout the 1980s and into the twenty-first century, Stevie Wonder has been active performing duets with a number of well-known performers, including Julio Iglesias, Frank Sinatra, Tony Bennett, Paul McCartney, and others. Among the lesser-known of these pairings, but a very intriguing one, was a performance with Julian Lennon, son of the former Beatle John Lennon, on the song "Time Will Teach Us All," from the 1985 musical *Time*. The musical itself was written by Dave Clark, the former drummer and leader of one of the best-loved of the "British Invasion" bands of the 1960s, the Dave Clark Five.

IN SQUARE CIRCLE

Hot on the heels of his commercial success with *The Woman in Red*, Wonder recorded and released the 1985 album *In Square Circle*. All in all, the album was another commercial success; it reached No. 1 on the *Billboard* R&B charts and was Wonder's last top 10 pop album to date. As noted by *All Music*'s Ron Wynn, many listeners equated the hit single "Part-Time Lover" with the album, even though a few of the album tracks were, at least in Wynn's eyes, better compositions and performances than "Part-Time Lover."[10] Despite the commercial success of *In Square Circle*, overall the album suffers from a uniform, nearly generic, mid-1980s production style that obscures Wonder's customary creativeness to an extent not heard on any of his other mature albums. In short, the drum machines, sequencers, and pop dance sound could have come from any one of a large number of 1980s musicians (like *The Woman in Red* all over again, but even more so). The stylistic, melodic, harmonic, and rhythmic eclecticism of Wonder's best-written, best-arranged, and best-produced albums of the 1972–1976 period (*Talking Book, Innervisions, Fulfillingness' First Finale,* and *Songs in the Key of Life*) is regretfully absent; there is no clear reference to the great torch songs of the 1940s, no sense of true funkiness, and not much outside of "Part-Time Lover" that even smacks of top 40 pop. The album also pales in comparison with Wonder's 1990s albums *Music from the Movie "Jungle Fever"* and *Conversation Peace*. Generic-sounding dance tracks simply do not make a great Stevie Wonder album. What *In Square Circle* does have in its favor—besides the big hit single—is the political song "It's Wrong (Apartheid)," and some very interesting melodic connections between songs—a unifying factor that becomes clearer with repeated hearings of the album.

In Square Circle begins with "Part-Time Lover," the big hit single, and the song with arguably the strongest melodic hook of any of the 10 songs on the album. One can tell, however, that there was a basic problem with American popular music in the mid-1980s when the best-remembered song on this album by one of the most important American singer-songwriters of the second half of the twentieth century is a fluffy little pop dance ditty about married people having affairs. Of course, the problem was not just in the popular taste of the time period, but also in the way in which Stevie Wonder indulged in it on *In Square Circle*.

Although the story of deceit of "Part-Time Lover" is at odds with the snappy music of the piece, the music itself is an example of good pop music: the melody of each section is logical and memorable; the harmonies are standard for pop songs; and Wonder's performance shows off his voice to good effect. The recording also benefits from the guest appearance of singer Luther Vandross. But there is something odd about the disconnection between music and lyrics. Certainly, pop singers have made material work that is even more conflicted in this regard than "Part-Time Lover." Bobby Darin's famous recording of Brecht and Weill's "Mack the Knife" is perhaps the ultimate example. Maybe Darin's recording works better because it is *so* extreme, so over the top. The Darin finger-snapping, big-band take on the Brecht and Weill song serves to heighten the irony already built into the song by the writers. Wonder's pop tale of part-time lovers sneaking around only to find that they have themselves been cheated on falls a bit flat. The other, unsettling thing about the song is how the line "part-time lover" can be misunderstood, in part because of the way in which Wonder places the lead vocal into the mix and his use of 1980s artificial studio reverb. As with John Fogerty's oft-misunderstood line, "There's a bad moon on the rise" (often misheard as "There's a bathroom on the right") from the song "Bad Moon Rising," if one is not paying particularly close attention, one might think that Wonder is singing about an "apartheid lover"—truly eerie considering Wonder's public statements and demonstrations against the racist South African institution.[11] With all that, if the listener tunes out the words, the song works wonderfully.

"I Love You Too Much" follows "Part-Time Lover." This 5–1/2-minute dance track features some of the interesting chromatic harmonic shifts that had been a staple of Stevie Wonder's compositional style since the 1960s. Melodically, though, the chorus section meanders a little too much, and finds Wonder sounding a little forced in the upper part of his singing range, thereby negating some of the strength of the melody of the verses. Wonder's inventive vocal improvisations on the long run-out coda, along with his multitracked backing vocal harmonies, are the high points of the recording. As is typical on the up-tempo songs on *In Square Circle*, however, the reverb and rhythm-forward production make some of the lyrics of the verses difficult to understand. The listener is left with many easily discernable repetitions of the main idea of the song in the coda section, but a fair chunk of the detail of Wonder's poetry is lost along the way.

"Whereabouts" is one of two slow songs on the album. The other, "Overjoyed," plays the role of the traditional ballad. "Whereabouts," however, finds Wonder in search of the "missing person that [he has] just got to find." It turns out the missing person is himself, or at least the part of his soul that was lost when he lost the person to whom the song is addressed. The theme is not new, but Wonder succeeds in framing it in an unusual way, using a serious form of wordplay that is not all that common in his songs. What he does is to describes this missing person in the abstract and gradually narrow the focus until it becomes clear that he is the missing person. It effectively communicates the feeling, and the lyrics find themselves wrapped in some lovely musical writing. Perhaps part of the self-alienation Wonder expresses in the song comes from the fact that the styles that defined his earlier masterpieces of the 1970s are lacking in some of his work of the mid-1980s. Be that as it may, "Whereabouts" comes off as thoroughly sincere without being self-pitying; The beauty and clarity of Wonder's musical setting balances the potential for self-pity that the lyrical theme suggests.

The vaguely Caribbean-sounding "Stranger on the Shore of Love" follows. Even though the keyboards and percussion sound a tad electronic (read "unnatural"), it is a pleasant enough song in which Wonder's exclamation that he does not want to be a broken-hearted stranger on the shore of love sums up the basic message. The really intriguing thing about "Stranger on the Shore of Love" is found in the arrangement, and in the harmonic and melodic motivic connections it shares with the album's next track, "Never in Your Sun."

"Never in Your Sun" is a moderately fast-paced pop song in which much of the poetic detail is obscured by the electronic processing of Wonder's voice. He dusts off the harmonica for a solo. It is effective, making up for the listless effort in "That Girl" from a few years before, but it is not an extended outpouring of inventiveness like Wonder's harmonica work on "Isn't She Lovely" in *Songs in the Key of Life*. "Never in Your Sun" also finds Wonder approaching this earlier style, constructing the melody through a sequential treatment of motives, and through the somewhat quirky upward melodic skips and rhythm of the chorus. These traits also make the song easily identifiable and move it far beyond the generic.

"Spiritual Walkers" does not stand alongside the more memorable songs on *In Square Circle*. For one thing, the rhythmic match of words and music is a little awkward at times: in particular, the phrase "spiritual walkers," which is unusual enough when spoken, seems as though it is forced into a melody that does not quite fit it. The song also suffers more than most from the production treatment of the vocal track.

"Land of La La" calls to mind the 1980s new wave/techno music of Oingo Boingo and some of David Bowie's dance music. Wonder's lyrics deal with what happens when young people from small towns move to Los Angeles, the "Land of La La" of the song's title, and discover the reality of urban life. Compared with the graphic story and more fully developed characters of "Living for the City," however, this song is considerably more lightweight in nature.

Musically, "Go Home" is one of the more interesting songs on *In Square Circle*. Here, Wonder returns to a procedure he had used effectively in the

1970s: that of blending acoustic and electronic-sounding instruments to give a greater richness of texture. The brass lines are not particularly complicated, but they help to balance some of the other more electronic-sounding timbres that pervade the album. The album's ballad, "Overjoyed," also includes an interesting mix of timbres and sound effects. Wonder includes some of the tasty harmonic shifts for which he was famous in this straightforward love song. Compared with the best of his ballads, however, "Overjoyed" suffers from the production techniques Wonder employs throughout *In Square Circle*. Here, the reverberation of the entire soundscape makes Wonder's lead vocal lose the sense that this is a song directed at one character from one other character. Wonder becomes a ballad singer in a cabaret, singing the song to an audience instead of to the one who has brought him such joy. A greater sense of intimacy and of rhetorical focus would have been possible with a clearer, drier treatment of the lead vocal.

Wonder had been quite vocal in his protests of South Africa's system of apartheid earlier in the year 1985. His song "It's Wrong (Apartheid)," on *In Square Circle* carries on the anti-apartheid theme. Wonder combines a very sequenced techno-sounding backing track with his pseudo–South African lead vocal and backing vocals that sound as if they came right out of the South African townships of the mid-1980s. Although Paul Simon, with *Graceland*, became possibly the best-known American pop singer-songwriter to merge American and South African styles in an attempt to expose the richness of black South African culture (as manifested in its music and lyrics), Stevie Wonder's "It's Wrong (Apartheid)" predated the songs of Simon's album.

CHARACTERS

The 1987 album *Characters* represented something of a musical hybrid for Wonder: on one hand, the dance rhythms and sometimes synthetic percussion and sequencer sounds of *In Square Circle* were still around, albeit in thankfully muted form, but on the other hand, the funkiness and bluesy emotion that largely had been missing since the 1980 album *Hotter Than July* made a welcome return. Although *Characters* did well enough commercially on the R&B charts—it hit No. 1—it only reached No. 17 on the *Billboard* pop charts. The less overtly pop-dance feel of the album may be to blame, but I suspect that it had at least as much to do with the disappointment longtime Wonder fans may have felt as a result of its immediate predecessor, and indeed with some of Wonder's other recordings of the first half of the 1980s. Another contributing factor, however, certainly was the lack of a major hit pop single to support and draw attention to the album.[12] And although several of the songs are successful to superb in their own right, and although Wonder develops two main themes throughout the album, *Characters* does not hold together as a unified album to quite the same extent as the megahits of 1972–1974.

Characters leads off with "You Will Know," a pleasant ballad that seems to anticipate the ballad-oriented songs to come out of the group Boyz II Men a few years later. The song has a fairly pedestrian melody (except for the memorable chorus) with a fairly anonymous instrumental backing. In fact, the most notable feature is Wonder's interesting use of truncated phrases that end up suggesting an occasional shift from quadruple meter (four pulses per measure) to duple meter (two pulses per measure) at the end of each stanza just as the chorus section begins. Also of interest is his use of deceptive cadences in the harmonies near the end of the chorus sections. In these places, Wonder builds up the expectation that a musical phrase will end on the tonic chord (built on the first scale degree), and then he ends the phrase on a non-tonic built on the sixth scale degree. Wonder's lyrics address the problems of those who are chemically dependent and those who are single parents by suggesting that through prayer they will find the answers. Wonder takes up these themes of societal/political problems and spirituality again in later songs on the album, sometimes by themselves, but more often in tandem.

"Dark 'n' Lovely" is a rare collaboration between Wonder and Gary Byrd. Wonder and Byrd deal with terrible tragedies of war, ethnic cleansing, starvation, and terrorism in South Africa under apartheid. The basic premise is that the white South African political structure (South African President P. W. Botha is mentioned by name) is effecting this violence against people simply because they are "dark 'n' lovely." The *Characters* subtheme of spirituality returns as Wonder and Byrd assure those who are being tortured, starved, and killed that God will "stop this reign." The melody of "Dark 'n' Lovely" is remarkable for its simplicity: each of the three main sections features its own tune, but each of the tunes is built on repetitions of one unique short phrase. The accompaniment is also very focused on an almost ostinato-like effect. Ultimately, this enables the message—the lyrics—to shine through. In the hands of lesser writers this could become very dull very quickly; however, the short phrases that generate the three melodic sections contrast with each other enough and are engaging enough that the song never becomes boring. The accompaniment lends a somber tone to the song, but the tempo suggests that good will ultimately triumph over evil in this politically charged situation. "Dark 'n' Lovely" is not one of Stevie Wonder's better-known songs, but it ranks among his better political songs, and is very effective in this context.

Despite all that Stevie Wonder had achieved after his 21st birthday (*Talking Book, Songs in the Key of Life, Innervisions,* etc.), the next track on *Characters,* "In Your Corner," suggests that he still held a place in his heart for the material he co-wrote with his old Motown staff collaborators and recorded back in the 1960s. In fact, as with some of the work that Billy Joel has done over the years, there even are hints at the musical styles of the 1950s. Although some of the specific lyrical images are more the product of the 1980s, the overall theme of a guy who is part of the "in crowd" (Wonder's character) taking one of his buddies who is *not* part of the in crowd to his favorite hangout to enjoy "fine women" and "lots of liquor" would not be out of place in the world of the late 1950s or early 1960s. The shuffle rhythmic style of the song—and particularly the early Motown-influenced baritone saxophone solo—set the time period. It is a wonderful character piece that sounds like it should have been in a film soundtrack set in the *Happy Days/American Graffiti* era. It counterbalances the love ballads and the serious songs of *Characters,* but in standing so far away in temperament and musical style from the rest of the songs on the album, also somehow seems out of place. The really ironic part of this sense of disconnection is that "In Your Corner" is one of the few songs on the album in which Stevie Wonder is *clearly* playing an actor's role. Therefore, it is one of the few songs on *Characters* that actually completely jibes with the title of the package and the cover art, which shows Wonder standing in front of busts holding an actor's mask.

The lyrics of "With Each Beat of My Heart" express, purely and simply, a proposal of marriage. It is a pretty ballad, and although not one of Wonder's classic love songs, it serves as a reminder of just how effortlessly he seems to be able to write and perform this type of song. The next track on *Characters,* "One of a Kind," continues the theme, but with lyrics that move even more in the direction of the cliché. "With Each Beat of My Heart" is more interesting musically and conceptually.

"Skeletons" concerns the proverbial "skeletons in the closet" that everyone has. For one of his songs of social and personal consciousness, Wonder is uncharacteristically oblique about the exact nature of these skeletons, except that in the end, they all amount to, in his word, "lies." Musically, "Skeletons" owes a debt of gratitude to "You Haven't Done Nothin'," Wonder's anti-Nixon funk track from *Fulfillingness' First Finale.* The track features one of Wonder's most soulful funk vocals and was a highly successful song on the various R&B charts when it was released as a single. Despite its stylistic resemblance to "You Haven't Done Nothin'," "Superstition," and maybe even "Living for the City," the song manages to sound contemporary, especially because of Wonder's vocals and the arrangement of the synthesizer parts.

"Get It," a duet with Michael Jackson, follows "Skeletons." The lyrics are about "Miss Lady Girl" who refuses to love any man. Wonder and Jackson, however, are convinced that she will love each of them; well, really "him," because the two singers essentially take turns acting out the role of the same character. Jackson is superfluous—Wonder gets the best melodic lines to sing—and the song does not add much to the album. The song might have made more sense had it been a product of 1982, when duets were the rage, with Paul McCartney and Wonder recording "Ebony and Ivory," and McCartney and Michael Jackson recording "Say, Say, Say" and the unfortunate "The Girl Is Mine." "Get It" is more distinguished than the latter Jackson/McCartney project, but it is about half a decade too late to be part of the heyday of the male superstar duet.

After a few seconds of pseudo-galactic electronic noise, the next track on *Characters* begins: "Galaxy Paradise." This is anything but the typical Stevie Wonder love song; rather, it's more along the lines of "men are from Earth, women are from UFOs." Wonder's lyrics express the fact that she is unpredictable, while he is not. Musically, it is little more than filler, nearly 4 minutes' worth. Given that *Characters* was an all-digital recording in the early days of the compact disc, when, in order to compete, albums suddenly had to be approximately 25 percent longer than they could comfortably be in the vinyl/analog age, it is perhaps understandable that there might be more filler on Wonder's albums of the day than on his big-hit, single-vinyl-disc, 40-minute albums of the 1970s. Unfortunately, this song is so out of character for the album in lyrical content, and of so little musical interest, that it seems clearly there just to be there.

"Cryin' through the Night" does not offer much in the way of lyrical interest, but—and this is a big "but"—it is a tuneful, danceable track. Wonder's character has discovered that his lover has left him for his best friend, and his vocal performance is replete with bluesy melodic licks that reflect the pain his character feels.

"Free" is one of the rare examples of the influence of Hispanic music in Stevie Wonder's output. There has been the occasional "Don't You Worry 'bout a Thing," but "Free" sounds not so much like Wonder doing Latino music as it does Wonder more fully integrating Latin American influences. The fact that it is such a good piece makes up in part for the less-inspired examples of filler material that precede it. Wonder's lyrics express the feeling of freedom his character has found in his life (the reason for this feeling is never directly divulged, though). He rekindles the album's subtheme of spirituality by acknowledging that this freedom can only exist, however, until his "father God has called." Clearly, this is a song in which Wonder is playing the role of a character: the singer of the song has found this freedom despite the fact that he has few if any possessions. Wonder's use of minor tonality with a chord progression and melodic shape is appropriate within the historical Hispanic popular song tradition. From a conceptual standpoint, the accompaniment sounds to be guitar-based, which fits entirely within the Latin American musical framework.

One of the maddening things about *Characters* is that printed liner material is so sparse. It would be nice to be able to read Wonder's lyrics, especially because the old 1960s Motown and mid-1980s *In Square Circle* echo returns on some of the tracks. It also would be nice to know what guest artists joined Wonder on the album (besides Michael Jackson, whose guest appearance on "Get It" appears in type as large as the song's title itself). So the listener must rely on Wonder's mention of B. B. King in the lyrics of "Come Let Me Make Your Love Come Down" to figure out that the blues legend must be the guest electric guitar soloist on the song. Or is he? In any case, the song is a sort of funky, bluesy love song about a woman who is "about 4'10''" and who keeps him satisfied in every way. It is enjoyable lyrically and musically, although not one of Wonder's greatest songs.

In terms of its memorable melodic hook and its hints of some of the funkiness of mid-1970s Stevie Wonder, the final track on *Characters,* "My Eyes Don't Cry," is a true highlight. It is an up-tempo dance track, but sounds more like a band jam than some of the highly programmed (on a sequencer, that is) dance music of Wonder's previous couple of recordings. In short, "My Eyes Don't Cry" maybe the best example of the great Stevie Wonder single that never was. It should have been released as a single, as it is at least as good as other successful 1987 singles by other artists, and it is a better song with more probable commercial appeal than the *Characters* singles that actually were issued: "You Will Know" and "Skeletons." Musically, "My Eyes Don't Cry" has a thoroughly memorable melody, just enough of the old Wonder chromatic harmony quirks, and some tasty open-interval vocal harmonies to make it both a clear part of the Wonder tradition of 1970s funky standards and a convincingly contemporary 1980s dance track. One of the things that makes the song so memorable is the way in which the verse starts away from the tonal center of the song—with the effect that the verse has a strong, choruslike hook all its own. Although the songs are quite different in rhythmic style, the effect is similar to that achieved in "If You Really Love Me," a song that actually starts with the chorus. The lyrics speak of an exuberance Wonder feels with a new love that caused his eyes to cease their tears, and the music fits them perfectly. To top it off, Wonder's lead vocal is filled with more energy than that shown in many of the rest of the album's tracks.

Interestingly, "My Eyes Don't Cry" is one of the few Stevie Wonder lyrics that is clearly autobiographical as it alludes to the singer's (or his character's) blindness. Although this might add a degree of poignancy to the text, the lyric's reference could also be understood as a metaphorical blindness. The beauty of this text is that it is so straight to the point. This brings up one of the features of Wonder's lyrics that is often not acknowledged: he has the ability to write equally well from a variety of viewpoints, and can use the English language in a wide variety of styles effectively. For example, the text of "My Eyes Don't Cry" is entirely different in character from the Tin Pan Alley use of clichés in "All In Love Is Fair," but both are highly effective. Throughout the years, he has written not only in these styles, but has written using the language of the street, the King's English, and every style in between. About the only thing that Wonder could possibly have done to propel this song to an even higher level would have been to record a scorching harmonica solo. Everything else about the composition and the recording says "classic."

All in all, *Characters* seems to fall into place as the logical follow-up album to Wonder's 1980 opus *Hotter Than July.* Rather than focusing on pop material and overly synthesized dance material as he had through the first two-thirds of the 1980s, Wonder returned to the eclecticism that had brought about his breakthrough as an album artist back in 1972. There was some obvious filler, but this, the first of Wonder's fully digital, made-for-compact disc albums, found him clearly back on course.

A native of Michigan, Wonder considered running for mayor of the heavily African American city of Detroit in 1988. Although he did not run, the fact that he mentioned publicly that he was considering it suggests his commitment to enacting social change from within the system. He continued to be associated with various political and social causes into the twenty-first century.

Because Stevie Wonder had made his first impact as a recording artist in 1962 and had been one of the most important recording artists in popular music in the 1970s, it was appropriate that he would be one of the fairly early inductees into the Rock and Roll Hall of Fame. His induction came in 1989. The accolades continued the following year when the National Urban League honored Wonder at its April 1990 gala in Los Angeles.

Wonder had been interested in and active in addressing international social and political issues for years. In 1990, he appeared in the *Nelson Mandela: 70th Birthday Tribute* video. Unfortunately, the video did not garner particularly great reviews, particularly from *Rolling Stone* critic Jim Farber.[13] Wonder's international concern was also highlighted by his October 1990 announcement that he planned to donate proceeds from his next recording to UNICEF.

JUNGLE FEVER

Film director Spike Lee has been known for tackling important and frequently controversial social issues in his movies. His 1991 film *Jungle Fever* dealt with the topic of interracial relationships. Stevie Wonder provided a soundtrack for the film that renewed his longstanding pattern of writing and performing music of highly diverse styles, an eclecticism that had been absent from some of his albums of the 1980s. In the *Jungle Fever* soundtrack, Wonder was able to combine early 1990s styles such as hip-hop with jazz, funk, and ballads. In short, Stevie Wonder was fully back from the techno and dance craziness of the mid-1980s.

The *Jungle Fever* soundtrack album opens with "Fun Day," which is regretfully one of Wonder's few straightforward jazz compositions and performances. The lyrics tell of a fun day, a day of celebration—while not exactly the stuff of great consequence, these lyrics set a celebratory mood. The real meat of the piece is in Wonder's arrangement in the style of CTI Records, his performance, and his production. Creed Taylor's CTI label came into prominence in the 1970s with pop-jazz artists such as Hubert Laws, Dave Grusin, Bob James, and Grover Washington, Jr. The music associated with CTI was highly accessible, rhythmically reflective of the pop music of the period, and usually featured improvisations that stayed clearly in a key (as opposed to the free jazz of the 1960s avant-garde). The Wonder song resembles a mix of the CTI style and that of jazz guitarist-singer George Benson, whose vocal style, incidentally, has been compared with that of Wonder. For someone who is as gifted an instrumentalist as Wonder, it is curious that the bulk of the extended improvised solos he has recorded have been on the harmonica. "Fun Day" includes a harmonica solo, but significantly, also features Wonder on a piano solo. Wonder proves that he is a first-rate jazz piano stylist. His singing, too, includes a touch of 1990s jazz scat. All this is entirely in keeping with the carefree nature of the lyrics.

"Queen in the Black" is a hip-hop-oriented celebration of a black woman about whom Wonder's character fantasizes. Wonder refers to her as a queen and "Miss Ebony." Lyrically, this song represents something of a departure for Wonder, who generally does not dwell on the race or ethnicity of the object of his (or the character he is portraying) desire in love songs. Of course, given the focus of the film on interracial relationships and the placement of the song in the film's context, the focus on the racial-ethnic identity of the woman is entirely appropriate. Curiously, Wonder does not define *his* character in the lyrics: he might be white or black. There is nothing in the lyrics to suggest whether this is a black man celebrating a black woman about whom he fantasizes or a white man fantasizing about "the other." Musically, "Queen in the Black" represents one of Wonder's first forays into the world of hip-hop. And this is strictly found in his drum playing. The rest of the composition and arrangement sounds like good contemporary (for 1991) R&B. Notable, however, is the fact that unlike some of Wonder's 1980s up-tempo songs, here Stevie Wonder the producer puts the lead vocal well forward in the mix: the lyrics are never obscured by 1980s-style production.

"These Three Words" is a pop ballad piece in which Wonder sings of the importance of verbally expressing love. He mentions that parents and children, husbands and wives, and siblings need to tell each other "I love you," and his chorus mentions the power of "these three words" in cementing relationships and in healing wounds. Outside of the context of the film, this is the sort of ballad about which Wonder's critics have complained since the 1980s. The simple love-conquers-all philosophy may not succeed with critics, but it has remained a staple of pop music for decades. In the context of the Spike Lee film, in which the love of generations of family members and of lovers is severely challenged by racism on several levels, the song's lyrical statement is poignant. The song's harmonies feature the type of chromatic voice leading and shifts that set the best of Stevie Wonder's 1970s ballads apart from the bulk of top 40 pop material. The melody generally is strong, although curiously the verses are more distinctive than the somewhat meandering chorus and "middle eight."[14] Wonder's jazz- and gospel-influenced vocal extemporizations serve to prove that Wonder, the master interpretative singer, is also back from the disco/techno 1980s.

"Make Sure You're Sure" is the soundtrack's jazz-oriented ballad. Although the song is thoroughly contemporary, as a composition and as a vocal and instrumental performance it owes a huge debt of gratitude to the types of ballads sung by such jazz performers as Billie Holiday and Nat "King" Cole. It is more sophisticated perhaps than the more poppish ballad "These Three Words." The earlier song, however, makes much better use of the strongest qualities of Wonder's voice and is also more melodically memorable than "Make Sure You're Sure."

Jazz and pop ballads, however, are just two of the styles Wonder explores in his *Jungle Fever* soundtrack. Notable is his latching onto and making his own a somewhat muted version of hip-hop style. Although there are elements of this early 1990s R&B style in Wonder's drum performance on "Queen in the Black," "Each Other's Throats" incorporates the style more thoroughly. This denouncement of the evil that people work against each other even contains a three-stanza rap by Wonder. The song is an especially interesting one to review in the twenty-first century. The 1990s eventually saw the explosion of gangsta rap, a hip-hop style that glorifies the very sort of violence that Wonder dismisses in "Each Other's Throats." The song is a breath of fresh air amid the direction some, if not most, of rap turned in the years after the release of *Jungle Fever*. It also, with its fast tempo and a fair amount of syncopation and rhythmic intensity in the instrumental and vocal lines, defies stereotypes of what songs that dismiss hate and violence "should" sound like. Because of how it defies these stereotypes—unlike some of Wonder's other material in the soundtrack—it is also an especially effective setting of its message: it resists complacent listening.

One who has not heard the track "Each Other's Throats" might wonder about Stevie Wonder's ability to incorporate the new hip-hop style, especially his ability to rap. Granted, given his age (40 at the time of the recording of *Jungle Fever*) and his long association with styles that did not have street credibility in the 1990s, one could dismiss a song like "Each Other's Throats" as a curiosity—a desperate attempt to be "hip." The song, however, is not that—it is authentic, somewhat youthful, and in hindsight, it set the stage for additional hip-hop work on the 1995 album *Conversation Peace*.

Guest artist Kimberly Brewer provides lead vocals on Wonder's composition "If She Breaks Your Heart." It is a song that fits a cinematic situation and is not one of the strongest efforts on the soundtrack album. In particular, Wonder's use of hip-hop rhythms in this ballad context sound labored, and the singsong nature of the melody also made it difficult for the work to hold much interest independently from the film. "If She Breaks Your Heart" is, however, typical of the prevailing pop R&B/top 40 crossover material of the early 1990s.

The majority of the songs on the *Jungle Fever* soundtrack album are longer than 4 minutes. As Stevie Wonder worked into the compact disc age, he adjusted his arrangements to add increasing amounts of musical space, generally in the form of extended instrumental introductions, instrumental interludes that establish rhythmic grooves, and longer coda sections. In these respects, "Gotta Have You," which exceeds 6 minutes, is something of a look into the future: it anticipates the regularly 6-minutes-plus songs of his next album, *Conversation Peace*.[15] "Gotta Have You" is not one of Wonder's best-remembered compositions and recordings, but it does feature a fine funky, blues-infused lead vocal melody in the verses, recalling his songs of two decades earlier, such as "Superstition."

"Jungle Fever" is one of the catchiest songs on the soundtrack album. This song, in which Wonder's character has gone "white-girl hazy" while the object of his desire has gone "black-boy crazy," makes for interesting study in the way that it deals with a long-held taboo in American society: interracial relationships. In the 1960s the subject was treated with intense seriousness, as in the film *Guess Who's Coming to Dinner*, in which there is little hope of the relationship surviving, and in Janis Ian's song "Society's Child (Baby, I've Been Thinking)." Or it's been handled in a humorous mock shock manner, as in the songs "Black Boys" and "White Boys" from the musical *Hair*. In contrast to these approaches, Wonder's song is playful and optimistic, while thumbing its nose at the "ignorant people" who are filled with prejudice on both sides of the racial divide. Speaking of thumbing his nose, Wonder does so by using some mildly explicit language of the street, telling those who disapprove of the relationship purely on the basis of race that they "don't know jack shit." The street speak might not be even close to the level of gangsta rap, or Prince's "Sexy M.F.," in which the singer-songwriter's description of himself as a "sexy motherfucker" flows like the most natural phrase in the world, but in the context of the entire corpus of the compositions of Stevie Wonder, the street speak of "Jungle Fever" is unique. In a clear show of decorum, the expletive used by Wonder is not included in the lyrics in the compact disc's program notes: it is replaced with a dashed line. And it is not even the expletive itself that seems most unnatural coming from Stevie Wonder; it is the thumbing-his-nose-at-the-ignorant negativism that seems most strange coming from an artist who has devoted practically his entire lyrics-writing career to delivering optimistic, positive messages. But then, there was a cinematic context within which Wonder was working for this entire collection of songs. The playful part of the "Jungle Fever" equation also comes from the deliberately singsong chorus and from Wonder's unexpected spoken acknowledgments of the percussionists on the recording, which actually happens twice.

"I Go Sailing" follows the title track. This gentle ballad finds Wonder's heartbroken character trying to find "a way to smile again" and coming to the conclusion that he will heed a wise man's advice that he find his happiness within himself—he does this by going sailing in his mind. This is a melodically pleasant song with some of Wonder's expectedly (from having done it now in four different decades) unexpected harmonic shifts. Ultimately, however, it is a mood piece for the film soundtrack and not one of his most memorable compositions. The performance is likewise low-key.

"Chemical Love" perhaps is one of the better-known songs from *Jungle Fever* and is the one soundtrack song with lyrics by someone other than Wonder: Stephanie Andrews wrote them. Her lyrics speak of drug addiction as a "chemical love." She concludes that the only way to achieve a true high is from "spiritual love," which she describes as a "natural miracle drug." Wonder's musical setting is an understated, moderate-tempo piece in a mild techno style. Wonder the producer treats Wonder the singer's voice to an effective artificial-sounding reverb and electronic timbre alteration. The ostinato nature of the backing instrumental tracks is unusual in the Wonder corpus, but works well in the context of this warning to the drug abuser. The reason for the effectiveness of the backing tracks and the mild electronic processing of Wonder's voice is that it creates the impression of a kind of soulless detachment—the kind of lack of human spirit or soul that might come from chemical addiction.

Stevie Wonder's natural voice returns for the final song on the *Jungle Fever* soundtrack album, "Lighting Up the Candles." This rock ballad about "lighting up the candles" of "our love" resembles the other ballads on the album in being pleasant enough, but not as memorable as Wonder's classic ballads. The mood of the song is consistent, however, and fits into its cinematic context (as a celebration of a love that will overcome all odds) perhaps better than it works as a purely aural experience.

Wonder's soundtrack for Spike Lee's *Jungle Fever* was an important piece of work for the musician for a number of reasons. First, Wonder proved himself capable of scoring a commercial film. His CD liner notes thank Lee for this. Wonder writes to the filmmaker, "I was able to see this project well enough to write the songs, even though you gave me the rough version in black & white!!!"[16] Second, and more important, Wonder proved that he could again be relevant, taking up the new rhythmic and structural styles of early 1990s popular music and merging them into his always-growing bag of tricks. Perhaps his first steps into the inclusion of hip-hop influence into his overall style were not as well realized as they would be on 1995's *Conversation Peace*, but these steps were mostly successful in the *Jungle Fever* soundtrack. The other important feature of the soundtrack was that it found Wonder exploring a wider range of emotions and musical styles than he had through the 1980s.

CONVERSATION PEACE

With a few exceptions, once he took total control of his recordings, by writing or co-writing all of the songs, singing all or nearly all of the vocal tracks, playing all or nearly all of the instruments, and producing, Stevie Wonder took a few years to release each new studio album. Wonder had mentioned the upcoming *Conversation Peace* album in interviews for several years leading up to 1995; however, it was finally released only in March of that year, nearly four years after his soundtrack to *Jungle Fever.* He had not been entirely absent from the music industry—Wonder appeared on Frank Sinatra's album *Duets II* (Capitol CDP 8281932) in 1994, singing his old hit from the 1960s "For Once in My Life" with Sinatra and Gladys Knight.

Conversation Peace is an album dedicated to finding peace in a world full of mistrust, hate, and violence. This theme, in one form or another, can be found on virtually all of Wonder's albums, even going back to the early 1960s. Never, though, had the focus been so strong, nor the result so much like a concept album. By focusing on an important social and political issue, Wonder met with more critical approval than he had in a decade and a half. For example, the *Wall Street Journal*'s critic Jim Fusilli gave *Conversation Peace* a favorable review,[17] and *All Music Guide*'s Stephen Thomas Erlewine praised Wonder's attempts at integrating the contemporary hip-hop style more thoroughly in the album.[18] The critics, however, were not unanimous in their praise of Wonder's adoption of hip-hop rhythms. *People Weekly*'s Andrew Abrahams, for example, complained that on *Conversation Peace,* Wonder "too often winds up slamming out pedestrian songs lacking his usual celebratory bounce" because of his attempt "to sound au courant" by incorporating hip-hop style.[19] Contrary to Abrahams's assessment, however, the lack of bounce was probably attributable more to the weightiness of the social, spiritual, and political commentary of the album than to the incorporation of hip-hop per se.

Conversation Peace hit No. 2 on the *Billboard* R&B album charts and No. 16 on the magazine's pop album charts. Although Wonder had not recaptured his tremendous sales appeal of the first half of the 1970s, he had returned to relevance (especially, if the sales statistics figures are any indication, among black listeners) after the uncertain 1980s. The words and music of *Conversation Peace* and the *Jungle Fever* soundtrack were more eclectic and interesting than anything Wonder had produced since *Hotter Than July* more than a decade earlier (even if *Characters* had shown that Wonder was no longer *In Square Circle,* as it were, in 1987).

Conversation Peace opens with the sound of a thunderstorm, which does an immediate segue into "Rain Down Your Love," a completely contemporary mid-1990s hip-hop infused R&B track. Except that, unlike the stereotype of the hip-hop genre, this song is a prayer asking God to rain his love down to wash our minds and our spirits. The reasons that this prayer—which makes up the song's chorus—and this cleansing is needed are enumerated in the verses, in which Wonder talks about the psychological illness that causes humanity to ignore the Creator's master plan. Wonder provides all of the song's instrumental and vocal parts, thereby demonstrating that he has thoroughly absorbed the contemporary R&B style of the mid-1990s as writer, producer, instrumentalist, and singer. The change in his rhythmic approach as a drummer is especially remarkable: he no longer is the heavily jazz-influenced improviser of *Talking Book* and *Innervisions,* as he now lays down an unrelenting hip-hop beat. This is something of a double-edged sword: on one hand it shows Wonder's creativity in being able to keep current; on the other hand, it means that the measure-by-measure and phrase-by-phrase creative jamming of Wonder's instrumental work of 20 years prior is almost entirely absent not only on this song but throughout *Conversation Peace*. Given the seriousness of the subject matter, and the heartfelt way in which Wonder's lyrics address those subjects, perhaps it is only appropriate that he forsakes musical virtuosity—for the style of a song like "Rain Down Your Love" and the bulk of *Conversation Peace* places the listener's attention more squarely on the lyrics. The hip-hop drum track cuts out before the last repetitions of the chorus. This textural change is unexpected and brings the listener's attention back to the music, where it belongs.

The song "Taboo to Love" is the first recorded example of the collaboration between Stevie Wonder and Dr. Henry Panion III, a music professor associated with the University of Alabama, Birmingham.[20] Wonder had never done his own string arrangements, even though some of his recordings contained decidedly stringlike synthesizer arrangements, and thus, he contacted this conductor, composer, arranger, and orchestrator, based on his knowledge of Panion's previous work for other artists. Panion provides a full orchestral treatment to "Taboo to Love," a song that finds Wonder and his would-be companion concluding that the taboo to their love—the exact nature of which is not fully explained—can ultimately be overcome. In fact, the orchestration is one of the most interesting features of the composition. On his past recordings, Wonder had had the assistance of Motown stalwarts such as Paul Riser to do orchestral arrangements—they worked well enough—but Panion's mixture of classical and pop actually works better in some respects than the work of Wonder's previous orchestrators: it is lush without being heavy handed (though some might find it somewhat "schmaltzy"). As for the lyrics, this is a love ballad; however, the nature of the story (love overcoming the artificial taboos society places on certain relationships—interracial, perhaps?) fits right into the overall concept of *Conversation Peace*.

Throughout his songwriting career—or more appropriately, throughout his lyrics-writing career—Stevie Wonder has returned to the theme of a universal, agape-type love time after time. "Take the Time Out" is such a song, and in some respects is reminiscent lyrically of the 1970 Diana Ross hit "Reach Out and Touch (Somebody's Hand)." Wonder here urges the listener to "take the time out to love someone," and especially the poor, the lonely, and the homeless. He emphasizes that "we are all one underneath the sun," and to underscore the message, Wonder is joined on the background vocals by the famed South African vocal group Ladysmith Black Mambazo. Although the relatively low-energy level of the arrangement and tempo makes the song seem overly long and repetitious—it is, after all, one of the 10 (out of 13) songs on the album to clock in at more than 5 minutes, and the chorus does repeat quite a few times—Wonder's melody is catchy and memorable, and the verse and chorus melody stand in an appealingly stark contrast to each other. In fact, this melodic contrast is notable for its text painting: the verses, which enumerate all the people with serious problems who are in need of help and love, are set to short melodic phrases in a narrow range, while the chorus, which requests that the listener show his or her love, is set to a wider range, a higher vocal tessitura, and features a few more skips than the verses.

Wonder plays all the instruments on "Take the Time Out," and that is worth noting. Further, careful listening to his synthesized bass and other synthesizer parts reveals the extent to which technology had evolved from his first "all-Stevie" recordings of 1971 to 1995. The synth bass sounds like an authentic electric bass, and the guitarlike lines certainly do not have the kind of fake sound that was evident in some of Wonder's early 1970s recordings. It is also important to note that Wonder plays the synthesized bass lines like a fine electric bass player would: he has absorbed the electric bass idiom, as evidenced by his melodic approach on the track.

"I'm New" is a love song with a twist, and it is with that twist that the song fits squarely into the programmatic theme of *Conversation Peace*'s emphasis on spirituality. Here, Wonder sings that his newfound love—for which gift Wonder's character thanks "him" (God)—makes him feel completely new. He goes so far as to compare this feeling to the sense of newness felt by a born-again Christian. It is, then, a song that explores the notion of romantic love as a spiritual gift that itself has a deeply spiritual (in addition to physical and emotional) nature. A later album track, "Sensuous Whisper," celebrates the physical, sensuous side of love with an appropriately funkier rhythmic groove. Wonder's piano playing and the sax/trumpet horn lines suggest the contemporary popular jazz of the era. The track that follows "Sensuous Whisper," "For Your Love," is a gentle ballad that celebrates the emotional, romantic side of love. By looking at love in these decidedly contrasting ways—lyrically and musically—Wonder presents a more fully rounded-out view of love than on many of his albums. Incidentally, "For Your Love," not be confused with the 1960s Yardbirds hit of the same title, is the closest song on *Conversation Peace* to Wonder's great ballads of the 1970s: there is a touch of soul, a slight touch of Tin Pan Alley, and a touch of the old jazz influence in Wonder's piano and drum playing.

In an interesting turn of rhetorical style, "My Love Is with You" finds Wonder portraying two separate characters that have been murdered with handguns. As might be expected, the entire point of the song is to make a plea for the banning of handguns and to strengthen the message by providing the two concrete examples of the result of their use. Wonder uses the hip-hop musical style of the 'hood, as well as the *musique concrète* sounds of the killings. The *concrète* recordings that come after the music itself fades out add significantly to the chilling effect of the song, and had Wonder not included that surprise, the song would have seemed too pedestrian to be completely effective. "My Love Is with You" serves an important function on *Conversation Peace* by dealing with the real everyday violence of the American city streets.

Stephanie Andrews, who had collaborated with Wonder on the song "Chemical Love" from the *Jungle Fever* soundtrack, provided the lyrics for "Treat Myself." Interestingly, her lyrics are considerably more sparse than any of the others on *Conversation Peace*. In a sense, one of the immediate commercial weaknesses of the album is that, aside from this song and "Conversation Peace," the majority of the songs are so densely packed lyrically that it is a real challenge for the listener to take them all in. Wonder was addressing societal issues that had meant—and continue to mean—the world to him over the years, and he seems to have wanted to address them from every possible angle over the course of the one-hour-plus album. Consequently, Stephanie Andrews's poetry ends up having a more focused feel than some of the other songs. The lyrics suggest that one should conjure up "pretty places" in his or her head when his or her "life's in a place" that is unbearable. Without saying it directly, she suggests that one's emotional state is basically under one's control. Wonder's musical setting highlights the sharp distinctions between the world as the character actually experiences it and the world of imagination through his high degree of melodic-shape and harmonic contrast between the verses (the cruelty of the world) and the chorus (the sunny world of the imagination). Also highlighting the lyrical contrast are Wonder's harmonica solos over the top of the numerous repetitions of the chorus.

"Tomorrow Robins Will Sing" is a Jamaican-groove love song featuring "chatting" by Edley Shine. It is a pleasant mood piece, but in the larger thematic context of *Conversation Peace*, it is less than essential. In a way, it comes off as something of a reversion back to the occasionally anonymous Wonder songs of the 1980s.

After the twin celebrations of love that come approximately two-thirds of the way through *Conversation Peace*—"Sensuous Whisper" and "For Your Love"—Wonder explores the theme of broken relationships. The first of these two songs, "Cold Chill," is a funky piece that keeps the subwoofer thumping. This sonic effect, along with the background vocal arrangement, and the melodic and harmonic style resemble some of Prince's music of the 1980s and 1990s, and to some extent, Michael Jackson's recordings of the same period as well. The main difference is that, in contrast to the lustiness of some of Prince's lyrics, the lust is more implicit here. And ultimately, Wonder's character never has the chance to act on his fantasies, as the object of his desire gives him a "cold chill" of rejection.

Although Stevie Wonder managed to integrate newer pop and R&B rhythmic and structural styles into his songs of the 1990s, and particularly those with muted hip-hop references on *Conversation Peace*, not all of his musical focus was on sounding completely new and contemporary just for the sake of doing so. "Sorry" provides ample evidence of this. Curiously, this song incorporates musical elements that are reminiscent of Wonder's work from the 1960s through the 1990s. Harmonically and (particularly) melodically—both in the "written" melody and in Wonder's extemporizations—"Sorry" sounds like one of the easily recognizable, strong hook–focused Wonder singles of the 1960s and pre–*Talking Book* 1970s ("Signed, Sealed, Delivered [I'm Yours]" or "Uptight [Everything's Alright]," for example). Once the lead vocal line enters, the song's structure also reads like a page from the 1960s; however, like virtually every song on *Conversation Peace,* "Sorry" begins with a long introduction, something rarely found in Wonder's recordings of 20 or 30 years earlier. Of course, back in the mid-1960s, the primary form of expression in the world of popular music was the 2–1/2-minute single record. Wonder's backing instrumental tracks—he plays all of the instruments on this song—contain just a twinge of 1990s hip-hop, but a little bit more than just a twinge of early 1980s British new wave/techno, a la Orchestral Manoeuvers in the Dark or the Human League. This may sound like a strange mix of stylistic references, but "Sorry," the second *Conversation Peace* song to deal with a troubled love relationship, works very well. The reason is that Wonder fully integrates all of the stylistic references in such a way that the recording becomes just a Stevie Wonder song, and not a derivative work nor a chaotic mixture of sounds. The lyrical theme could have been a product of the 1960s: Wonder told his lover lies; she left him; now he is expressing his sorrow and begging for forgiveness. Although this is not the sort of higher philosophy that Wonder explores on other *Conversation Peace* songs, and although the situation is a pop song cliché, it is an everyday occurrence around the world, and fits entirely within the album's grand scheme of exploring the things that tear people apart and the need for healing and peace on many levels.

The lyrical treatment in both the verses and in the chorus of "Conversation Peace" has a somewhat parlando (speechlike rhythms) feel, in part because of the asymmetrical lengths of the lines of text. Given that this happens within an easygoing pop/hip-hop/gospel feel—and given the upfront placement of the lead vocal line in the recording's mix—it focuses the listener's attention right in on the words. Wonder's message of "all for one, one for all" as the only way to avoid repeating the atrocities of the past (such as the "holocaust of six million Jews and a hundred and fifty million blacks during slavery") is greatly enhanced by the rich background vocal harmonies of the group Sounds of Blackness. This is a millennial song: a call to allow conversation and remembrance of the past to usher in a new age of the global connection of all humanity. Although this theme has been at the background of more than a few past Wonder songs and certainly at the background of his social activism throughout the years, "Conversation Peace" is perhaps the clearest, most focused, and concise single statement of Wonder's overall life philosophy. Not necessarily among his best-known compositions or recordings, it is nonetheless one of his most effective philosophical/spiritual songs.

Conversation Peace was a remarkable achievement for Stevie Wonder. Of all of the musicians who had made their recording debuts back in 1962, only a very few were still active in 1995. But the most impressive aspect of the album and how it defines Wonder's work is that he is pretty close to being alone among musicians who had debuted in 1962 but whose mid-1990s work had evolved along with prevailing stylistic trends. And for the most part, *Conversation Peace* does indeed sound like a very good, topical (though a little bit muted) mid-1990s R&B album, done by a contemporary musician fluent in the styles, issues, and language of the day.

Perhaps even more important than the fact that *Conversation Peace* is a very good example of mid-1990s R&B is that it provided an opportunity for Stevie Wonder to focus as a lyricist on weightier subjects over the course of an hour-and-a-quarter-length piece. It becomes, in this way, his most complete testament to the social, political, and spiritual concerns of his work as a musician.

Perhaps as natural a follow-up to the *Conversation Peace* album as any of Wonder's philanthropic activities was his 1995 establishment of an annual series of concerts to benefit needy children. The Annual House Full of Toys Benefit Concerts raised money to purchase toys so that underprivileged children would be able to enjoy the same holiday cheer as children from more affluent homes. The concerts have continued into the twenty-first century. The sixth annual event, held December 15, 2001, was notable for its sponsorship by Yahoo!, which made possible a live broadcast on the World Wide Web.

NATURAL WONDER

Dr. Henry Panion, III, who had orchestrated "Taboo to Love" on the May 1995 album *Conversation Peace,* was contracted to orchestrate Wonder's music for the subsequent 1995 album and concert tour project *Natural Wonder.* Because the project involved working with symphony orchestras and Wonder had not done string arrangements in the past, he sought out someone whose work he respected. As a skilled conductor, Panion, in addition to the arrangements and orchestrations[21] that he did for the project, also directed the Tokyo Philharmonic Orchestra for the recording.

More than anything else, what Panion did when it came to some of Wonder's older songs, was to take Wonder's arrangements and translate them into a full symphonic context. For example, the *Natural Wonder* version of "Village Ghetto Land," a Stevie Wonder–Gary Byrd composition from *Songs in the Key of Life,* uses real orchestral strings in place of the 1976 recordings synthesized strings. The eighteenth-century chamber orchestra style of Wonder's original arrangement is further enhanced by the use of the orchestral instruments, creating a heightening of the striking sense of ironic disconnection between the lyrics' description of scenes from a poverty-stricken slum and the musical settings' association with late eighteenth-century European aristocracy. Panion's orchestration of this song makes use of the resources of live stringed instruments, but the arrangement itself (just exactly what melodic lines the instruments play) is remarkably similar to Wonder's earlier "synthestration."

This is true not just on "Village Ghetto Land" but also on the other older material on *Natural Wonder*. The arrangements are not all that different from the definitive Wonder recordings of the past. There is a reason for the retention of Wonder's original arrangements even within the broader symphony orchestra context of this particular recording. As rock guitarist-composer Frank Zappa wrote:

> On a record, the overall timbre of the piece (determined by equalization of individual parts and their proportions in the mix) tells you, in a subtle way, *WHAT* the song is about. The orchestration provides *important information* about what the composition *IS* and, in some instances, assumes a greater importance than *the composition itself*.[22]

Although Zappa uses the term *orchestration,* one could substitute *arrangement* in the context of Stevie Wonder's music. Musicologist Albin J. Zak III, in a spring 2005 article in *American Music,* quotes Zappa and goes even farther in essentially defining the "text" of a pop song—the artifact itself—as the definitive recording of the song. In other words, a song is not the melody, harmony, instrumentation, arrangement, but also includes the studio mixing, and the entire vinyl or compact disc experience.[23] If one is to accept Zappa and Zak's definition in its strictest form, then re-arranging, re-orchestrating, or even just re-recording a "song" results in a new "song." In that he was the one to make the contact with Panion, Stevie Wonder apparently did not think of the new orchestrations of the original arrangements as creating fundamentally different, new "songs." It is entirely legitimate to define Wonder's compositions in terms of the definitive recordings. And *Natural Wonder* seems in a sense to confirm this: Henry Panion basically took what were almost totally studio-conceived pieces and adapted them for live performance while retaining the essential character of the original versions.

The late 1990s and early twenty-first century saw Stevie Wonder receiving more awards and accolades. In 1996, he not only received two Grammy Awards, but was also the recipient of Grammy's Lifetime Achievement Award. In 1999, Wonder became the youngest honoree up to that time to be recognized by the Kennedy Center for the Performing Arts. The Dr. Martin Luther King, Jr. Center for Nonviolent Social Change, Inc., honored Wonder at its January 13, 2001, "Salute to Greatness Awards" dinner. Wonder became only the third-ever recipient of the Ivor Novello Awards' Special International Prize; he traveled to London to accept this major award for composers. And, in 2002, Wonder was elected to the Songwriters Hall of Fame. The hall also presented him with the Sammy Cahn Lifetime Achievement Award.

The twentieth century ended with Motown issuing the 4-compact disc set *At the Close of a Century*. The collection consists of most of Wonder's hit singles (although "Workout Stevie, Workout" and "Hey Harmonica Man," both pop top 40 singles, are absent) along with some well-chosen album tracks ("Isn't She Lovely," for example, is a particularly well-known Wonder song that strangely was never released as a single). Motown would release a couple of additional Stevie Wonder compilations in the early twenty-first century, each with a focus on presenting Wonder as a writer and performer who excelled in many diverse styles. Although the company could have easily issued a funk album or a ballad collection, fortunately it has not done so—for to compartmentalize Wonder is to do his career a disservice.

Wonder's guest appearances to raise money for philanthropic causes also continued into the twenty-first century. For example, he appeared in September 2000 at School Night '00, an event that raised more than $6 million for scholarships to enable underprivileged Washington, D.C.–area children to attend private or parochial schools. In April 2001, Wonder performed at the Eighth Annual RACE To Erase MS. In addition to performing at benefits to fight multiple sclerosis, he has also performed at numerous events to raise AIDS awareness and to raise funds to combat the disease.

In 2001, Wonder appeared on Tony Bennett's album *Playin' with My Friends* (RPM Records CK85833). The two musicians with excellent jazz credentials performed "Everyday (I Have the Blues)." Wonder was also one of the featured performers in July 2001 during the celebrations of the 300th birthday of the city of Detroit, Michigan.

The early twenty-first century has not been entirely bright for Stevie Wonder, however. In October 2001, his longtime girlfriend, Angela McAfee, sued the musician, claiming that he had broken his promise to maintain her in his Los Angeles home for the rest of her life, even if the couple broke up. According to the $30-million lawsuit, Wonder transmitted herpes to her, moved out, and stopped paying rent. Wonder countersued, claiming that McAfee had taken more than $160,000 worth of furniture, exercise equipment, musical instruments, and other property that belonged to Wonder from the house.

Adding to the turmoil of Wonder's personal life in 2002 was the release of Dennis Love and Stacy Brown's book *Blind Faith: The Miraculous Journey of Lula Hardaway*. This biography of Wonder's mother has created controversy on several levels. First, some critics have questioned the book's focus on Wonder himself at the expense of the purported subject of the book, Lula Hardaway. Second, Stevie Wonder has questioned the book's details on his mother being forced into prostitution. Regarding Wonder's concerns, it should be noted that Lula Hardaway has cooperated fully with the authors of *Blind Faith* by appearing in radio and television interviews to promote the book.

Despite the acrimony between Wonder and McAfee and controversy created by the details of the early life of Lula Hardaway, the years 2002 through the present have for the most part seen Wonder coming back into the fore-front of American pop and R&B music through important compact disc com-pilations from Motown, and his appearances at benefits, and his receiving and presenting prestigious awards. Motown released *Stevie Wonder: The Defini-tive Collection,* a single CD, in 2002. Although this collection is more limited than the massive 4-disc *At the Close of a Century* collection that Motown had issued in 1999, *The Definitive Collection* was the first single-disc greatest hits collection that covered what looked to be his entire career. The year 2003 found Wonder presenting the 2003 Century Award to Sting, with the two musicians seeming to form a mutual admiration society with their onstage banter.

On June 10, 2004, Stevie Wonder received the prestigious Johnny Mercer Award from the National Academy of Popular Music/Songwriters Hall of Fame. The Chairman of the Hall of Fame, famed lyricist Hal David, referred to Wonder as "a 'songwriters' songwriter,'" acknowledging that Stevie Wonder's "music is known and loved around the world and has made a difference in the lives of so many."[24]

On the subject of great American popular songs, Wonder performed on the 2004 album *Stardust: The Great American Songbook III.* He sang the song "What a Wonderful World" in a version that pays tribute to the famous Louis Armstrong recording of the 1960s, but that included some highly virtuosic harmonica figures. Wonder's harmonica solos emphasize that the melody of "What a Wonderful World" essentially is a reworking/expansion of the children's song "Twinkle, Twinkle Little Star." As one might imagine, the fact that the song is based on visual images makes the choice of Stevie Wonder as the performer ironic, and the fact that the musician's pseudonym is part of the title is also ironic. Far from being some sort of joke, though, the recording truly is a fitting tribute to Armstrong, even though the easy listen-ing material is not something that one might ordinarily associate with Stevie Wonder. And the harmonica solo, despite its technical brilliance, strips this very naïve song of some of its heartfelt sincerity because of Wonder's insistence on emphasizing the childlike nature of the song's "Twinkle, Twinkle"–based melody. Those little matters aside, listeners who liked Louis Armstrong's ver-sion of "What a Wonderful World" will appreciate Stevie Wonder's version as well. Hard-core Wonder fans, though, probably will not. Even so, Wonder's emphasis on "Twinkle, Twinkle, Little Star" recalls his incorporation of "Mary Had a Little Lamb" on his first smash recording—the live recording of "Fingertips" more than four decades earlier.

Unfortunately, Wonder had to endure some personal losses in 2004. Inter-views with Ray Charles and with Stevie Wonder suggest that the two blind singer-songwriter-keyboard players were never particularly close—they were, after all, of completely different generations and ultimately created music that had only the most surface similarities—but it must be remembered that one of the early attempts by Motown to define Little Stevie Wonder was as a sort of new Ray Charles. Wonder not only commented favorably on the music of Charles with the musician's passing in 2004, he also led a jam session at the Radisson Hotel in Los Angeles to celebrate the life and music of Charles. The performers who joined Wonder included members of Charles's recording and road bands, the Raylettes, Ellis Hall, and several other musicians.

Undoubtedly, Stevie Wonder suffered an even greater personal loss with the death of his former wife and writing partner Syreeta Wright, who passed away from bone cancer on July 6, 2004. In addition to being married from 1970–1972, Wright and Wonder co-wrote several songs that appeared on Wonder's albums and on Wright's 1972 album *Syreeta*. Wonder and Wright continued to compose together, including the material on Wright's 1974 album *Stevie Wonder Presents Syreeta*, which as the title implies, was produced by Wonder. Wright and Wonder had remained friends in later years.

The end of 2004 and the beginning of 2005 found Stevie Wonder in the news once again. This time, he expressed his support for his legally embattled friend Michael Jackson by criticizing the latest music video by white rapper Eminem, who appears in the video dressed like Jackson, with young boys cavorting with him on a bed. Wonder took the rapper to task for making money off of an African American music style, while mocking the important African American artist Jackson and failing to give the former King of Pop, one of the commercially successful musicians of the 1980s, the presumption of innocence.

On a totally unrelated front, Wonder was back in the media spotlight with his appearance at the January 15, 2005 Tsunami Relief Telethon, which involved not only longtime important musicians such as Wonder and Elton John, but also many well-known film and television actors. His charity work continued through spring 2005 with a performance at Tiger Jam, a fund-raiser for the Tiger Woods Foundation.

A TIME TO LOVE

Because he is a perfectionist, and because on his post-1970 albums Stevie Wonder typically plays all or nearly all of the instruments, he has been notoriously slow at releasing new material. The 10 years that have elapsed between the 1995 album *Conversation Peace* and the 2005 album *A Time to Love*, however, are a dubious record for Stevie Wonder. Considerable expectation was built throughout 2004 and the first half of 2005 as both unofficial and official release dates were publicized, canceled, and changed. The question on the minds of both reviewers and fans was, "Would it be worth the wait?"

The first hints of the potential impact of Wonder's new material were impressive enough. In early May 2005, it was announced that Wonder's new song, "So What the Fuss," would be issued as the first-ever music video for the blind. The song, with vocals by Wonder and En Vogue, and an appearance by guest guitarist Prince, features narration that will be accessible on the secondary audio track of modern televisions. This narration, performed by rapper Busta Rhymes, describes what is taking place in the visual action of the video so that blind individuals can better experience the medium of music video.[25]

Finally, in October 2005, *A Time to Love* made it to record stores, both virtual and actual. Critics have praised the album, making it and Paul McCartney's *Chaos and Creation in the Backyard* close competitors for comeback album of the year. Perhaps significantly, McCartney makes a guest appearance on *A Time to Love* as a guitarist, as does the aforementioned Prince, singers India.Arie, Kim Burrell, and Aisha Morris (Wonder's daughter of "Isn't She Lovely" fame), as well as the well-known jazz flutist Hubert Laws. Add to that Doug E. Fresh performing as human beatbox, Bonnie Raitt, Busta Rhymes, G. Patrick Gandy and Paul Riser's orchestral arrangements, and a host of highly skilled instrumentalists and background singers, and *A Time to Love* certainly boasts the personnel capable of producing one Wonder's best albums in decades. And Wonder's singing, songwriting, arranging, instrumental, and production skills are more than up to the task.

These songs are not the catchy, instantly infectious tunes common to Stevie Wonder's work up to the mid-1970s. And, as Allmusic.com critic Rob Theakston notes, they also are not the middle-of-the-road ballads of the 1980s.[26] Nor are the songs of *A Time to Love* the nearly anonymous dance pieces of *In Square Circle*. They are solid, contemporary sounding, and show that Wonder has aged very well, especially as a lyricist.

The one not-so-obvious area in which *A Time to Love* exhibits Stevie Wonder's continuing growth as a composer is in his use of space and proportion. Wonder's longer songs of the late 1960s and early 1970s often were extended funk workouts; the length was largely a result of an extended instrumental groove. As the music industry moved from the vinyl age into the compact disc age through the 1980s, Stevie Wonder adapted by increasing the average length of his songs, usually through extended introductions and fadeouts. Even to a greater extent than on his previous album (1995's *Conversation Peace*) Wonder's twenty-first-century work includes even longer songs. Unlike his extended-length album cuts of the 1970s and 1980s, however, a song like "A Time to Love," which clocks in at over nine minutes, owes its length to both the use of instrumental space and a more sophisticated, larger-scale song structure. One senses the presence of an ongoing variation technique in "A Time to Love," something that takes the song beyond the customary limits of pop song construction.

Another important feature on this album is the increased naturalness of Wonder's use of the parlando rhythms of hip-hop in delivering his texts. Critics have given Wonder's lyrics mixed reviews from the time he started to write his own lyrics in the early 1970s. This response seems to have been prompted by factors such as Wonder's use of soft rhymes instead of the hard rhymes of the Tin Pan Alley songwriters, the unusual turns of phrase that

Wonder sometimes employed to create a rhyme, his tendency to rely on cliché expressions (particularly in his love songs), and his tendency to write very long political and social commentaries into the texts of his songs. While he has been using the parlando rhythmic approach of hip-hop since his 1991 soundtrack to the film *Jungle Fever*, he seems to have fully integrated the approach on *A Time to Love*. This style allows him freedom from both the need to create artificial-sounding rhyme schemes and from the rather stricter syllable counts of traditional pop song structure. In addition, it provides him with a vehicle perfectly suited to his longer texts dealing with social issues. Also, the ease with which Wonder moves into the style on *A Time to Love* gives several of the songs a convincing, thoroughly contemporary sound.

Perhaps the one part of the overall texture that does not wear well is the approach to the incorporation of the strings. Wonder and Riser arrangements, and Riser and Gandy's orchestrations are generally presented in the mix in such a way as to sound artificially placed in the background. It is an approach that can be heard in some of the mid-1970s recordings of jazz saxophonist Stanley Turrentine. I much prefer Wonder's presentation of synthesized strings and acoustic orchestral strings in earlier albums like the studio masterpiece *Songs in the Key of Life* and the live recording *Natural Wonder*. One track, however, on which Wonder's string arrangement succeeds completely is "If Your Love Cannot Be Moved," but here (unlike a song such as "Sweetest Somebody I Know") the strings are in the forefront of the texture, sort of like a "Pastime Paradise" for the twenty-first century. Another area on *A Time to Love* that is something of a double-edged sword is Wonder's approach as an instrumentalist. His keyboard and percussion virtuosity of the 1970s is largely absent from this album, which helps him place greater emphasis on the lyrics but can be a little disappointing to fans of Stevie Wonder the former instrumental wizard. Because the lyrics (both his own and those of his collaborators) stand up quite well, this approach succeeds; it would have been nice, nonetheless, to hear a bit more instrumental funk and jamming.

Conclusion: Stevie Wonder's Songs as Recorded by Other Performers

Throughout the years, a wide variety of musicians has performed Stevie Wonder's compositions. Jazz musicians, in particular, have been drawn to his more harmonically adventuresome works of the 1970s. Although the focus of this book is on the recordings of Stevie Wonder, the singer-songwriter-multi-instrumentalist, it is also important to study Stevie Wonder, the songwriter who provided material for other recording artists. Most of these are cover versions of songs that Wonder himself made famous—such as the standard "You Are the Sunshine of My Life"—but one notable song—"The Tears of a Clown"—was a Wonder composition that was made famous by Smokey Robinson and the Miracles. Among the popular songwriters of the second half of the twentieth century, Stevie Wonder is notable for the enormous stylistic range of artists who have recorded his work.

Stevie Wonder's earliest collaborative compositions were not commercially successful enough to generate a great deal of interest among other artists. Even though Wonder had made a significant impression as a performer as early as 1962, many artists probably thought of him strictly as Little Stevie Wonder, the child prodigy, and not necessarily as a significant pop musician with whom a connection (through performances or recording of his compositions) might generate increased record sales.

Although he was only 16 at the time, Stevie Wonder's first "mature" smash hit was "Uptight (Everything's Alright)." Several well-known artists covered the song, including Brenda Lee, who recorded it in 1966, the same year in which Wonder's version hit the charts. Lee had herself been a recording artist since she was 13 years old and was a major star by 1966, having racked up a dozen pop top 10 hits.[1] She recorded "Uptight" on her album *Coming On Strong* (Decca DL 74825).

Another intriguing recording of "Uptight (Everything's Alright)" took place in 1968 when soul vocalist Jackie Wilson joined with the Count Basie Orchestra to record Benny Carter's arrangement of the song on the album

Manufacturers of Soul (Brunswick BL 54134). Wilson and Basie's band also included the song "I Was Made to Love Her" on the same album. Basie had long supported musical genres that were not strictly swing jazz. For example, the blues-based pieces he recorded with vocalist Joe Williams were certainly closer to roots blues music than blues form pieces recorded by many of the big bands. However, there is an undeniable tie between urban blues and jazz. The *Manufacturers of Soul* album highlights the fact that—in part through blues style—there is also a relationship between soul, and even the Motown version of soul, and jazz. That two songs associated with Stevie Wonder appeared on the album was not an accident: the influence of jazz can be heard in the vocal and instrumental work of Wonder more so than in the work of just about any 1960s soul musician.

Unquestionably, the most important 1960s recording of a Stevie Wonder composition by someone other than Wonder himself was done by Motown legends Smokey Robinson and the Miracles. Ironically, this was not even a cover of a Wonder recording, but rather, a song that was never commercially released by Wonder: "The Tears of a Clown." The song, a musical collaboration of Wonder and Henry Cosby, with lyrics by Robinson,[2] is based upon a very old premise, that of the tragic clown. For example, Ruggiero Leoncavallo's opera *I Pagliacci* ("The Clowns"), a popular work from the late nineteenth century, was based on a true story of tragic clowns, as was Austrian composer Arnold Schönberg's famous 1912 atonal chamber song cycle *Pierrot lunaire*. Incidentally, both Leoncavallo and Schönberg based their compositions on clowns that were considerably more tragic than the clown of the Wonder, Cosby, and Robinson song. Robinson's text mentions "Pagliacci," in reference to the character Canio in the Leoncavallo opera. This operatic character is best known for his soliloquy, "Vesti la giubba," a tune that might be familiar to baby boomers as a result of its use a couple of decades ago in a television commercial for Rice Krispies cereal.

Given the rocking Motown soul nature of many of Wonder's up-tempo songs of the 1967 period, it is difficult to imagine how his version of "The Tears of a Clown" might have sounded, had he actually released a recording of the song. The 1967 recording by Robinson and the Miracles was issued on their album *Make It Happen*. The recording was eventually issued as a single by Tamla (the Motown imprint used by the Miracles and Wonder) in 1970, but only after a Motown executive in the United Kingdom convinced the company's American executives of the commercial potential of the recording. It went very quickly to the top of the pop and R&B charts. And it sounded nothing like a Stevie Wonder recording, with the circus band orchestration (the only example of a combined soul piccolo and soul bassoon timbre the listener is likely to experience in his or her lifetime!), added to the omnipresent Motown backing band, and topped off with Smokey Robinson's vulnerable, falsetto vocal.[3]

Musically, "The Tears of a Clown" features a riff-oriented verse, which sounds much like many of Wonder's compositions of the period, and especially the songs he wrote in 1968. The chorus begins with a chromatic harmonic shift using a secondary dominant chord, creating almost a gospel-like harmonic motion. The real genius of the piece, however, is in the arrangement—especially the thinning of the instrumental texture to the circuslike instrumentation on the last line of the chorus when Robinson explains just what one of the saddest things known to man is: "The tears of a clown when there's no one around"—and in Smokey Robinson's text. Robinson's words fit the music perfectly and exhibit a higher level of thematic and poetic sophistication than that typically found in Stevie Wonder's collaborative compositions of the period. Admittedly, the song has nothing of the depth of feeling and pathos of Canio's soliloquy in *I Pagliacci*—Wonder and Cosby's music is far too upbeat for that—however, Robinson's text does rise above much of what Wonder was setting to music (or what was being set to Wonder's music) at the time.

There is a touch of irony in that Smokey Robinson's text and his falsetto delivery paints the singer—the clown—as such a vulnerable and pathetic figure, while the music is so upbeat. In a very real sense, this apparent conflict between the materials of the song gets at the very heart of the conflict within Canio between his public smile and his inner frown. Perhaps the ultimate irony of this rare collaboration between Robinson and Wonder, however, is that what started out as album filler became master composer Smokey Robinson's biggest hit and Stevie Wonder's first No. 1 song as a composer.

It was not until Wonder recorded his album masterpieces *Talking Book, Innervisions,* and *Fulfillingness' First Finale* in 1972–1974 that his compositions began to be covered in earnest. "You Are the Sunshine of My Life," in particular, became a favorite of jazz instrumentalists and mainstream pop singers. Some of the musicians who recorded Wonder's best-known composition over the years include pianist Lincoln Mayorga; pianist George Shearing; a small group that included Gerald Wiggins, Major Holley, Ed Thigpen, and Oliver Jackson; Rob McConnell and the Boss Brass; and guitarist Joe Pass and his Trio. "You Are the Sunshine of My Life" has an interesting enough melody and jazz-styled harmonic changes that it has been a near-ideal piece for instrumentalists. The song became so well known, both through record sales and through heavy radio airplay, that it instantly became part of American popular culture. It was also ideal cover material for mainstream singers because it sounded contemporary, yet it was solidly pop (as opposed to soul) and harmonically tied to the sophistication of older jazz styles.

Although Wonder exhibited fewer overt ties to the black church as a singer than did performers such as James Brown and Aretha Franklin, by the early 1970s, he was incorporating religious references—and sometimes specifically Christian references—in his lyrics in addition to musical references to black gospel music. It could, therefore, be argued that one of the finest tributes to the success of Wonder's relatively late assumption of elements of the gospel style was the fact that the Dixie Hummingbirds recorded his song "Jesus Children of America" in 1973, shortly after the release of the song on Wonder's *Innervisions*. The Dixie Hummingbirds also included their recording of the song on their 2002 greatest hits album; this was significant because this black male gospel quartet had been around since the late 1930s. They had performed for sold-out houses in the 1940s and 1950s and had been particularly well received at the 1966 Newport Folk Festival. In addition to recording "Jesus Children of America" in 1973, they were also heard in that year on radio stations across the country as backing singers on Paul Simon's song "Loves Me Like a Rock." This was in many respects the cream of the crop of black gospel vocal groups, and they chose to record Wonder's song.

Wonder also received other forms of tribute in 1973. Among the most touching, and in some respects, the strangest, was that from Paul McCartney. When McCartney's fans purchased his band Wings' latest album, *Red Rose Speedway*, upon its release in early May 1973, they were probably initially baffled by the raised dots on the back of the gatefold album cover. Those bumps actually formed the expression "We love you" in Braille. McCartney has been widely quoted as saying that he did it as a tribute to Stevie Wonder. Of course, Wonder and McCartney became collaborators in the 1980s when the two recorded McCartney's "Ebony and Ivory" and their joint composition "What's That You're Doing."

Stevie Wonder's *Music of My Mind* had not been a package that yielded much in the way of commercially successful material. In fact, the album itself had not sold particularly well, especially compared to some of Wonder's 1960s material and his two successive albums: *Talking Book* and *Innervisions*. There was, however, some good music to be found on the album. In 1974, jazz tenor saxophonist Stanley Turrentine recorded Wonder's "Evil" on his *Pieces of Dreams* album. Turrentine enjoyed a run of commercial success in the mid-1970s with covers of R&B, gospel, funk, and pop material. He captured the gospel-flavored intensity of "Evil" well, including the surprise ending. Although a fair number of notable jazz albums from the 1960s and 1970s did not find their way into the digital era, Turrentine's *Pieces of Dreams* has been reissued by Fantasy Records on compact disc. Stanley Turrentine's 1975 album *In the Pocket*, incidentally, included Wonder and Ivy Hunter's song "Loving You Is Sweeter Than Ever."

The year 1975 was the real breakthrough year in terms of covers of Stevie Wonder material. The impressive commercial success of his 1972–1974 albums *Talking Book, Innervisions,* and *Fulfillingness' First Finale* contributed to this, but possibly his recovery from a near-death experience contributed as well. Another factor was that Wonder himself did not release an album of new material in 1975. Not only were a variety of artists recording cover versions of Wonder songs, but some were even incorporating Wonder medleys into their concerts. Such was the case with the Osmonds, who, on their first world tour, included "Uptight (Everything's Alright)" "Higher Ground," "Signed, Sealed, Delivered (I'm Yours)," "Superstition," and "For Once in My Life." This popular brother act included their Stevie Wonder medley on the 1975 live album *Around the World, Live in Concert.*

Bert DeCoteaux recorded an entire album of Wonder material for his 1975 package *Bert DeCoteaux Plays a Stevie Wonder Songbook.* This RCA album was heavily weighted toward up-tempo material from 1970 through 1974 and included the following tracks: "Superstition," "Boogie On Reggae Woman," "If You Really Love Me," "My Cherie Amour," "You Are the Sunshine of My Life," "Girl Blue," "Signed, Sealed, Delivered (I'm Yours)," "You Haven't Done Nothin'," "Don't Worry 'bout a Thing," and "Living for the City."

Perhaps the most intriguing cover of Wonder material from 1975—and, indeed possibly the most intriguing cover of Wonder's songs ever—was Jack Mullane's Educational Activities release *Keep On Steppin'.* This album included a number of Wonder's up-tempo songs in which the lyrics were changed to better accompany physical fitness activities!

On the more serious side was well-known folksinger Joan Baez's recording of "Never Dreamed You'd Leave in Summer." The track was included on the Baez album *Diamonds and Rust,* one of her best-known collections of the 1970s.

The song "Visions" had originally set the thematic stage for Wonder's *Innervisions* album. However, an arrangement of the song by John Howell found its way into 1976 performances by the Belles of Indiana, a women's vocal ensemble at Indiana University. A live recording of the group's performance, which was conducted by Howell, is archived at Indiana University. The almost classical nature of the song is also highlighted by the fact that it appeared as a vocal solo on at least one Bachelor of Music degree recital: that of Devin Sanders at the University of Oregon in 2002.

Stevie Wonder's 1976 album *Songs in the Key of Life* ratcheted up the interest in covering his songs to a still higher level. The album contained several hugely successful singles and well-known album tracks. Given the near-epic size of the album—two albums, plus a "bonus" extended-play disc—the collection included more stylistic diversity than even Wonder's albums from earlier in the 1970s.

Although the song was never released as a single—perhaps one of Motown's greatest missed commercial opportunities—Wonder's "Isn't She Lovely" generated a great deal of airplay and was one of the best-known songs on *Songs in the Key of Life.* One of the notable features of this album track was Wonder's inventive, extended harmonica solo at the end of the recording, and as the song became an instant hit, it was a natural selection for instrumental jazz musicians. The popular jazz guitarist Lee Ritenour, who had been doing some recording work with Stanley Turrentine, included "Isn't She Lovely" on his 1977 album *Captain Fingers.* That same year, keyboardist

Victor Feldman and his ensemble included the song on the album *The Artful Dodger*. Larger jazz big bands have also turned to "Isn't She Lovely." Famed clarinetist and saxophonist Woody Herman's band included the song on the 1978 album *Fatha Herman & His Thundering Herd* and the well-known jazz arranger/bandleader Bill Holman included "Isn't She Lovely" on the 1987 JVC album *The Bill Holman Band*.

It was not just "Isn't She Lovely," however, that generated interest among musicians in the late 1970s and into the 1980s. Trumpeter Blue Mitchell performed "As," a popular *Songs in the Key of Life* album track, on his 1977 album *African Violet*. Motown eventually released Wonder's own recording of "As" as a single in November 1977, more than a year after the *Songs in the Key of Life* album had first hit the charts. The year 1977 also found the Michigan State University Spartan Marching Band performing a "Music of Stevie Wonder" halftime show.

After the commercial impact of Wonder's *Songs in the Key of Life*, several artists returned to his slightly earlier material. Among the bigger names to do so were Diana Ross and Stan Kenton. Ross recorded "Too Shy to Say," a song from Wonder's *Fulfillingness' First Finale*, as the B-side to her 1977 single "You Got It" and also included the track on her album *Baby It's Me*. Although he had made his strongest impact in the 1950s, big band leader Stan Kenton was still recording in the late 1970s. He also turned to "Too Shy to Say," and included an arrangement of the song on his 1979 album *Street of Dreams*.

Because Wonder's recording career was considerably more sporadic in the late 1970s through the 1980s, and because his releases from the period were not as well received by critics or by fans as his 1972–1976 recordings, cover versions of Wonder's material trailed off a bit through the period. Jazz musicians continued to be the primary musicians to include Wonder's songs. For example, the Joe Pass Trio recorded "You Are the Sunshine of My Life" on their 1981 album *The Joe Pass Trio Live at Donte's*, and vibraphonist Cal Tjader and singer Carmen McRae included "All in Love Is Fair" on their 1982 album *Heat Wave*. Pianist Marian McPartland also recorded "All in Love Is Fair" on her 1985 album *Willow Creek and Other Ballads*.

Certainly, one of the most intriguing jazz covers of Stevie Wonder material in the 1980s was the jazz-rock fusion violinist Jean Luc Ponty's recording of "As" on his *Mystical Adventures* album in 1982. It is a testimony to the importance of Wonder as a composer that this is the only piece on the album not composed by Ponty himself. Nigel Kennedy, another unconventional violinist, recorded "Isn't She Lovely" for his 1984 classical-jazz crossover album with pianist Peter Pettinger, *Strad Jazz*.

After Wonder had made a comeback with his work on the soundtrack of *The Woman in Red* in 1984, several musicians covered "I Just Called to Say I Love You." The stylistic range of these musicians attests to the purely pop nature of the song. For example, Mr. Acker Bilk, the British clarinetist best known for his No. 1 1962 easy listening instrumental hit "Stranger on the Shore," released "I Just Called to Say I Love You" on his 1986 album *Magic Serenade*. The ultimate indication that the song became an easy listening standard was its appearance on orchestra leader Mantovani's 1988 album *Incomparable* (LaserLight 15 082).

Jazz guitar virtuoso Stanley Jordan enjoyed a great deal of popularity in the 1980s, including an appearance in the Bruce Willis film *Blind Date*. Jordan recorded "Send One Your Love" for his 1986 *Standards, Vol. 1* album (Jazz Heritage 513368X). That a major jazz figure like Jordan would label "Send One Your Love" as a standard is significant. It is not Stevie Wonder's best-known composition, but Jordan's choice of the song for the album suggests the esteem in which he held the song, and it also underscores the stylistic connection of the song with the great American songbook of the first half of the twentieth century.

Some of Wonder's compositions translated more easily into the style of diverse performers than others. The funkier pieces, such as "Superstition," were covered less frequently than more pop-oriented songs such as "You Are the Sunshine of My Life." One of the rare, and very fortunate, exceptions was blues-rock guitarist Stevie Ray Vaughan's recording of "Superstition" on the 1986 album *Stevie Ray Vaughan and Double Trouble Live*. Its intensity has rarely been matched, and it continues to rank as one of the best covers of a Stevie Wonder composition ever. One recording (again by a blues-rock musician) that matched the Vaughan recording was Eric Clapton's early twenty-first century recording of "Higher Ground" on the album *Conception: An Interpretation of Stevie Wonder's Songs*, which will be discussed later.

Jazz tenor saxophonist Stanley Turrentine enjoyed popularity in the 1970s and 1980s, largely through the funkiness of both his playing and the material he performed, as well as the romantic string arrangements that sweetened the funk on his recordings. In 1987, Turrentine issued an entire album of Stevie Wonder material. *Wonderland* (Blue Note BT-85140) included "Bird of Beauty," "Creepin'," "You and I (We Can Conquer the World)," "Living for the City," "Boogie On Reggae Woman," "Rocket Love," "Don't You Worry 'bout a Thing," and "Sir Duke."

Contrasting jazz vocal inflections of Wonder's songs could be heard in Abbey Lincoln's performance of "Golden Lady" on the 1987 album *Painted Lady* (Intercord 1987) and disco diva/jazz singer Chaka Khan's recording of "Signed, Sealed, Delivered (I'm Yours)" on her 1988 album *C.K.* (Warner Brothers 9 25707–1). Abbey Lincoln's combo on *Painted Lady* included noted avant-garde jazz saxophonist Archie Shepp.

Many different artists covered Stevie Wonder songs in the 1990s, but those years also found Wonder's own recordings of his songs appearing in the soundtracks to popular Hollywood films. Among the soundtracks that used at least one Stevie Wonder composition and/or Stevie Wonder performance from the past were *High Fidelity, Get On the Bus, Wild Wild West,*

Writer's Block, You've Got Mail, Bamboozled, Mulan, Now and Then, A Smile Like Yours, Dead Presidents, The Adventures of Pinocchio, and *Mr. Holland's Opus.* In addition to films, Wonder's recordings appeared in the soundtracks of some television programs, including *The Wonder Years* and *Northern Exposure.*

The diversity of performers who turned to the Stevie Wonder songbook in the 1990s and early twenty-first century was at least as wide as it had been in the 1980s. For example, conductor/arranger Peter Nero and the Fort Worth Symphony Pops included "Isn't She Lovely" on their *My Way* album (Intersound Entertainment CDS 3455, 1993); Jodeci released "Lately" as a single in 1993; the Red Hot Chili Peppers included "Higher Ground" on their album *Mother's Milk* (EMI E2–2152, 1989); jazz flutist Najee covered a number of Wonder selections on *Najee Plays Songs from the Key of Life* (EMI E2–35704, 1995); an all-star jazz combo consisting of Herbie Hancock, Michael Brecker, John Scofield, Dave Holland, Jack DeJohnette, and Don Alias recorded "You've Got It Bad Girl" on the album *The New Standard* (Jazz Heritage 514518Z, 1997); Keb Mo' recorded "Isn't She Lovely" on the 2001 children's album *Big Wide Grin;* and BeBe Winans (with an assist from guest performers Marvin L. Winans and Stevie Wonder) covered "Jesus Children of America" on the 2002 EMI album *WOW Gospel.*

It was not just established acts that turned to the Stevie Wonder songbook in the 1990s. R. Kelly & Public Announcement covered Wonder's "Hey Love" on their new jack swing debut album *Born into the 90's* in 1992. Kelly and company's recording brought Wonder's old 1960s material squarely into a youth-oriented, urban, 1990s context. In fact, because of his huge early success in the record industry, Kelly's recording of "Hey Love" probably brought the sound of Stevie Wonder's compositions into the ears of more young people than Wonder's own soundtrack to *Jungle Fever* of the year before.

Even musical ensembles associated with the U.S. military covered Wonder's compositions. The 2000 compact disc *Listen to the Music* by the U.S. Air Force Band of Flight and their rock music ensemble Systems Go included "I Wish," and the 2000 compact disc *Choices,* an anti–drug abuse album by the Band of the U.S. Air Force Reserve, included "Higher Ground."

One of the more intriguing albums of recent years that focused on the Wonder songbook was Nnenna Freelon's 2002 album *Tales of Wonder* (Concord CCD-2107–2). Music critic Steve Eddy described Freelon's *Tales of Wonder* as "consistently inventive." Interestingly, Freelon is quoted in Eddy's review as saying that she "tried to alter the chords" in some of the songs, but that they "fell apart in my hands. It seemed like he wrote those songs with the intention of that's the way it's going to be."[4] Freelon's statement suggests— as I have tried to make the case elsewhere in this study—that Wonder's works truly are fully realized compositions—they are not "jazz tunes" that can be altered with substitute chords as many jazz performers are wont to do.

The second half of the 1990s and the beginning of the twenty-first century saw no releases of new material from Stevie Wonder; however, Motown issued major, multi–compact disc compilations of Wonder's great recordings of the past. In 2003, Wonder's record label released *Conception: An Interpretation of Stevie Wonder's Songs* (Motown 440 067 314–2), a collection of performances by a diverse group of rock, R&B, and hip-hop artists. Despite the disparate styles of artists such as Eric Clapton (who is assisted by well-known keyboardist Billy Preston, well-known studio percussionist Jim Keltner, and others), Mary J. Blige, Musiq, Marc Anthony, and Joe (featuring rapper Mr. Cheeks), and all the others, the arrangements and performances remain remarkably true to the Stevie Wonder originals. Some of the recordings, such as Black Coffey's performance of "Rocket Love," and Mary J. Blige's performance of "Overjoyed,"[5] thump the stereo system's subwoofer to a far greater extent than Wonder's original recordings. Angie Stone and Jonathan Richmond's arrangement of "You Will Know" for Stone's performance places a greater emphasis on spoken text than Wonder's original, but the "meta-flavor" (to coin an expression) of the entire compact disc is that of other singers doing slightly updated versions of not only Stevie Wonder's songs, but of his classic recorded versions of the songs.

Ultimately, what the arrangements of *Conception* suggest is the extent to which Stevie Wonder is a composer rather than a songwriter. By this I mean that Wonder's songs are not words, melody, rhythm, and harmony like a musician might see on a jazz lead sheet, or like one might find in a popular piano-vocal collection of songs at a music store. The arrangements—and Wonder's recordings of those arrangements—are a key part of the overall effect of virtually all of Stevie Wonder's songs. In part, this may be the result of Wonder's distinctive voice and vocal style, but it is also because of the highly distinctive nature of his post-1970 arrangements.

One of the highlights of *Conception: An Interpretation of Stevie Wonder's Songs* is Stephen, Julian, Damian "Jr. Gong," and Kymani Marley's performance of "Master Blaster (Jammin')." The significance of this performance is that the Wonder song was based on a tribute to Bob Marley. Another highlight is Eric Clapton's blistering, bluesy performance of "Higher Ground." None of the renditions, however, can be labeled as clear-cut improvements on Wonder's original performances, and in several cases, the singing frankly is not as good as what Wonder committed to tape years before. The sole non-Wonder composition on the album is India.Arie's song "Wonderful." Arie's song is a tribute to Wonder and incorporates lines from Wonder's songs. Harmonically and melodically, her song also vaguely resembles the Wonder style, minus the strong pop hook of the most commercially successful of Wonder's works. However, this heartfelt tribute presents a bit of a problem: given that Stevie Wonder (the object of the tribute) happens to be one of the co-producers of the CD, the inclusion of the track comes off as being self-serving. Almost certainly, this was not the intent of co-producers

Kedar Massenburg and Wonder, but some listeners may get the uncomfortable feeling that "this is me celebrating me" when they hear the song in this context.

One of the most recently released covers of a Stevie Wonder song is Celine Dion's recording of "I Wish" on her 2004 album *A New Day: Live in Las Vegas* (Sony 92680). This is also one of the most curious Stevie Wonder covers ever, given the highly autobiographical nature of Wonder's lyrics. Dion does not change the lyrics either, beginning the song with the line, "Thinking back to when I was a little nappy headed boy," just as Wonder had done nearly 20 years before. Although Wonder's song may provide a funky, rhythmically interesting showcase for Dion's voice in her popular Las Vegas show, her performance of the song as is completely strips it of its most interesting lyrical feature: its autobiographical tale of growing up poor, black, and male in the ghetto. The longing for the simplicity of life before fame rings true when the song is sung by Celine Dion, but that is only a small part of the overall significance of "I Wish."

All of the covers mentioned in this chapter were of Wonder compositions that Stevie Wonder the performer made popular, with the exception of "The Tears of a Clown." Over the years, Wonder actually wrote many songs that he never recorded: songs that were really meant for others. Among the acts who benefited from Stevie Wonder the independent songwriter were jazz musicians George Benson, Ramsey Lewis, Lionel Hampton, and Quincy Jones; Motown legends Smokey Robinson, Jermaine Jackson, Michael Jackson, the Supremes, Martha Reeves & the Vandellas, Marvin Gaye, and the Four Tops; rock musicians Jeff Beck and the Beach Boys; and other artists as diverse as Syreeta Wright, Dionne Warwick, the Flying Burrito Brothers, and John Denver.

CONCLUSION

For more than 40 years, Stevland Morris has been a professional musician using the moniker Stevie Wonder. And he has been and remains a wonder. There are but a handful of pop music artists who have made a commercial and social impact in every decade from the 1960s to the present, and perhaps less than a handful who have the iconic status of Stevie Wonder. Even in 2005, when I mention a pop or R&B musician from the 1960s in my college classes on music in America or music and the Vietnam Conflict, some of the students will know the musician's songs—or at least a couple of them—and some students can identify the musician from a photograph without prompting. When it comes to Stevie Wonder, however, a musician who made his first commercial impact as early as 1963, twenty-first-century college students can name several of the songs, they can pick him out from a photograph, and many have even seen him performing live on television.

Perhaps many years from now history will recall that Stevie Wonder was an incredibly gifted singer, harmonica player, keyboard player, and a composer without peer. Perhaps recordings such as "You Are the Sunshine of My Life," "Superstition," "Living for the City," "Happy Birthday," "Signed, Sealed, Delivered (I'm Yours)," "Sir Duke," "Higher Ground," and "My Cherie Amour" will still grace radio airwaves and will still be available in some yet-to-be-invented audio file format. Even so, future generations should also recall that Stevie Wonder was one of the first Motown artists to record songs of social commentary, and that he was one of the strongest proponents of a national holiday to honor the Rev. Dr. Martin Luther King, Jr. They should recall that Stevie Wonder was one of the first musicians ever to control every note of a song on a recording by writing the music and lyrics, singing all the vocal lines, playing all the instruments, and producing the session, and that he was perhaps the most adaptable musician of his time, fully integrating rock, R&B, blues, pop, gospel, hip-hop, and jazz in recording after recording. Further, they should know that Stevie Wonder was among the most highly respected composers and performers by his peers, having had an usually wide range of recording artists cover his songs; and winning an Academy Award, more than 20 Grammy Awards, as well as Grammy's Lifetime Achievement Award, the National Academy of Popular Music/Songwriters Hall of Fame's prestigious Johnny Mercer Award, the Ivor Novello Awards' Special International Prize, and election to the Rock and Roll Hall of Fame and Songwriters Hall of Fame. Perhaps most important, they should know that Stevie Wonder was a tireless champion of equal rights for all human beings, and a champion for the economically disadvantaged and the ill, in the songs he wrote and recorded, in his public statements, and in the dozens of benefit concerts at which he performed. The musician who began his career under the name "Little" Stevie Wonder became one of the biggest figures ever in American popular culture.

Discography

THE ALBUMS OF STEVIE WONDER

The Jazz-Soul of Little Stevie. Stevie Wonder, vocals, harmonica, drums; various assisting instrumentalists and vocalists. "Fingertips" (Clarence Paul, Henry Cosby); "Square" (Nettie Glynn, Clarence Paul); "Soul Bongo" (Clarence Paul, Marvin Gaye); "Manhattan at Six" (Clarence Paul, Henry Cosby); "Paulsby" (Clarence Paul, Henry Cosby); "Some Other Time" (Clarence Paul, Henry Cosby); "Wondering" (Clarence Paul, Joey DiBenedetto); "Session No. 112" (Stephen Judkins, Clarence Paul); "Bam" (Berry Gordy, Jr.). 33–1/3 rpm phonodisc. Tamla 233, 1962.

Tribute to Uncle Ray. Stevie Wonder, vocals; various assisting instrumentalists and vocalists. "Hallelujah I Love Her So" (Ray Charles); "Ain't That Love" (Ray Charles); "Don't You Know" (Ray Charles); "(I'm Afraid) The Masquerade Is Over" (Herbert Magidson, Allie Wrubel); "Frankie and Johnny" (Clarence Paul); "Drown in My Own Tears" (Henry Glover); "Come Back Baby" (Ray Charles); "Mary Ann" (Ray Charles); "Sunset" (Clarence Paul, Stephen Judkins); "My Baby's Gone" (Berry Gordy, Jr.). 33–1/3 rpm phonodisc. Tamla 232, 1962.

Recorded Live—The 12 Year Old Genius. Stevie Wonder, vocals, harmonica, piano, drums, bongos, organ; various assisting instrumentalists and vocalists. "Fingertips" (Clarence Paul, Henry Cosby); "Soul Bongo" (Clarence Paul, Marvin Gaye); "La La La La La" (Clarence Paul); "(I'm Afraid) The Masquerade Is Over" (Herbert Magidson, Allie Wrubel); "Hallelujah I Lover Her So" (Ray Charles); "Drown in My Own Tears" (Henry Glover); "Don't You Know" (Ray Charles). 33–1/3 rpm phonodisc. Tamla 240, 1963.

With a Song in My Heart. Stevie Wonder, vocals; various assisting instrumentalists and vocalists. "With a Song in My Heart" (Richard Rodgers, Lorenz Hart); "When You Wish Upon a Star" (Leigh Harline, Ned Washington); "Smile" (Charlie Chaplin); "Make Someone Happy" (Betty Comden, Adolph Green, Jule Styne); "Dream" (Johnny Mercer); "Put On a Happy Face" (Lee Adams, Charles Strouse); "On the Sunny Side of the Street" (Dorothy Fields, Jimmy McHugh); "Get Happy" (Harold Arlen, Ted Koehler); "Give Your Heart a Chance" (Ron

Miller, Orlando Murden); "Without a Song" (Billy Rose, Edward Eliscu, Vincent Youmans). 33–1/3 rpm phonodisc. Tamla 250, 1963.

Stevie at the Beach. Stevie Wonder, vocals, harmonica; various assisting instrumentalists and vocalists. "Castles in the Sand" (Hal Davis, Frank Wilson, Marc Gordon, Mary M. O'Brien); "Ebb Tide" (Robert Maxwell, Carl Sigman); "Sad Boy" (Dorsey Burnette, Gerald Nelson); "Red Sails in the Sunset" (Wilhelm Grosz, James B. Kennedy); "The Beachcomber" (Bobby Darin); "Castles in the Sand" [instrumental version] (Hal Davis, Frank Wilson, Marc Gordon, Mary M. O'Brien); "Happy Street" (Ben Peters); "The Party at the Beach House" (Frank Wilson); "Hey Harmonica Man" (Marty Cooper, Lou Josie); "Beach Stomp" (Hal Davis, Frank Wilson); "Beyond the Sea" (Jack Lawrence, Charles Trenet). 33–1/3 rpm phonodisc. Tamla 255, 1964.

Uptight. Stevie Wonder, vocals, piano, harmonica; various assisting instrumentalists and vocalists. "Love a Go Go" (Beth Beatty, Ernie Shelby); "Hold Me" (Morris Broadnax, Wonder, Clarence Paul); "Blowin' in the Wind" (Bob Dylan); "Nothing's Too Good for My Baby" (Sylvia Moy, Henry Cosby, William Stevenson); "Teach Me Tonight" (Sammy Cahn, Gene De Paul); "Uptight (Everything's Alright)" (Sylvia Moy, Henry Cosby, Wonder); "Ain't That Asking for Trouble" (Sylvia Moy, Wonder, Clarence Paul); "I Want My Baby Back" (Cornelius Grant, Eddie Kendricks, Norman Whitfield); "Pretty Little Angel" (Clarence Paul, Mike Valvano, Wonder); "Music Talk" (Ted Hull, Wonder, Clarence Paul); "Contract on Love" (Janie Bradford, Lamont Dozier, Brian Holland); "With a Child's Heart" (Vicki Basemore, Henry Cosby, Sylvia Moy). 33–1/3 rpm phonodisc. Tamla 268, 1966. Reissued on compact disc with *For Once in My Life,* Tamla TCD08025TD, 1986.

Down to Earth. Stevie Wonder, vocals; various assisting instrumentalists and vocalists. "A Place in the Sun" (Ron Miller, Bryan Wells); "Bang Bang" (Sonny Bono); "Down to Earth" (Ron Miller, William O'Malley, Avery Vandenberg); "Thank You Love" (Wonder, Henry Cosby, Sylvia Moy); "Be Cool, Be Calm (and Keep Yourself Together)" (Sylvia Moy, Henry Cosby, Wonder); "Sylvia" (Sylvia Moy, Henry Cosby, Wonder); "My World Is Empty without You" (Brian Holland, Lamont Dozier, Eddie Holland, Jr.); "The Lonesome Road" (Gene Austin, Nat Shilkret); "Angel Baby (Don't You Ever Leave Me)" (Henry Cosby, Sylvia Moy, Angelica Moy); "Mr. Tambourine Man" (Bob Dylan); "Sixteen Tons" (Merle Travis); "Hey Love" (Wonder, Clarence Paul, Morris Broadnax). 33–1/3 rpm phonodisc. Tamla 272, 1966.

I Was Made to Love Her. Stevie Wonder, vocals, keyboards, harmonica; various assisting instrumentalists and vocalists. "I Was Made to Love Her" (Lula Hardaway, Sylvia Moy, Wonder, Henry Cosby); "Send Me Some Lovin'" (John Marascalco, Leo Price); "I'd Cry" (Sylvia Moy, Wonder); "Everybody Needs Somebody (I Need You)" (Morris Broadnax, Clarence Paul, Wonder); "Respect" (Otis Redding); "My Girl" (William ["Smokey"] Robinson, Jr., Ronald White); "Baby Don't You Do It" (Brian Holland, Lamont Dozier, Eddie Holland, Jr.); "A Fool for You" (Ray Charles); "Can I Get a Witness" (Brian Holland, Lamont Dozier, Eddie Holland, Jr.); "I Pity the Fool" (Don Robey); "Please, Please, Please" (James Brown, Johnny Terry); "Every Time I See You I Go Wild" (Sylvia Moy, Wonder, Henry Cosby). 33–1/3 rpm phonodisc. Tamla 279, 1967.

Someday at Christmas. Stevie Wonder, vocals; various assisting instrumentalists and vocalists. "Someday at Christmas" (Ron Miller, Bryan Wells); "Silver Bells" (Ray Evans, Jay Livingston); "Ave Maria" (Franz Schubert); "The Little Drummer Boy" (Katherine Davis, Henry Onorati, Harry Simeone); "One Little Christmas Tree" (Ron Miller, Bryan Wells); "The Day That Love Began" (Ron Miller, Deborah Miller); "The Christmas Song" (Mel Tormé, Robert Wells); "Bedtime for Toys" (Ron Miller, Orlando Murden); "Christmastime" (Sol Selegna); "Twinkle Twinkle Little Me" (Ron Miller, William O'Malley); "A Warm Little Home on a Hill" (Ron Miller, Bryan Wells); "What Christmas Means to Me" (Anna Gordy Gaye, Horgay Gordy, Allen Story). 33–1/3 rpm phonodisc. Tamla 281, 1967. Reissued on compact disc as *The Best of Stevie Wonder: The Christmas Collection,* Motown 80002831–02, 2004. *Note:* The compact disc reissue includes the bonus tracks "The Miracles of Christmas" (Ron Miller, Aurora Miller) and "Everyone's a Kid at Christmas Time" (Ron Miller, Aurora Miller).

Stevie Wonder's Greatest Hits. Stevie Wonder, vocals, harmonica, piano; various assisting instrumentalists and vocalists. "Uptight (Everything's Alright)" (Sylvia Moy, Henry Cosby, Wonder); "I'm Wondering" (Sylvia Moy, Wonder, Henry Cosby); "I Was Made to Love Her" (Henry Cosby, Lula Hardaway, Wonder, Sylvia Moy); "Hey Love" (Wonder, Clarence Paul, Morris Broadnax); "Blowin' in the Wind" (Bob Dylan); "A Place in the Sun" (Ron Miller, Bryan Wells); "Contract on Love" (Janie Bradford, Lamont Dozier, Brian Holland); "Workout Stevie, Workout" (Clarence Paul, Henry Cosby); "Fingertips, Part 2" (Henry Cosby, Clarence Paul); "Castles in the Sand" (Hal Davis, Frank Wilson, Marc Gordon, Mary M. O'Brien); "Hey Harmonica Man" (Marty Cooper, Lou Josie); "Nothing's Too Good for My Baby" (Sylvia Moy, Henry Cosby, William Stevenson). 33–1/3 rpm phonodisc. Tamla 282, 1968. Contains previously released material.

Eivets Rednow. Stevie Wonder, harmonica; various assisting instrumentalists. "Alfie" (Burt Bacharach, Hal David); "More Than a Dream" (Henry Cosby, Wonder); "A House Is Not a Home" (Burt Bacharach, Hal David); "How Can You Believe" (Wonder); "Never My Love" (Don Addrisi, Dick Addrisi); "Ask the Lonely" (Ivy Hunter, William Stevenson); "Ruby" (Michell Parish, Heinz Roemheld); "Which Way the Wind" (Wonder); "Bye Bye World" (Wonder); "Grazing in the Grass" (Harry J. Elston, Philemon Hou). 33–1/3 rpm phonodisc. Gordy 932, 1968.

For Once in My Life. Stevie Wonder, vocals, keyboards, harmonica; various assisting instrumentalists and vocalists. "For Once in My Life" (Ron Miller, Orlando Murden); "Shoo-Be-Doo-Be-Doo-Da-Day" (Henry Cosby, Sylvia Moy, Wonder); "You Met Your Match" (Don Hunter, Wonder, Lula Hardaway); "I Wanna Make Her Love Me" (Henry Cosby, Lula Hardaway, Sylvia Moy, Wonder); "I'm More Than Happy (I'm Satisfied)" (Henry Cosby, Cornelius Grant, Sylvia Moy, Wonder); "I Don't Know Why" (Don Hunter, Lula Hardaway, Wonder, Paul Riser); "Sunny" (Bobby Hebb); "I'd Be a Fool Right Now" (Henry Cosby, Wonder, Sylvia Moy); "Ain't No Lovin'" (Paul Riser, Don Hunter, Wonder, Lula Hardaway); "God Bless the Child" (Arthur Herzog, Jr., Billie Holiday); "Do I Love Her" (Wonder, Sylvia Moy); "The House on the Hill" (Allen Story, Horgay Gordy, Lawrence Brown). 33–1/3 rpm phonodisc. Tamla 291, 1968.

Reissued on compact disc with *Uptight*, Tamla TCD08025TD, 1986. Reissued on compact disc, Motown 3746352342.

My Cherie Amour. Stevie Wonder, vocals, harmonica, keyboards; various assisting instrumentalists and vocalists. "My Cherie Amour" (Wonder, Henry Cosby, Sylvia Moy); "Hello Young Lovers" (Richard Rodgers, Oscar Hammerstein); "At Last" (Henry Cosby); "Light My Fire" (John Densmore, Robbie Krieger, Ray Manzarek, Jim Morrison); "The Shadow of Your Smile" (Johnny Mandel, Paul Francis Webster); "You and Me" (Henry Cosby); "Pearl" (Richard Morris); "Somebody Knows, Somebody Cares" (Henry Cosby, Lula Hardaway, Sylvia Moy, Wonder); "Yester-Me, Yester-You, Yesterday" (Ron Miller, Bryan Wells); "Angie Girl" (Henry Cosby, Sylvia Moy, Wonder); "Give Your Love" (Henry Cosby); "I've Got You" (Sylvia Moy, Wonder). 33–1/3 rpm phonodisc. Tamla 296, 1969. Reissued on compact disc, Motown MOTD-5179, 1990.

Stevie Wonder Live at the Talk of the Town. Stevie Wonder, vocals, harmonica, keyboards; various assisting instrumentalists and vocalists. "Pretty World" (Antonio Adolfo, Tiberio Gasper, Alan Bergman, Marilyn Bergman); "Sunny" (Bobby Hebb); "Love Theme from *Romeo and Juliet* (A Time for Us)" (Larry Kusik, Nino Rota, Rinaldi Rota, Eddie Snyder); "Shoo-Be-Doo-Be-Doo-Da-Day" (Henry Cosby, Sylvia Moy, Wonder); "Everybody's Talking" (Fred Neil); "My Cherie Amour" (Henry Cosby, Sylvia Moy, Wonder); "Yester-Me, Yester-You, Yesterday" (Ron Miller, Bryan Wells); "I've Gotta Be Me" (Walter Marks); "A Place in the Sun" (Ron Miller, Bryan Wells); "Down to Earth" (Ron Miller, William O'Malley, Avery Vandenberg); "Blowin' in the Wind" (Bob Dylan); "By the Time I Get to Phoenix" (Jimmy Webb); "Ca' purange" (Mussapere); "Alfie" (Burt Bacharach, Hal David); "For Once in My Life" (Ron Miller, Orlando Murden); "Thank You Love" (Wonder, Henry Cosby, Sylvia Moy). Tamla 298, 1970.

Signed, Sealed & Delivered. Stevie Wonder, vocals, harmonica, keyboards; various assisting instrumentalists and vocalists. "Never Had a Dream Come True" (Bryan Wells, Ron Miller); "We Can Work It Out" (John Lennon, Paul McCartney); "Signed, Sealed, Delivered (I'm Yours)" (Wonder, Lee Garrett, Syreeta Wright, Lula Hardaway); "Heaven Help Us All" (Ron Miller); "You Can't Judge a Book by Its Cover" (Henry Cosby, Sylvia Moy, Wonder); "Sugar" (Don Hunter, Wonder); "Don't Wonder Why" (Leonard Caston); "Anything You Want Me to Do" (Lula Hardaway, Don Hunter, Paul Riser, Wonder); "I Can't Let My Heaven Walk Away" (Joe Hinton, Pamela Sawyer); "Joy (Takes Over Me)" (B. Browner); "I Gotta Have a Song" (Wonder, Don Hunter, Lula Hardaway, Paul Riser); "Something to Say" (Lula Hardaway, Don Hunter, Paul Riser, Wonder). 33–1/3 rpm phonodisc. Tamla 304, 1970. Reissued on compact disc, Motown 3746351762, 1990.

Where I'm Coming From. Stevie Wonder, vocals, keyboards, harmonica; various assisting instrumentalists and vocalists. "Look Around" (Wonder, Syreeta Wright); "Do Yourself a Favor" (Syreeta Wright, Wonder); "Think of Me as Your Soldier" (Wonder, Syreeta Wright); "Something Out of the Blue" (Wonder, Syreeta Wright); "If You Really Love Me" (Wonder, Syreeta Wright); "I Wanna Talk to You" (Wonder, Syreeta Wright); "Take a Course in Happiness" (Wonder, Syreeta Wright); "Never Dreamed You'd Leave in Summer" (Wonder, Syreeta Wright); "Sunshine in Their Eyes" (Wonder, Syreeta Wright). 33–1/3 rpm phonodisc. Tamla 308, 1971. Reissued on compact disc, Motown 530 223–2, 1993.

Stevie Wonder's Greatest Hits, Vol. 2. Stevie Wonder, vocals, keyboards, harmonica; various assisting instrumentalists and vocalists. "Shoo-Be-Doo-Be-Doo-Da-Day" (Sylvia Moy, Wonder, Henry Cosby); "Signed, Sealed, Delivered (I'm Yours)" (Wonder, Lee Garrett, Syreeta Wright, Lula Hardaway); "If You Really Love Me" (Wonder, Syreeta Wright); "For Once in My Life" (Ron Miller, Orlando Murden); "We Can Work It Out" (John Lennon, Paul McCartney); "You Met Your Match" (Don Hunter, Wonder, Lula Hardaway); "Never Had a Dream Come True" (Bryan Wells, Ron Miller); "Yester-Me, Yester-You, Yesterday" (Ron Miller, Bryan Wells); "My Cherie Amour" (Henry Cosby, Sylvia Moy, Wonder); "Never Dreamed You'd Leave in Summer" (Syreeta Wright, Wonder); "Travelin' Man" (Ron Miller, Bryan Wells); "Heaven Help Us All" (Ron Miller). 33–1/3 rpm phonodisc. Tamla 313, 1971.

Music of My Mind. Stevie Wonder, vocals, keyboards, harmonica, synthesizers, drums, percussion; various assisting instrumentalists and vocalists. "Love Having You Around" (Wonder, Syreeta Wright); "Superwoman (Where Were You When I Needed You)" (Wonder); "I Love Every Little Thing about You" (Wonder); "Sweet Little Girl" (Wonder); "Happier Than the Morning Sun" (Wonder); "Girl Blue" (Wonder, Yvonne Wright); "Seems So Long" (Wonder); "Keep On Running" (Wonder); "Evil" (Wonder, Yvonne Wright). 33–1/3 rpm phonodisc. Tamla 314, 1972. Reissued on compact disc, Motown 012 157 353–2, 2000.

Talking Book. Stevie Wonder, vocals, keyboards, harmonica, synthesizers, drums, percussion; various assisting instrumentalists and vocalists. "You Are the Sunshine of My Life" (Wonder); "Maybe Your Baby" (Wonder); "You and I (We Can Conquer the World)" (Wonder); "Tuesday Heartbreak" (Wonder); "You've Got It Bad Girl" (Yvonne Wright, Wonder); "Superstition" (Wonder); "Big Brother" (Wonder); "Blame It On the Sun" (Syreeta Wright, Wonder); "Lookin' for Another Pure Love" (Syreeta Wright, Wonder); "I Believe (When I Fall in Love It Will Be Forever)" (Yvonne Wright, Wonder).[1] 33–1/3 rpm phonodisc. Tamla 319, 1972. Reissued on compact disc, Motown 012 157 354–2, 2000.

Innervisions. Stevie Wonder, vocals, piano, keyboards, harmonica, synthesizers, drums, percussion; various assisting instrumentalists and vocalists. "Too High" (Wonder); "Visions" (Wonder); "Living for the City" (Wonder); "Golden Lady" (Wonder); "Higher Ground" (Wonder); "Jesus Children of America" (Wonder); "All in Love Is Fair" (Wonder); "Don't You Worry 'bout a Thing" (Wonder); "He's Misstra Know-It-All" (Wonder). 33–1/3 rpm phonodisc. Tamla 326, 1973. Reissued on compact disc, Motown 3746303262, 1992; Motown 012 157 355–2, 2000.

Fulfillingness' First Finale. Stevie Wonder, vocals, keyboards, synthesizers, harmonica, drums, and percussion; various assisting instrumentalists and vocalists. "Smile Please" (Wonder); "Heaven Is 10 Zillion Light Years Away" (Wonder); "Too Shy to Say" (Wonder); "Boogie On Reggae Woman" (Wonder); "Creepin'" (Wonder); "You Haven't Done Nothin'" (Wonder); "It Ain't No Use" (Wonder); "They Won't Go When I Go" (Wonder, Yvonne Wright); "Bird of Beauty" (Wonder); "Please Don't Go" (Wonder). 33–1/3 rpm phonodisc. Tamla 332, 1974. Reissued on compact disc, Motown 012 157 581–2, 2000.

Songs in the Key of Life. Stevie Wonder, vocals, keyboards, synthesizers, harmonica, drums, and percussion; various assisting instrumentalists and vocalists. "Love's in Need of Love Today" (Wonder); "Have a Talk with God" (Wonder, Calvin Hardaway); "Village Ghetto Land" (Wonder, Gary Byrd); "Contusion" (Wonder);

"Sir Duke" (Wonder); "I Wish" (Wonder); "Knocks Me Off My Feet" (Wonder); "Pastime Paradise" (Wonder); "Summer Soft" (Wonder); "Ordinary Pain" (Wonder); "Isn't She Lovely" (Wonder); "Joy Inside My Fears" (Wonder); "Black Man" (Wonder, Gary Byrd); "Ngiculela—Es Una Historia—I Am Singing" (Wonder); "If It's Magic" (Wonder); "As" (Wonder); "Another Star" (Wonder). The following tracks were included on a special bonus record: "Saturn" (Wonder, Mike Sembello); "Ebony Eyes" (Wonder); "All Day Sucker" (Wonder); "Easy Goin' Evening (My Mama's Call)" (Wonder). 2 33–1/3 rpm phonodiscs (plus bonus extended-play disc). Tamla 340, 1976. Reissued on 2 compact discs, Motown 012 157 357–2, 2000.

Looking Back. Stevie Wonder, vocals, harmonica, keyboards, piano, drums, percussion; various assisting instrumentals and vocalists. "Thank You (For Loving Me All the Way)" (Clarence Paul, Eddie Holland, Jr., William Stevenson); "Contract on Love" (Janie Bradford, Lamont Dozier, Brian Holland); "Fingertips (Part 2)" (Henry Cosby, Clarence Paul); "Workout Stevie, Workout" (Clarence Paul, Henry Cosby); "Castles in the Sand" (Hal Davis, Frank Wilson, Marc Gordon, Mary M. O'Brien); "Hey Harmonica Man" (Marty Cooper, Lou Josie); "High Heel Sneakers" (Robert Higginbotham); "Uptight (Everything's Alright)" (Sylvia Moy, Henry Cosby, Wonder); "Nothing's Too Good for My Baby" (Sylvia Moy, Henry Cosby, William Stevenson); "Blowin' in the Wind" (Bob Dylan); "Ain't That Asking for Trouble" (Clarence Paul, Wonder, Sylvia Moy); "I'd Cry" (Sylvia Moy, Wonder); "A Place in the Sun" (Ron Miller, Bryan Wells); "Sylvia" (Sylvia Moy, Henry Cosby, Wonder); "Down to Earth" (Ron Miller, William O'Malley, Avery Vandenberg); "Thank You Love" (Wonder, Henry Cosby, Sylvia Moy); "Hey Love" (Clarence Paul, Morris Broadnax, Wonder); "Travelin' Man" (Ron Miller, Bryan Wells); "Until You Come Back to Me (That's What I'm Gonna Do)" (Wonder, Clarence Paul, Morris Broadnax); "I Was Made to Love Her" (Henry Cosby, Lula Hardaway, Wonder, Sylvia Moy); "I'm Wondering" (Sylvia Moy, Wonder, Henry Cosby); "Shoo-Be-Doo-Be-Doo-Da-Day" (Sylvia Moy, Wonder, Henry Cosby); "You Met Your Match" (Don Hunter, Wonder, Lula Hardaway); "I'd Be a Fool Right Now" (Sylvia Moy, Wonder, Henry Cosby); "Alfie" (Hal David, Burt Bacharach); "More Than a Dream" (Wonder, Henry Cosby); "For Once in My Life" (Ron Miller, Orlando Murden); "Angie Girl" (Sylvia Moy, Wonder, Henry Cosby); "My Cherie Amour" (Henry Cosby, Sylvia Moy, Wonder); "Don't Know Why I Love You" (Paul Riser, Don Hunter, Wonder, Lula Hardaway); "If I Ruled the World" (Leslie Bricusse, Syral Ornadel); "Yester-Me, Yester-You, Yesterday" (Ron Miller, Bryan Wells); "Never Had a Dream Come True" (Wonder, Henry Cosby, Sylvia Moy); "Signed, Sealed, Delivered (I'm Yours)" (Lula Hardaway, Wonder, Syreeta Wright, Lee Garrett); "Heaven Help Us All" (Ron Miller); "I Gotta Have a Song" (Wonder, Don Hunter, Lula Hardaway, Paul Riser); "Never Dreamed You'd Leave in Summer" (Syreeta Wright, Wonder); "If You Really Love Me" (Syreeta Wright, Wonder); "Something Out of the Blue" (Syreeta Wright, Wonder); "Do Yourself a Favor" (Syreeta Wright, Wonder). 3 33–1/3 rpm phonodiscs. Motown M804-LP3, 1977. Consists of previously released material (all pre-1972).

Journey Through the Secret Life of Plants. "Earth's Creation" (Wonder); "The First Garden" (Wonder); "Voyage to India" (Wonder); "Same Old Story" (Wonder); "Venus' Flytrap and the Bug" (Wonder); "Ai No, Sono" (Wonder); "Seasons" (Wonder);

"Power Flower" (Wonder, Michael Sembello); "Send One Your Love" [instrumental version] (Wonder); "Race Babbling" (Wonder); "Send One Your Love" (Wonder); "Outside My Window" (Wonder); Black Orchid (Wonder, Yvonne Wright); "Ecclesiastes" (Wonder); "Kesse Ye Lolo De Ye (Wonder); "Come Back as a Flower" (Wonder, Syreeta Wright); "A Seed's a Star and Tree Medley" (Wonder, Stephanie Andrews); "The Secret Life of Plants" (Wonder); "Tree" (Wonder); "Finale" (Wonder). 2 33–1/3 rpm phonodiscs. Tamla T13–371C2, 1979. Reissued on compact disc, Motown 374636127, 1992.

Hotter Than July. Stevie Wonder, vocals, keyboards, synthesizers, harmonic, drums, percussion; various assisting instrumentalists and vocalists. "Did I Hear You Say You Love Me" (Wonder); "All I Do (Is Think about You)" (Wonder, Morris Broadnax, Clarence Paul); "Rocket Love" (Wonder); "I Ain't Gonna Stand for It" (Wonder); "As If You Read My Mind" (Wonder); "Master Blaster (Jammin')" (Wonder); "Do Like You" (Wonder); "Cash in Your Face" (Wonder); "Lately" (Wonder); "Happy Birthday" (Wonder). 33–1/3 rpm phonodisc. Tamla 373, 1980. Reissued on compact disc, Tamla 012 157 363–2, 2000.

Stevie Wonder's Original Musiquarium I. Stevie Wonder, vocals, keyboards, synthesizers, harmonica, drums, percussion; various assisting instrumentalists and vocalists. "Superstition" (Wonder); "You Haven't Done Nothin'" (Wonder); "Living for the City" (Wonder); "Front Line" (Wonder); "Superwoman (Where Were You When I Needed You)" (Wonder); "Send One Your Love" (Wonder); "You Are the Sunshine of My Life" (Wonder); "Ribbon in the Sky" (Wonder); "Higher Ground" (Wonder); "Sir Duke" (Wonder); "Master Blaster (Jammin')" (Wonder); "Boogie On Reggae Woman" (Wonder); "That Girl" (Wonder); "I Wish" (Wonder); "Isn't She Lovely" (Wonder); "Do I Do" (Wonder). 2 33–1/3 rpm phonodiscs. Tamla 6002, 1982. Contains principally previously released material. Reissued on 2 compact discs (available separately), Tamla 61113TD2 1990, and reissued as Motown 37463–6002–2, 2000.

The Woman in Red. Stevie Wonder, vocals, piano, keyboards, harmonica, drums, percussion; Dionne Warwick, vocals; various assisting instrumentalists and vocalists. "The Woman in Red" (Wonder); "It's You" (Wonder); "It's More Than You" (Ben Bridges); "I Just Called to Say I Love You" (Wonder); "Love Light in Flight" (Wonder); "Moments Aren't Moments" (Wonder); "Weakness" (Wonder); "Don't Drive Drunk" (Wonder). 33–1/3 rpm phonodisc. Motown 6108, 1984. Reissued on compact disc, Motown 3746361082, 1992.

In Square Circle. Stevie Wonder, vocals, keyboards, synthesizers, percussion; various assisting instrumentalists and vocalists. "Part-Time Lover" (Wonder); "I Love You Too Much" (Wonder); "Whereabouts" (Wonder); "Stranger on the Shore of Love" (Wonder); "Never in Your Sun" (Wonder); "Spiritual Walkers" (Wonder); "Land of La La" (Wonder); "Go Home" (Wonder); "Overjoyed" (Wonder); "It's Wrong (Apartheid)" (Wonder). Compact disc. Tamla 3746361342, 1985.

Love Songs: 20 Classic Hits. Stevie Wonder, vocals, harmonica, piano, keyboards, drums, percussion; various assisting instrumentalists and vocalists. "Contract on Love" (Janie Bradford, Lamont Dozier, Brian Holland); "My Cherie Amour" (Henry Cosby, Sylvia Moy, Wonder); "Until You Come Back to Me" (Wonder, Morris Broadnax, Clarence Paul); "Yester-Me, Yester-You, Yesterday" (Ron Miller, Bryan Wells); "Never Had a Dream Come True" (Wonder, Henry Cosby, Sylvia Moy); "If You Really Love Me" (Wonder, Syreeta Wright); "Heaven Help Us All" (Ron Miller); "Never Dreamed You'd Leave in Summer" (Wonder, Syreeta

Wright); "A Place in the Sun" (Ron Miller, Bryan Wells); "Alfie" (Hal David, Burt Bacharach); "Hey Love" (Morris Broadnax, Clarence Paul, Wonder); "For Once in My Love" (Ron Miller, Orlando Murden); "We Can Work It Out" (John Lennon, Paul McCartney); "I Was Made to Love Her" (Lula Hardaway, Sylvia Moy, Wonder, Henry Cosby); "Don't Know Why I Love You" (Paul Riser, Don Hunter, Wonder, Lula Hardaway); "Blowin' in the Wind" (Bob Dylan); "Shoo-Be-Doo-Be-Doo-Da-Day" (Sylvia Moy, Wonder, Henry Cosby); "I'm Wondering" (Sylvia Moy, Wonder, Henry Cosby); "Nothing's Too Good for My Baby" (Sylvia Moy, Henry Cosby, William Stevenson); "Signed, Sealed, Delivered (I'm Yours)" (Wonder, Lee Garrett, Syreeta Wright, Lula Hardaway). Compact disc. Tamla MCD 0950MD, 1985. Contains previously issued material.

Essential Stevie Wonder. Stevie Wonder, vocals, harmonica, piano, keyboards, drums, percussion; various assisting instrumentalists and vocalists. "I Was Made to Love Her" (Lula Hardaway, Sylvia Moy, Wonder, Henry Cosby); "Thank You Love" (Wonder, Henry Cosby, Sylvia Moy); "Until You Come Back to Me (That's What I'm Gonna Do)" (Wonder, Clarence Paul, Morris Broadnax); "I'm Wondering" (Sylvia Moy, Wonder, Henry Cosby); "Shoo-Be-Doo-Be-Doo-Da-Day" (Sylvia Moy, Wonder, Henry Cosby); "Angie Girl" (Henry Cosby, Sylvia Moy, Wonder); "More Than a Dream" (Henry Cosby, Wonder); "For Once in My Life" (Ron Miller, Orlando Murden); "You Met Your Match" (Don Hunter, Wonder, Lula Hardaway); "Don't Know Why I Love You" (Paul Riser, Don Hunter, Wonder, Lula Hardaway); "Yester-Me, Yester-You, Yesterday" (Ron Miller, Bryan Wells); "My Cherie Amour" (Henry Cosby, Sylvia Moy, Wonder); "If You Really Love Me" (Wonder, Syreeta Wright); "We Can Work It Out" (John Lennon, Paul McCartney); "Signed, Sealed, Delivered (I'm Yours)" (Wonder, Lee Garrett, Syreeta Wright, Lula Hardaway); "Never Had a Dream Come True" (Wonder, Henry Cosby, Sylvia Moy); "Something Out of the Blue" (Wonder, Syreeta Wright); "Heaven Help Us All" (Ron Miller); "Do Yourself a Favor" (Syreeta Wright, Wonder); "Fingertips" (Clarence Paul, Henry Cosby); "Workout Stevie, Workout" (Clarence Paul, Henry Cosby); "Hey Harmonica Man" (Marty Cooper, Lou Josie); "Kiss Me Baby" (Clarence Paul, Stevie Judkins); "High Heel Sneakers" (Robert Higginbotham); "Happy Street" (Ben Peters); "Castles in the Sand" (Hal Davis, Frank Wilson, Marc Gordon, Mary M. O'Brien); "Contract on Love" (Janie Bradford, Lamont Dozier, Brian Holland); "I Call It Pretty Music, but the Old People Call It the Blues, Part 1" (Berry Gordy, Jr., Clarence Paul); "Uptight (Everything's Alright)" (Sylvia Moy, Henry Cosby, Wonder); "Music Talk" (Ted Hull, Wonder, Clarence Paul); "Ain't That Asking for Trouble" (Clarence Paul, Wonder, Sylvia Moy); "Love a Go Go" (Beth Beatty, Ernie Shelby); "Be Cool, Be Calm (and Keep Yourself Together)" (Sylvia Moy, Henry Cosby, Wonder); "Nothing's Too Good for My Baby" (Sylvia Moy, Henry Cosby, William "Mickey" Stevenson); "I'd Cry" (Sylvia Moy, Wonder); "Travelin' Man" (Ron Miller, Bryan Wells); "A Place in the Sun" (Ron Miller, Bryan Wells); "Blowin' in the Wind" (Bob Dylan). 2 compact discs. Motown 530 047–2, 1987. Contains previously released material.

Characters. Stevie Wonder, vocals, keyboards, drums, percussion; various assisting instrumentalists and vocalists. "You Will Know" (Wonder); "Dark 'n' Lovely" (Wonder, Gary Byrd); "In Your Corner" (Wonder); "With Each Beat of My

Heart" (Wonder); "One of a Kind" (Wonder); "Skeletons" (Wonder); "Get It" (Wonder); "Galaxy Paradise" (Wonder); "Cryin' Through the Night" (Wonder); "Free" (Wonder). Compact disc. Motown 6248, 1987.

Music from the Movie "Jungle Fever." Stevie Wonder, vocals, piano, keyboards, drums, percussion; various assisting instrumentalists and vocalists. "Fun Day" (Wonder); "Queen in the Black" (Wonder); "These Three Words" (Wonder); "Each Other's Throat" (Wonder); "If She Breaks Your Heart" (Wonder); "Gotta Have You" (Wonder); "Make Sure You're Sure" (Wonder); "Jungle Fever" (Wonder); "I Go Sailing" (Wonder); "Chemical Love" (Wonder, Stephanie Andrews); "Lighting Up the Candles" (Wonder). Compact disc. Motown 374636291–2, 1991.

Conversation Peace. Stevie Wonder, vocals, keyboards, drums, percussion. "Rain Your Love Down" (Wonder); "Edge of Eternity" (Wonder); "Taboo to Love" (Wonder); "Take the Time Out" (Wonder); "I'm New" (Wonder); "My Love Is with You" (Wonder); "Treat Myself" (Wonder, Stephanie Andrews); "Tomorrow Robins Will Sing" (Wonder, Edley Shine [rap]); "Sensuous Whisper" (Wonder); "For Your Love" (Wonder); "Cold Chill" (Wonder); "Sorry" (Wonder); "Conversation Peace" (Wonder). Compact disc. Motown 314530238–2, 1995.

Natural Wonder. Stevie Wonder, vocals, harmonica, keyboards; Tokyo Philharmonic Orchestra; Henry Panion III, conductor; various assisting instrumentalists and vocalists. "Dancing to the Rhythm" (Wonder); "Love's in Need of Love Today" (Wonder); "Master Blaster (Jammin')" (Wonder); "Stevie Ray Blues" (Wonder); "Higher Ground" (Wonder); "Rocket Love" (Wonder); "Stay Gold" (Wonder, Carmine Coppola); "Ribbon in the Sky" (Wonder); "Pastime Paradise" (Wonder); "If It's Magic" (Wonder); "Ms. & Mr. Little Ones" (Wonder); "Village Ghetto Land" (Wonder, Gary Byrd); "Tomorrow Robins Will Sing" (Wonder); "Overjoyed" (Wonder); "My Cherie Amour" (Henry Cosby, Sylvia Moy, Wonder); "Signed, Sealed, Delivered (I'm Yours)" (Wonder, Lee Garrett, Syreeta Wright, Lula Hardaway); "Living for the City" (Wonder); "Sir Duke" (Wonder); "I Wish" (Wonder); "You Are the Sunshine of My Life" (Wonder); "Superstition" (Wonder); "I Just Called to Say I Love You" (Wonder); "For Your Love" (Wonder); "Another Star" (Wonder). 2 compact discs. Motown 314530546–2, 1995. Recorded live in concert in Osaka and Tel Aviv.

Song Review: A Greatest Hits Collection. Stevie Wonder, vocals, harmonica, piano, keyboards, drums, percussion; various assisting instrumentalists and vocalists. "Part-Time Lover" (Wonder); "I Just Called to Say I Love You" (Wonder); "Superstition" (Wonder); "Sir Duke" (Wonder); "My Cherie Amour" (Henry Cosby, Sylvia Moy, Wonder); "I Was Made to Love Her" (Lula Hardaway, Sylvia Moy, Wonder, Henry Cosby); "Overjoyed" (Wonder); "Hey Love" (Morris Broadnax, Clarence Paul, Wonder); "Signed, Sealed, Delivered (I'm Yours)" (Wonder, Lee Garrett, Syreeta Wright, Lula Hardaway); "You Are the Sunshine of My Life" (Wonder); "Ribbon in the Sky" (Wonder); "Master Blaster (Jammin')" (Wonder); "Living for the City" (Wonder); "Uptight (Everything's Alright)" (Sylvia Moy, Henry Cosby, Wonder); "Lately" (Wonder); "Do I Do" (Wonder); "Send One Your Love" (Wonder); "Ebony and Ivory" (Paul McCartney); "All I Do" (Morris Broadnax, Clarence Paul, Wonder); "That Girl" (Wonder); "For Your Love" (Wonder); "I Wish" (Wonder); "You Will Know" (Wonder); "Boogie On Reggae Woman" (Wonder); "Higher Ground" (Wonder); "These Three

Words" (Wonder); "Stay Gold" (Wonder, Carmine Coppola); "Love Light in Flight" (Wonder); "Kiss Lonely Good-Bye" (two versions) (Wonder); "Redemption Song" (Bob Marley). 2 compact discs. Motown 530767, 1996.

At the Close of a Century. Stevie Wonder, vocals, harmonica, piano, keyboards, drums, percussion; various assisting instrumentalists and vocalists. "Fingertips" (Clarence Paul, Henry Cosby); "Uptight (Everything's Alright)" (Sylvia Moy, Henry Cosby, Wonder); "Nothing's Too Good for My Baby" (Sylvia Moy, Henry Cosby, William "Mickey" Stevenson); "Blowin' in the Wind" (Bob Dylan); "A Place in the Sun" (Ron Miller, Bryan Wells); "Hey Love" (Wonder, Clarence Paul, Morris Broadnax); "I Was Made to Love Her" (Sylvia Moy, Henry Cosby, Wonder, Lula Hardaway); "Until You Come Back to Me (That's What I'm Gonna Do)" (Wonder, Morris Broadnax, Clarence Paul); "I'm Wondering" (Sylvia Moy, Henry Cosby, Wonder); "Shoo-Be-Doo-Be-Doo-Da-Day" (Sylvia Moy, Wonder, Henry Cosby); "You Met Your Match" (Wonder, Don Hunter, Lula Hardaway); "For Once in My Life" (Ron Miller, Orlando Murden); "I Don't Know Why" (Don Hunter, Lula Hardaway, Wonder, Paul Riser); "My Cherie Amour" (Henry Cosby, Sylvia Moy, Wonder); "Yester-me Yester-you, Yesterday" (Ron Miller, Bryan Wells); "Never Had a Dream Come True" (Bryan Wells, Ron Miller),[2] "Signed, Sealed, Delivered (I'm Yours)" (Wonder, Lee Garrett, Syreeta Wright, Lula Hardaway); "Heaven Help Us All" (Ron Miller); "We Can Work It Out" (John Lennon, Paul McCartney); "If You Really Love Me" (Wonder, Syreeta Wright); "Never Dreamed You'd Leave in Summer" (Wonder, Syreeta Wright); "Superwoman (Where Were You When I Needed You)" (Wonder); "I Love Every Little Thing about You" (Wonder); "Superstition" (Wonder); "You Are the Sunshine of My Life" (Wonder); "You and I (We Can Conquer the World)" (Wonder); "I Believe (When I Fall in Love It Will Be Forever)" (Yvonne Wright, Wonder); "Too High" (Wonder); "Visions" (Wonder); "Living for the City" (Wonder); "Golden Lady" (Wonder); "Higher Ground" (Wonder); "All in Love Is Fair" (Wonder); "Don't You Worry 'bout a Thing" (Wonder); "He's Misstra Know-It-All" (Wonder); "You Haven't Done Nothin'" (Wonder); "Heaven Is 10 Zillion Miles Away" (Wonder); "Too Shy to Say" (Wonder); "Boogie On Reggae Woman" (Wonder); "Creepin'" (Wonder); "Sir Duke" (Wonder); "I Wish" (Wonder); "Knocks Me Off My Feet" (Wonder); "Pastime Paradise" (Wonder); "Isn't She Lovely" (Wonder); "Ngiculela—Es una Historia—I Am Singing" (Wonder); "If It's Magic" (Wonder); "As" (Wonder); "Another Star" (Wonder); "Send One Your Love" (Wonder); "All I Do (Is Think about You)" (Wonder, Clarence Paul, Morris Broadnax); "Rocket Love" (Wonder); "I Ain't Gonna Stand for It" (Wonder); "Master Blaster (Jammin')" (Wonder); "Lately" (Wonder); "Happy Birthday" (Wonder); "That Girl" (Wonder); "Ribbon in the Sky" (Wonder); "Do I Do" (Wonder); "Love Light in Flight" (Wonder); "I Just Called to Say I Love You" (Wonder); "Overjoyed" (Wonder); "Part-Time Lover" (Wonder); "Go Home" (Wonder); "You Will Know" (Wonder); "Skeletons" (Wonder); "Gotta Have You" (Wonder); "These Three Words" (Wonder); "For Your Love" (Wonder); "How Come, How Long" (Babyface, Wonder). 4 compact discs. Motown 012 153 992–2, 1999. Contains previously released material.

The Definitive Collection. Stevie Wonder, vocals, harmonica, piano, keyboards, drums, percussion; various assisting instrumentalists and vocalists. "Superstition"

(Wonder); "Sir Duke" (Wonder); "I Wish" (Wonder); "Master Blaster (Jammin')" (Wonder); "Isn't She Lovely" (Wonder); "I Just Called to Say I Love You" (Wonder); "Ebony and Ivory" (Paul McCartney); "As" (Wonder); "Never Had a Dream Come True" (Wonder, Henry Cosby, Sylvia Moy); "I Was Made to Love Her" (Henry Cosby, Lula Hardaway, Wonder, Sylvia Moy); "Heaven Help Us All" (Ron Miller); "Overjoyed" (Wonder); "Lately" (Wonder); "For Your Love" (Wonder); "If You Really Love Me" (Wonder, Syreeta Wright); "Higher Ground" (Wonder); "Do I Do" (Wonder); "Living for the City" (Wonder); "Part-Time Lover" (Wonder); "For Once in My Life" (Ron Miller, Orlando Murden); "Uptight (Everything's Alright)" (Sylvia Moy, Henry Cosby, Wonder); "We Can Work It Out" (John Lennon, Paul McCartney); "Signed, Sealed, Delivered (I'm Yours)" (Wonder, Lee Garrett, Syreeta Wright, Lula Hardaway); "Yester-Me, Yester-You, Yesterday" (Ron Miller, Bryan Wells); "I'm Wondering" (Sylvia Moy, Wonder, Henry Cosby); "My Cherie Amour" (Henry Cosby, Sylvia Moy, Wonder); "You Are the Sunshine of My Life" (Wonder); "Don't Know Why I Love You" (Paul Riser, Don Hunter, Wonder, Lula Hardaway); "A Place in the Sun" (Ron Miller, Bryan Wells); "Blowin' in the Wind" (Bob Dylan); "Send One Your Love" (Wonder); "Pastime Paradise" (Wonder); "I Ain't Gonna Stand for It" (Wonder); "Fingertips" (Henry Cosby, Clarence Paul); "Boogie On Reggae Woman" (Wonder); "You Haven't Done Nothin'" (Wonder); "He's Misstra Know-It-All" (Wonder); "Happy Birthday" (Wonder). 2 compact discs. UTV Records/Motown 066503–2 and 066504–2, 2002. Contains previously released material.

A Time to Love. Stevie Wonder, vocals, keyboards, harmonica, drums, percussion; various assisting vocalists and instrumentalists. "If Your Love Cannot Be Moved" (Wonder); "Sweetest Somebody I Know" (Wonder); "Moon Blue" (Wonder, Akosua Busia); "From the Bottom of My Heart" (Wonder); "Please Don't Hurt My Baby" (Wonder); "How Will I Know" (Wonder); "My Love Is on Fire" (Wonder); "Passionate Relationships" (Wonder); "Tell Your Heart I Love You" (Wonder); "True Love" (Wonder); "Shelter in the Rain" (Wonder); "So What the Fuss" (Wonder); "Can't Imagine Love Without You" (Wonder); "Positivity" (Wonder); "A Time to Love" (Wonder, India.Arie). Compact disc. Motown B0002402–2, 2005.

THE SINGLES OF STEVIE WONDER

"I Call It Pretty Music, but the Old People Call It the Blues, Parts 1 and 2" (Berry Gordy, Jr., Clarence Paul). 45 rpm phonodisc. Tamla 54061, 1962.

"Little Water Boy" (Clarence Paul, Stephen Judkins); "La La La La La" (Clarence Paul). 45 rpm phonodisc. Tamla 54070, 1962.

"Contract on Love" (Janie Bradford, Lamont Dozier, Brian Holland); "Sunset" (Clarence Paul, Stephen Judkins). 45 rpm phonodisc. Tamla 54074, 1962.[3]

"Fingertips, Parts 1 and 2" (Clarence Paul, Henry Cosby). 45 rpm phonodisc. Tamla 54080, 1963.

"Workout Stevie, Workout" (Clarence Paul, Henry Cosby); "Monkey Talk" (Clarence Paul). 45 rpm phonodisc. Tamla 54086, 1963.

"Castles in the Sand" (Hal Davis, Frank Wilson, Marc Gordon, Mary M. O'Brien); "Thank You (for Loving Me All the Way)" (Clarence Paul, Eddie Holland, Jr., William Stevenson). 45 rpm phonodisc. Tamla 54090, 1964.

"Hey Harmonica Man" (Marty Cooper, Lou Josie); "This Little Girl" (Henry Cosby, Eddie Holland, Jr., William Stevenson). 45 rpm phonodisc. Tamla 54096, 1964.

"Happy Street" (Ben Peters); "Sad Boy" (Dorsey Burnette, Gerald Nelson). 45 rpm phonodisc. Tamla 54103, 1964.

"Kiss Me Baby" (Clarence Paul, Stevie Judkins); "Tears in Vain" (Clarence Paul). 45 rpm phonodisc. Tamla 54114, 1965.

"High Heel Sneakers" (Robert Higginbotham); "Funny How Time Slips Away" (Willie Nelson). 45 rpm phonodisc. Tamla 54119, 1965. Some copies include "Music Talk" as the B-side.

"Uptight (Everything's Alright)" (Sylvia Moy, Henry Cosby, Wonder); "Purple Rain Drops" (Ted Hull). 45 rpm phonodisc. Tamla 54124, 1965.

"Nothing's Too Good for My Baby" (Sylvia Moy, Henry Cosby, William Stevenson); "With a Child's Heart" (Vicki Basemore, Henry Cosby, Sylvia Moy). 45 rpm phonodisc. Tamla 54130, 1966.

"Blowin' in the Wind" (Bob Dylan); "Ain't That Asking for Trouble" (Clarence Paul, Wonder, Sylvia Moy). 45 rpm phonodisc. Tamla 54136, 1966.

"A Place in the Sun" (Ron Miller, Bryan Wells); "Sylvia" (Sylvia Moy, Henry Cosby, Wonder). 45 rpm phonodisc. Tamla 54139, 1966.

"Someday at Christmas" (Ron Miller, Bryan Wells); "The Miracles of Christmas" (Aurora Miller, Ron Miller). 45 rpm phonodisc. Tamla 54142, 1966.

"Travelin' Man" (Ron Miller, Bryan Wells); "Hey Love" (Clarence Paul, Morris Broadnax, Wonder). 45 rpm phonodisc. Tamla 54147, 1967.

"I Was Made to Love Her" (Henry Cosby, Lula Hardaway, Wonder, Sylvia Moy); "Hold Me" (Morris Broadnax, Wonder, Clarence Paul). 45 rpm phonodisc. Tamla 54151, 1967.

"I'm Wondering" (Sylvia Moy, Wonder, Henry Cosby); "Every Time I See You I Go Wild" (Henry Cosby, Sylvia Moy, Wonder). 45 rpm phonodisc. Tamla 54157, 1967.

"Shoo-Be-Doo-Be-Doo-Da-Day" (Sylvia Moy, Wonder, Henry Cosby); "Why Don't You Lead Me to Love" (Henry Cosby, Lula Hardaway, Sylvia Moy, Wonder). 45 rpm phonodisc. Tamla 54165, 1968.

"You Met Your Match" (Don Hunter, Wonder, Lula Hardaway); "My Girl" (William ["Smokey"] Robinson, Jr., Ronald White). 45 rpm phonodisc. Tamla 54168, 1968.

"Alfie" (Hal David, Burt Bacharach); "More Than a Dream" (Henry Cosby, Wonder). 45 rpm phonodisc. Gordy 7076, 1968. Wonder's name is given as Eivets Rednow (Stevie Wonder backward) on this single release.

"For Once in My Life" (Ron Miller, Orlando Murden); "Angie Girl" (Sylvia Moy, Wonder, Henry Cosby). 45 rpm phonodisc. Tamla 54174, 1968.

"I Don't Know Why" (Don Hunter, Lula Hardaway, Wonder, Paul Riser); "My Cherie Amour" (Henry Cosby, Sylvia Moy, Wonder). 45 rpm phonodisc. Tamla 54180, 1969.

"Yester-Me, Yester-You, Yesterday" (Ron Miller, Bryan Wells); "I'd Be a Fool Right Now" (Henry Cosby, Wonder, Sylvia Moy). 45 rpm phonodisc. Tamla 54188, 1969.

"Never Had a Dream Come True" (Wonder, Henry Cosby, Sylvia Moy); "Somebody Knows, Somebody Cares" (Henry Cosby, Lula Hardaway, Sylvia Moy, Wonder). 45 rpm phonodisc. Tamla 54191, 1970.

"Signed, Sealed, Delivered (I'm Yours)" (Wonder, Lee Garrett, Syreeta Wright, Lula Hardaway); "I'm More Than Happy (I'm Satisfied)" (Henry Cosby, Cornelius Grant, Sylvia Moy, Wonder). 45 rpm phonodisc. Tamla 54196.

"Heaven Help Us All" (Ron Miller); "I Gotta Have a Song" (Wonder, Don Hunter, Lula Hardaway, Paul Riser). 45 rpm phonodisc. Tamla 54200, 1970.

"We Can Work It Out" (John Lennon, Paul McCartney); "Never Dreamed You'd Leave in Summer" (Syreeta Wright, Wonder). 45 rpm phonodisc. Tamla 54202, 1971.

"If You Really Love Me" (Wonder, Syreeta Wright); "Think of Me as Your Soldier" (Wonder, Syreeta Wright). 45 rpm phonodisc. Tamla 54208, 1971.

"What Christmas Means to Me" (Anna Gaye, Horgay Gordy, Shadee Hasan); "Bedtime for Toys" (Ron Miller, Orlando Murden). 45 rpm phonodisc. Tamla 54214, 1971.

"Superwoman (Where Were You When I Needed You)" (Wonder); "I Love Every Little Thing about You" (Wonder). 45 rpm phonodisc. Tamla 54216, 1972.

"Keep On Running" (Wonder); "Evil" (Wonder, Yvonne Wright). 45 rpm phonodisc. Tamla 54223, 1972.

"Superstition" (Wonder); "You've Got It Bad Girl" (Yvonne Wright, Wonder). 45 rpm phonodisc. Tamla 54226, 1972.

"You Are the Sunshine of My Life" (Wonder); "Tuesday Heartbreak" (Wonder). 45 rpm phonodisc. Tamla 54232, 1973.

"Higher Ground" (Wonder); "Too High" (Wonder). 45 rpm phonodisc. Tamla 54235, 1973.

"Living for the City" (Wonder); "Visions" (Wonder). 45 rpm phonodisc. Tamla 54242, 1973.

"Don't You Worry 'bout a Thing" (Wonder); "Blame It On the Sun" (Syreeta Wright, Wonder). 45 rpm phonodisc. Tamla 54245, 1974.

"You Haven't Done Nothin'" (Wonder); "Big Brother" (Wonder). 45 rpm phonodisc. Tamla 54252, 1974.

"Boogie On Reggae Woman" (Wonder); "Seems So Long" (Wonder). 45 rpm phonodisc. Tamla 54254, 1974.

"I Wish" (Wonder); "You and I" (Wonder). 45 rpm phonodisc. Tamla 54274, 1976.

"Sir Duke" (Wonder); "He's Misstra Know-It-All" (Wonder). 45 rpm phonodisc. Tamla 54281, 1977.

"Another Star" (Wonder); "Creepin'" (Wonder). 45 rpm phonodisc. Tamla 54286, 1977.

"As" (Wonder); "Contusion" (Wonder). 45 rpm phonodisc. Tamla 54291, 1977.

"Pops, We Love You" (Marilyn McLeod, Pamela Sawyer); Pops, We Love You" [instrumental version] (Marilyn McLeod, Pamela Sawyer). 45 rpm phonodisc. Motown 1455, 1978. This recording is by Diana Ross, Marvin Gaye, Smokey Robinson, and Wonder.

"Send One Your Love" (Wonder); Send One Your Love" [instrumental version] (Wonder). 45 rpm phonodisc. Tamla 54303, 1979.

"Outside My Window" (Wonder); "Same Old Story" (Wonder). 45 rpm phonodisc. Tamla 54308, 1980.

"Master Blaster (Jammin')" (Wonder); "Master Blaster (Dub)" (Wonder). 45 rpm phonodisc. Tamla 54317, 1980.

"I Ain't Gonna Stand for It" (Wonder); "Knocks Me Off My Feet" (Wonder). 45 rpm phonodisc. Tamla 54320, 1980.

"Lately" (Wonder); "If It's Magic" (Wonder). 45 rpm phonodisc. Tamla 54323, 1981.

"Did I Hear You Say You Love Me" (Wonder); "As If You Read My Mind" (Wonder). 45 rpm phonodisc. Tamla 54328, 1981.

"That Girl" (Wonder); "All I Do (Is Think about You)" (Wonder, Morris Broadnax, Clarence Paul). 45 rpm phonodisc. Tamla 1602, 1981.

"Ebony and Ivory" (Paul McCartney); "Rainclouds" (Paul McCartney). Paul McCartney with Stevie Wonder. 45 rpm phonodisc. Parlophone 12R 6054/Columbia 02860, 1982. The B-side is performed by Paul McCartney.

"Do I Do" (Wonder); "Rocket Love" (Wonder). 45 rpm phonodisc. Tamla 1612, 1982.

"Ribbon in the Sky" (Wonder); "Black Orchid" (Wonder, Yvonne Wright). 45 rpm phonodisc. Tamla 1639, 1982.

"Used to Be" (Ron Miller, Ken Hirsch); "I Want to Come Back as a Song" (Ron Miller). 45 rpm phonodisc. Motown 1650, 1982. The A-side is performed by Charlene and Stevie Wonder. and the B-side is performed by Charlene.

"I Just Called to Say I Love You" (Wonder); "I Just Called to Say I Love You" [instrumental version] (Wonder). 45 rpm phonodisc. Motown 1745, 1984.

"Love Light in Flight" (Wonder); "It's More Than You" (Ben Bridges). 45 rpm phonodisc. Motown 1769, 1984.

"Don't Drive Drunk" (two versions) (Wonder); "Did I Hear You Say You Love Me" (Wonder). 12-inch 33–1/3 rpm extended-play single. Motown 4527MG, 1984.

"We Are the World" (Michael Jackson, Lionel Richie); "Grace" (Quincy Jones, Jeremy Lubbock). 45 rpm phonodisc. Columbia 04839, 1985. Wonder is the second of 21 solo singers on the A-side. The B-side of the recording is by Quincy Jones.

"Part-Time Lover" (Wonder); "Part-Time Lover" [instrumental version] (Wonder). 45 rpm phonodisc. Tamla 1808, 1985. Also released as a 12-inch 33–1/3 rpm extended-play phonodisc, Tamla 4548TG, 1985.

"That's What Friends Are For" (Burt Bacharach, Carole Bayer Sager); "Two Ships Passing in the Night" (Dionne Warwick). 45 rpm phonodisc. Arista 9422, 1985. The A-side is by Dionne [Warwick] & Friends (which includes Stevie Wonder), and the B-side is by Dionne Warwick.

"Go Home" (Wonder); "Go Home" [instrumental version] (Wonder). 45 rpm phonodisc. Tamla 1817, 1985.

"Overjoyed" (Wonder); "Overjoyed" [instrumental version] (Wonder). 45 rpm phonodisc. Tamla 1832, 1986.

"Land of La La" (Wonder); "Land of La La" [instrumental version] (Wonder). 45 rpm phonodisc. Tamla 1846, 1986.

"Skeletons" (Wonder); "Skeletons" [instrumental version] (Wonder). 45 rpm phonodisc. Motown 1907, 1987.

"You Will Know" (Wonder); "You Will Know" [instrumental version] (Wonder). 45 rpm phonodisc. Motown 1919, 1987.

"Get It" (Wonder); "Get It" [instrumental version] (Wonder). Stevie Wonder and Michael Jackson. 12-inch 33–1/3 rpm extended-play phonodisc. Motown 4604, 1988.

"Get It" (Wonder); "Get It" [instrumental version] (Wonder). Stevie Wonder and Michael Jackson. 45 rpm phonodisc. Motown 1930, 1988.

"My Love" (Wonder); "Words and Music" (Clifton Magness, Mark Edward Vieha). Julio Iglesias, featuring Stevie Wonder. 45 rpm phonodisc. Columbia 07781, 1988. Wonder performs only on the A-side.

"My Eyes Don't Cry" (Wonder); "My Eyes Don't Cry" [instrumental version] (Wonder). 45 rpm phonodisc. Motown 1946, 1988.

"With Each Beat of My Heart" (Wonder); "With Each Beat of My Heart" [instrumental version] (Wonder). 45 rpm phonodisc. Motown 1953, 1989.

"Keep Our Love Alive" (Wonder); "Keep Our Love Alive" [instrumental version] (Wonder). 45 rpm phonodisc. Motown 1990, 1990.

"Gotta Have You" (Wonder); "Feeding Off the Love of the Land" (Wonder). 45 rpm phonodisc. Motown 2081, 1991.

"Fun Day" (Wonder); "Fun Day" [instrumental version] (Wonder). 45 rpm phonodisc. Motown 2127, 1991.

"These Three Words" (Wonder); "These Three Words" [instrumental version] (Wonder). 45 rpm phonodisc. Motown 2143, 1991.

"We Didn't Know" (Wonder); "Lover for Life" (Sam L. Dees). The A-side is performed by Whitney Houston with Stevie Wonder, and the B-side is performed by Whitney Houston. Arista 12420, 1992.

"For Your Love" (Wonder); "For Your Love" [instrumental version] (Wonder). CD single. Motown 0290, 1995.

"Tomorrow Robins Will Sing" (Wonder, Edley Shine). CD single. Motown 0356, 1995.

"Treat Myself" (Wonder, Stephanie Andrews). CD single. Motown 0436, 1995.

"Kiss Lonely Goodbye" (Wonder). CD single. Motown 0476, 1996.

Notes

INTRODUCTION

1. Wonder's birth name is sometimes given as Steveland; he actually uses Stevland.

2. All chart data in this book has been checked in several sources, including the following: Liner notes to *Stevie Wonder: At the Close of a Century*, 4 compact discs, Motown 012 153 992–2, 1999; Joel Whitburn, *The Billboard Book of Top 40 Hits*, 6th ed. (New York: Billboard Books, 1996); Joel Whitburn, *Top Pop Singles, 1955–1996* (Menomonee Falls, Wis.: Record Research, Inc., 1997).

3. Whitburn, *Top Pop Singles, 1955–1996*, p. 840.

4. Robert Christgau's Web site, "Consumer Guide: Stevie Wonder," http://robertchristgau.com/get_artist.php?id=1328&name=Stevie+Wonder (accessed January 3, 2005).

CHAPTER 1

1. The recording was too long to be released on one side of a 45 rpm record, given the technology of the day; therefore, Motown split it between the two sides of the record.

2. In the early 1960s, Ray Charles recorded for Atlantic and then for ABC-Paramount.

3. Vladimir Bogdanov, John Bush, and Stephen Thomas Erlewine, eds., *All Music Guide to Soul* (Ann Arbor, Mich.: Backbeat Books, 2003), p. 764.

CHAPTER 2

1. Leonard Pitts, Jr., "Stevie Wonder," in liner notes to *At the Close of a Century*, 4 compact discs, Motown 012 153 992–2, 1999, p. 26.

2. "Uptight" was not Stevie Wonder's first published composition. He had collaborated with Clarence Paul for the 1962 songs "Little Water Boy" (a single A-side) and "Sunset" (a single B-side), and in 1965 he recorded another Clarence

Paul/Stevie Judkins collaboration, "Kiss Me Baby"; Judkins was Wonder's legal last name at the time.

3. Wonder's most notable work on this theme was his soundtrack for the Spike Lee film *Jungle Fever*, a movie about interracial relationships.

4. Kenneth J. Bindas and Craig Houston, "'Takin' Care of Business': Rock Music, Vietnam and the Protest Myth," *Historian* 52, November 1989, p. 16.

5. Steve Huey, "The Funk Brothers," in *All Music Guide to Soul*, ed. Vladimir Bogdanov, John Bush, and Stephen Thomas Erlewine (Ann Arbor, Mich.: Backbeat Books, 2003), p. 262.

CHAPTER 3

1. R. Eldridge, "Will Stevie Wonder Become Another Sammy Davis?" *Melody Maker* 44, 5 April 1969, p. 7.

2. Ibid.

3. By the 1960s, tap dancing was seen by some in the civil rights and Black Power movements as hearkening back to the embarrassing days of minstrelry.

4. The Motown 4–compact disc set *At the Close of a Century* (Motown 012 153 992–2, 1999) lists the songwriters as Bryan Wells and Ron Miller. Motown releases of the track also disagree on the arranger and the producer for the recording session. The official registration for the song with the American Society of Composers, Authors, and Publishers (ASCAP) confirms the credit to Wonder, Cosby, and Moy.

5. One might even say that the listing of five different arrangers on the back of the album cover suggests that all were in competition to see who could write the biggest "charts."

CHAPTER 4

1. John Bush, "*Where I'm Coming From*," in *All Music Guide to Soul*, ed. Vladimir Bogdanov, John Bush, and Stephen Thomas Erlewine (Ann Arbor, Mich.: Backbeat Books, 2003), p. 764.

2. Ibid.

3. "Superwoman (Where Were You When I Needed You Most)" is structured essentially like two disparate songs that have been combined, and not to particularly great effect.

4. John Bush, "*Music of My Mind*," in Bogdanov, Bush, and Erlewine, *All Music Guide to Soul*, p. 765.

5. Gail Hilson Woldu, "Contextualizing Rap," in *American Popular Music: New Approaches to the Twentieth Century*, ed. Rachel Rubin and Jeffry Melnick (Amherst: University of Massachusetts Press, 2001), pp. 173–91. Dr. Woldu has also presented papers on the historical contexts of rap at several regional conferences of the College Music Society.

6. The lyrics-music relationship in this song is unusual in that the chorus does not use the same text each time as is conventionally done. The chorus lyrics function like the second half of each stanza.

7. *All Music Guide* critic John Bush, for example, refers to it as "the first smash album of [Wonder's] career," and gives *Talking Book* the highest rating, five stars, in "*Talking Book*," Bogdanov, Bush, and Erlewine, *All Music Guide to Soul*, p. 765.

8. "Superstition" reached No. 1 on both *Billboard* magazine's pop and R&B charts. "You Are the Sunshine of My Life," which was released as a single later, reached No. 1 on the *Billboard* pop charts and No. 3 on the R&B charts.

9. Stevie Wonder, liner notes to *Talking Book,* compact disc reissue, Motown 012 157 354–2, 2000.

10. Tin Pan Alley is the name given to the grand American popular songwriting tradition that was centered largely in New York City from the 1880s through the start of the rock era in the early 1950s. Cole Porter, Irving Berlin, George and Ira Gershwin, and Sammy Cahn are among the best-known songwriters in this tradition.

11. Fake books are designed for the use of jazz musicians performing gigs. The arrangements are pared down to a melody and chord symbols so that a jazz combo can fake an arrangement on the spur of the moment. *The Real Book*, one of the best-known fake books of the 1970s and 1980s, was available in bootleg form; the composers, lyricists, and publishers of the songs contained in it were not paid royalties. *The Real Book* is now a legitimate publication of the Hal Leonard Publishing Company.

12. Note that the guitarist's name is given as Buzzy Feiton on other Stevie Wonder recordings on which he appeared.

13. I deal more with Wonder as a drummer in chapters 3 and 5 of this book. His work on "Superstition" shares traits with great jazz drummers of the past and with a few rock drummers (Keith Moon, for example) who treat the drum set as much more than a time keeper. A master of subtleties of improvisation in his singing and keyboard and harmonica playing, Wonder plays each drum fill in "Superstition" slightly differently and adds embellishments so that no two phrases are exactly alike.

14. An especially telling comparison is among the funk-based songs "Keep On Running" (*Music of My Mind*), "Superstition" and "Maybe Your Baby" (*Talking Book*), and "Higher Ground" and "Living for the City" (*Innervisions*). From the first of these to the last, Wonder exhibits an increased virtuosity, and the drums become increasingly prominent in the mix.

15. In discussing some of these heavily criticized songs in chapter 6, I will present an alternative view of the motivation behind and the effectiveness of Wonder's supposed naïve sappiness.

16. Unlike conventional sheet music publications of songs, which usually include a piano arrangement, the lead vocal line, lyrics, and guitar chord symbols, lead sheets include just the melody and chord symbols.

17. Robert Christgau's Web site, "Consumer Guide: Stevie Wonder," http://robertchristgau.com/get_artist.php?id=1328&name=Stevie+Wonder (accessed January 5, 2005).

18. See, for example, John Bush, "*Innervisions,*" in Bogdanov, Bush, and Erlewine.

19. See, for example, "The *Vibe* 100: *Innervisions,*" *Vibe* 7, December 1999–January 2000, p. 158; "Five Star Record," *Goldmine* 27, 9 February 2001, p. 77; and "The Rolling Stone 200: *Innervisions,*" *Rolling Stone* 15 May 1997, p. 82.

20. Leonard Pitts, Jr., "Stevie Wonder," in liner notes to *At the Close of a Century,* 4 compact discs, Motown 012 153 992–2, 1999, p. 41.

CHAPTER 5

1. Wonder, in fact, plays these parts on synthesizer.

2. Based on data in Joel Whitburn, *Top Pop Singles, 1955–1996* (Menomonee Falls, Wisc.: Record Research, Inc., 1997), p. 840.

3. In fact, one of the best iTunes folders I enjoy on my home computer consists of this impressive collection of songs.

4. I would argue that, on a song-by-song basis and as a unified package, *Innervisions* is superior to any other Stevie Wonder album to date.

5. Ben Wener, "Stevie Wonder Offers Songs in the Key of Healing," Knight Ridder/Tribune News Service, 28 September 2001. Wener heaps praise on Wonder for his appearance on the *America: A Tribute to Heroes* telethon, especially for his emotional performance of "Love's in Need of Love Today." In particular, he praises Wonder for proving that his music is still relevant and that he is more than a "Professional Legend."

6. Louis Chunovic, ed., *Chris-in-the-Morning: Love, Life, and the Whole Karmic Enchilada* (Chicago: Contemporary Books, 1993), p. 33.

7. Fred Bronson, "No One-Hit Wonder, Wonder Hits One," *Billboard* 111, 24 July 1999, p. 94.

8. Stephen Holden, "Machines as Collaborators," *The Atlantic* 253, June 1984, p. 102.

9. Ibid.

10. Sequencers are, essentially, digital multitrack recording devices. Sequencing software for the computer can be used to turn a computer into a multitrack recording studio for inputs from synthesizers.

11. The title is given on several Stevie Wonder collections as "All I Do"; however, the legally registered title with BMI is "All I Do Is Think About You."

12. Actually, Wonder does not mention the nature of Howard University's historical standing or the demographics of its student body; he leaves it up to the listener to know these facts.

13. The attacks of this synthesized bass, however, lack some of the punch of the acoustic pizzicato double bass.

14. See, for example, Bill Lane, "Stevie Wonder Tells Why Nation Needs MLK Holiday," *Sepia* 29, December 1980, p. 39ff.; "Birthday Celebration for M.L.K.: Stevie Wonder and More Than 100,000 Persons Rally for a National King Holiday," *Ebony* 36, March 1981, p. 126ff.; "Ambassador of Peace," *Sepia* 31, June 1982, p. 82; and "King 'Birthday Bill' Gains Strength as Date Nears," *Jet* 59 (January 15, 1981): 14.

15. Stevie Wonder, liner notes to *Hotter Than July*, Tamla 373, 1980.

CHAPTER 6

1. Rob Theakston, "*Hotter Than July*," in *All Music Guide to Soul*, ed. Vladimir Bogdanov, John Bush, and Stephen Thomas Erlewine (Ann Arbor, Mich.: Backbeat Books, 2003), p. 766.

2. There were a few mid- to late 1970s exceptions, such as Tom Paxton's "Born on the Fourth of July," a song that chronicled the life of Vietnam veteran Ron Kovic.

3. Woodwind player Andy Mackay played lyricon on the track and Paul McCartney, Linda McCartney, and Eric Stewart sang backing vocals.

4. "*The Woman in Red*," *People Weekly* 23, 25 February 1985, p. 23.

5. Christopher Connelly, "*The Woman in Red*," *Rolling Stone*, 8 November 1984, p. 73.

6. *All Music Guide* critic Stephen Thomas Erlewine referred to the song/recording as "sickening" in his 2003 comparison of Wonder's 1991 soundtrack to Spike Lee's film *Jungle Fever* with Wonder's mid-1980s work. "Jungle Fever" in Bogdanov, Bush, and Erlewine, *All Music Guide to Soul,* p. 766.

7. The McCartney song, credited to Mr. and Mrs. Paul McCartney, describes a female character's mundane daily existence in a musical setting that is just as generic as the character herself.

8. Robert Christgau's Web Site, "Never That Simple: Stevie Wonder," http://robertchristgau.com/xg/music/wonder-kc.php (accessed January 3, 2005).

9. See "Suit Says Wonder Stole Oscar-Winning Tune," *Jet* 77, 26 February 1990, p. 59; "Wonder Cleared in Recent Song Plagiarism Lawsuit," *Jet* 77, 12 March 1990, p. 61; and "Stevie Wonder Didn't Steal Song, Appeals Court Rules," *Jet* 82, 7 September 1992, p. 27, as examples of *Jet*'s coverage of the lawsuits over "I Just Called to Say I Love You."

10. Ron Wynn, "*In Square Circle,*" in Bogdanov, Bush, and Erlewine, *All Music Guide to Soul,* p. 766.

11. In fact, this mishearing of the lyrics of "Part-Time Lover" is included in several Internet sites devoted to the subject of misunderstood popular song lyrics; see *The Octopus's Garden—Misinterpreted Music Lyrics,* http://www.rareexception.com/Garden/Misinterpreted/Lyrics.php, and *Am I Right—Misheard Lyrics,* http://www.amiright.com/misheard (both accessed February 27, 2005).

12. The two most successful singles from *Characters,* "Skeletons" and "You Will Know," hit No. 1 on the *Billboard* R&B charts but enjoyed far less success on the pop charts.

13. Jim Farber, "*Nelson Mandela: 70th Birthday Tribute,*" *Rolling Stone,* , 6 April 1989, p. 75.

14. The "middle eight" is an eight-measure phrase that generally occurs only one time in a song.

15. Although some of Stevie Wonder's early songs had timed out at the 5- or 6-minute mark, the longer tracks on *Songs in the Key of Life* were structurally different from the long songs on *Jungle Fever* and *Conversation Peace.* For example, the songs "As" and "Isn't She Lovely" owe their length to instrumental solo sections, much like one might find in jazz pieces. Some of Wonder's longer songs of the 1970s owed their length to extended, nonsoloistic groove passages, but their presence was balanced by a higher percentage of songs in the 3- to 4-minute range than is found on *Conversation Peace.* The relatively high percentage of long songs on *Songs in the Key of Life* (as compared with Wonder's early 1970s albums) that did feature extended groove passages is possibly attributable to the nature of the double-album package: its temporal demands—like that of the compact disc—required a different kind of overall compositional approach than did the 40-minute LP.

16. Stevland Morris, liner notes to *Music from the Movie "Jungle Fever,"* compact disc, Motown 374636291-2, 1991.

17. Jim Fusilli, "*Conversation Peace,*" *Wall Street Journal,* 19 April 1995, p. A12.

18. Stephen Thomas Erlewine, "*Conversation Peace,*" in Bogdanov, Bush, and Erlewine, *All Music Guide to Soul,* p. 766.

19. Andrew Abrahams, "*Conversation Peace,*" *People Weekly* 43, 10 April 1995, p. 17.

20. Henry Panion III, "Do You Hear What They Hear?" Keynote address given at the Great Lakes Chapter Meeting of the College Music Society, Western Kentucky University, Bowling Green, Kentucky, 2 April 2005.

21. I make a fundamental distinction between arrangements and orchestrations in this discussion. Arrangements include vocal and instrumental details insofar as they include pitches, rhythms, and basic timbres. Orchestrations are herein defined as the assignment of specific instruments and/or groups of instruments in order to assign more specific timbres to an arrangement. For the *Natural Wonder* project, Henry Panion was called upon to provide some of each.

22. Frank Zappa, with Peter Occhiogrosso, *The Real Frank Zappa Book* (New York: Poseidon Press, 1989), p. 188 (capitalization and italics in the original). Quoted in Albin J. Zak III, "'Edition-ing' Rock," *American Music* 23, Spring 2005, p. 96.

23. Zak, "'Edition-ing' Rock," pp. 95–107.

24. Catherine Seifert, "Wonder to Receive Songwriting Award," America's Intelligence Wire, 16 April 2004.

25. "Busta Rhymes Narrates Stevie Wonder Video for Blind Fans," *MTV. com,* http://www.mtv.com/news/articles/1501542/20050509/wonder_stevie.jhtml?headlines=true (accessed May 12, 2005).

26. Rob Theakston, "A Time to Love," *Allmusic.com,* http://www.allmusic.com/cg/amg.dll?p=amg&sql=10:a96htr7tk16x (accessed October 25, 2005).

CONCLUSION

1. Brenda Lee was one of, if not the, most commercially successful solo female artist of the 1960s. For her to record a Stevie Wonder composition was an important outside validation of the worth of his songs as compositions and not just as vehicles for Wonder's vocal performances.

2. John Morthland, liner notes to *Sounds of the Seventies: 1970,* Time-Life Music SOO-01, 1989.

3. In fact, Smokey Robinson's voice is by far the biggest vocal contribution on the recording; the rest of the Miracles become little more than backing vocalists on "The Tears of a Clown."

4. Steve Eddy, "Nnenna Freelon's Latest CD Is a Labor of Love and a Tribute to a Hero," Knight-Ridder/Tribune News Service, 20 June 2002.

5. The heavy bass drum of the Blige recording can be directly attributed to the arranger of the track—none other than Stevie Wonder.

DISCOGRAPHY

1. The song is credited to Stevie Wonder alone on the 2000 compact disc reissue of *Talking Book.* It is credited to Yvonne Wright and Wonder on the original vinyl release and on other reissues, such as the multidisc collection *At the Close of a Century.*

2. Other releases of this song list the writers as Stevie Wonder, Henry Cosby, and Sylvia Moy. Registration information on the Web site of the American Society of Composers, Authors, and Publishers (ASCAP.com) confirms Wonder, Cosby, and Moy as the writers.

3. This single represents the first recording of a Stevie Wonder composition; note that Judkins was Wonder's legal last name at the time.

Annotated Bibliography

Abbott, Kingsley, ed. *Callin' Out around the World: A Motown Reader.* London: Helter Skelter, 2001.

This collection of essays contains a piece by John Rockwell on Stevie Wonder.

Abrahams, Andrew. "*Conversation Peace*." *People Weekly* 43, 10 April 1995, p. 17.

A lukewarm review of *Conversation Peace*, an album on which Wonder "too often winds up slamming out pedestrian songs lacking his usual celebratory bounce" because he is trying "to sound au courant" by using hip-hop beats. Abrahams, however, praises "I'm New" and "Sensuous Whisper."

———. "*Natural Wonder*." *People Weekly* 45, 22 January 1996, p. 23.

A highly favorable review of Wonder's live album. "Ribbon in the Sky" and the new song "Dancing to the Rhythm" receive special praise.

Albertson, Chris. "The Extraordinary Stevie Wonder." *Stereo Review* 38, January 1977, p. 94.

A favorable review of *Songs in the Key of Life*.

"Albums: Anthology." *Melody Maker* 52, 17 December 1977, p. 23.

A review of Wonder's *Looking Back* album.

"Albums: *Hotter Than July*." *Melody Maker* 55, 1 November 1980, p. 19.

A review of Wonder's *Hotter Than July* album.

"Albums: *Stevie Wonder's Journey Through the Secret Life of Plants*." *Melody Maker* 54, 3 November 1979, p. 27.

A review of Wonder's soundtrack album.

Aletti, V. "Riffs & Licks: Spiritual Walker." *The Village Voice* 30, 29 October 1985, p. 69.

———. "Signed, Sealed & Delivered." *Rolling Stone* no. 74, 21 January 1971, p. 48.

———. "*Where I'm Coming From*." *Rolling Stone* no. 88, 5 August 1971, pp. 43–44.

A review of Wonder's *Where I'm Coming From* album.

Am I Right—Misheard Lyrics. http://www.amiright.com/misheard (accessed February 27, 2005).

Contains references to "Part Time Lover."

"An All-Star Celebration Honoring Martin Luther King, Jr." *Variety* 322, 29 January 1986, p. 64.

A highly favorable review of the television special that Wonder hosted.

Allen, Zita. "*Hotter Than July.*" *Stereo Review* 46, January 1981, p. 104.
    A favorable review of Wonder's *Hotter Than July* album.
———. "*Journey Through the Secret Life of Plants.*" *Stereo Review* 44, February
    1980, p. 86.
    A favorable review of Wonder's soundtrack album.
———. "Steve Wonder." *Stereo Review* 44, May 1980, pp. 56–60.
    A feature biography of and interview with the mature Stevie Wonder.
———. "Wonder's Flourishing Plants." *Stereo Review* 44, February 1980, p. 86.
    A review of *Journey Through the Secret Life of Plants.*
Altman, Billy. "*Natural Wonder.*" *Rolling Stone* no. 726, 25 January 1996, p. 72.
    A favorable review of the *Natural Wonder* album.
Altman, Linda Jacobs. *Stevie Wonder: Sunshine in the Shadow.* St. Paul, Minn.: EMC
    Corp., 1976.
    A biography of Wonder for young readers.
"Ambassador of Peace." *Sepia* 31, June 1982, p. 82.
    A report on Wonder's political activities, particularly his work toward the
    establishment of a national holiday to honor Dr. Martin Luther King, Jr.
"American Express." *Advertising Age* 64, 29 November 1993, p. 33.
    An announcement that Stevie Wonder will appear in an advertisement pro-
    moting American Express' Charge Against Hunger campaign.
"Anomaly Unearthed in Ban on Wonder's Music." *Variety* 319, 19 June 1985, p. 89.
    A report on South African Broadcasting's ban on Stevie Wonder's music as a
    result of his anti-apartheid activity.
Arrington, Carl. "Airplay and Airports: For Stevie, It's a Wonderful Life." *People
    Weekly* 25, 3 March 1986, pp. 88ff.
    A feature-length article on Wonder's daily life, including his work in the stu-
    dio and how he handles his blindness.
"ASCAP Honors Most-Performed Songs: Lionel Richie, Stevie Wonder Are Big Win-
    ners." *Billboard* 98, 14 June 1986, pp. 3–4.
    This article serves as a reminder at how pervasive Wonder was in the record
    industry in 1985, composing and/or performing on three singles that hit No. 1
    on the *Billboard* pop and R&B charts: "Part-Time Lover," "We Are the World,"
    and "That's What Friends Are For."
"*At the Close of the* [*sic*] *Century.*" *Goldmine* 26, 11 February 2000, p. 58.
    A favorable review of Wonder's *At the Close of a Century* 4-disc set.
"Backbeat: *Characters.*" *High Fidelity* 38, March 1988, pp. 72–73.
    A retrospective review of Wonder's *Characters* album.
"Backside: Remembering Ella Fitzgerald (1918–1996)." *Musician* no. 215, October
    1996, p. 98.
    Stevie Wonder and Tony Bennett share their remembrances of the recently
    deceased jazz singer Ella Fitzgerald.
Barker, Karlyn. "Stevie Wonder Arrested in Apartheid Protest." *Washington Post,*
    15 February 1985, p. A8.
    A brief article about Wonder's arrest at the South African embassy.
Bauers, Sandy. "*Blind Faith* Surprisingly Well-Written for a Celebrity Biography."
    Philadelphia Inquirer, 18 November 2002.
    Bauers gives Dennis Love and Stacy Brown's book *Blind Faith* a favorable
    review.

Beyer, Mark T. *Stevie Wonder.* New York: Rosen Publishing Group, 2002.
    A biography of Wonder intended for juvenile readers.
Bindas, Kenneth J., and Craig Houston. "'Takin' Care of Business': Rock Music,
    Vietnam and the Protest Myth." *Historian* 52, November 1989, pp. 1–23.
    The article deals in part with the way in which songs of political and social
    protest were handled at Motown Records in the 1960s and the early 1970s.
"Birthday Celebration for M.L.K.: Stevie Wonder and More Than 100,000 Persons
    Rally for a National King Holiday." *Ebony* 36, March 1981, pp. 126ff.
    Wonder's contributions to the movement for a national holiday honoring
    Dr. Martin Luther King, Jr., are highlighted.
"Black Tie, Gloves Off at R'n'R Hall of Fame." *Musician* no. 126, April 1989, p. 11.
    A brief report that includes information on Wonder's induction into the Rock
    and Roll Hall of Fame.
"Blacks, Whites Unite to Fight for Beliefs King Lived and Died for." *Jet* 61, 4 February
    1982, p. 4ff.
    Wonder's work toward securing a national holiday to celebrate the birthday of
    Dr. Martin Luther King, Jr., is discussed.
"Blind Piano Player, 3, Visits Stevie Wonder." *Jet* 72, 22 June 1987, p. 18.
    This is a brief report on blind pianist Jermaine Gardner's visit with Stevie
    Wonder.
Bloom, Pamela. "*Characters.*" *High Fidelity* 38, March 1988, pp. 72ff.
    A favorable review of Wonder's album *Characters.*
Bogdanov, Vladimir, John Bush, and Stephen Thomas Erlewine, eds. *All Music Guide
    to Soul.* Ann Arbor, Mich.: Backbeat Books, 2003.
"Break Through: Stevie Wonder." *Crawdaddy* no. 83, April 1978, p. 27.
    An interview with Wonder.
Bronson, Fred. "No One-Hit Wonder, Wonder Hits One." *Billboard* 111, 24 July
    1999, p. 94.
    A report on one of Stevie Wonder's more interesting achievements as a song-
    writer: he is in "second place among songwriters with the longest span of chart-
    toppers in the rock era." His first No. 1 hit on the *Billboard* singles charts was
    "The Tears of a Clown," which he co-wrote for Smokey Robinson and the Mir-
    acles in 1970, and his latest was Will Smith's "Wild Wild West," which was based
    on Wonder's "I Wish," in 1999.
———. "Wonder Years: The Story So Far." *Billboard* 107, 13 May 1995, pp. 26–27.
    A feature-length profile of Wonder that praises his latest album, *Conversation
    Peace.*
Brower, W. A. "Soul Music Comes of Age: Stevie Wonder." *Down Beat* 48, May
    1981, pp. 15–17ff.
    A feature on Wonder's maturation and that of the soul music genre.
Brown, Geoff. "*Innervisions.*" *Melody Maker* 49, 2 February 1974, pp. 36–37ff.
    A review of the *Innervisions* album.
Brown, Joe. "Stevie Wonder." *Washington Post,* 16 January 1984, p. B11.
    A favorable review of Wonder's appearance at the Capital Centre, in
    Washington, D.C.
"Busta Rhymes Narrates Stevie Wonder Video for Blind Fans." *MTV.com.* http://www.
    mtv.com/news/articles/1501542/20050509/wonder_stevie.jhtml?headlines=
    true (accessed May 12, 2005).

A feature report on rapper Busta Rhymes's narration of Wonder's music video for the blind. Wonder discusses the genesis of the song "So What the Fuss," including guest guitarist Prince's impact on the arrangement.

Cain, Joy Duckett. "Stevie Wonder: Still Reaching for Higher Ground." *Essence* 15, December 1984, p. 66ff.

A feature biographical profile of Wonder.

Carrizosa, Philip. "Stevie Wonder Song Survives Appellate Test." *Los Angeles Daily Journal* 105, 18 August 1992, p. 1.

A brief report that the 9th Circuit Court found that the judge at Wonder's earlier plagiarism trial was not biased. Both trials revolved around charges that Wonder stole the song "I Just Called to Say I Love You."

Castellanos, Joaquín. *Stevie Wonder.* Barcelona: Edicomunicación, 1987.

A Spanish-language biography of Wonder.

"*Characters.*" *Creem* 19, March 1988, p. 29.

A review of Wonder's *Characters* album.

"*Characters.*" *Down Beat* 55, March 1988, p. 29.

A review of Wonder's *Characters* album.

"*Characters.*" *Musician* no. 112, February 1988, p. 114.

A review of Wonder's *Characters* album.

"*Characters.*" *Rolling Stone* no. 518, 28 January 1988, p. 47.

A review of Wonder's *Characters* album.

Chenault, Julie. "Black Music Month: Salute to Stevie Wonder." *Jet* 62, 14 June 1982, pp. 56ff.

A feature-length profile of Wonder.

Christgau, Robert. "Consumer Guide: Stevie Wonder." *Robert Christgau's Web Site.* http://robertchristgau.com/get_artist.php?id=1328&name=Stevie+Wonder (accessed January 3, 2005).

Christgau, a noted rock critic, provides reviews for Wonder's albums from 1967 to the present.

Christgau, Robert. "Never That Simple: Stevie Wonder." *Robert Christgau's Web Site.* http://robertchristgau.com/xg/music/wonder-kc.php (accessed January 3, 2005).

This article, by the dean of rock critics, was written for Stevie Wonder's Kennedy Center induction in 1999.

Chunovic, Louis, ed. *Chris-in-the-Morning: Love, Life, and the Whole Karmic Enchilada.* Chicago: Contemporary Books, 1993.

Contains quotations from the television program *Northern Exposure.*

Cioe, Crispin. "Stevie Wonder's *Journey Through the Secret Life of Plants.*" *High Fidelity/Musical America* 30, February 1980, p. 118.

A favorable review of Wonder's soundtrack album.

"Classic Album." Europe Intelligence Wire, 3 July 2003.

On the 30th anniversary of the release of *Talking Book,* the package receives a highly favorable review. This wire service review was originally published in the *Bristol Evening Post* in Great Britain.

"Cleffers Sue Wonder for Allegedly Stealing Song." *Variety* 320, 9 October 1985, p. 117.

A brief report on the lawsuit over the authorship of "I Just Called to Say I Love You."

"Close-Up." *Melody Maker* 51, 25 December 1976, p. 19.
 A report that *Songs in the Key of Life* was chosen as one of the magazine's albums of the year.
Cocks, Jay. "*Hotter Than July.*" *Time* 116, 22 December 1980, p. 90.
 A favorable review of Wonder's *Hotter Than July* album.
"*Conception: An Interpretation of Stevie Wonder's Songs.*" *Goldmine* 29, 27 June 2003, pp. 46–47.
 A report on the release of the album of covers of Wonder's songs.
Connelly, Christopher. "*The Woman in Red.*" *Rolling Stone,* 8 November 1984, p. 73.
 A lukewarm review of Wonder's contribution to the soundtrack of the film *The Woman in Red.*
———, Andrew Slater, and Debby Miller. "Give Peace a Chance." *Rolling Stone,* 22 July 1982, pp. 12ff.
 The antinuclear activism of Wonder, Bob Dylan, Graham Nash, Linda Ronstadt, Jackson Browne, and Joan Baez is detailed.
"*Conversation Peace.*" *Musician* no. 198, May 1995, pp. 86–87.
 A review of Wonder's *Conversation Peace* album.
"*Conversation Peace.*" *Stereo Review* 60, August 1995, pp. 78–79.
 A review of Wonder's *Conversation Peace* album.
"*Conversation Peace.*" *Stereoplay* no. 5, May 1995, p. 122.
 A review of Wonder's *Conversation Peace* album.
Daniels, Robert. "Comin' Home to Harlem." *Daily Variety* 275, 23 May 2002, p. 10.
 Daniels's review of a May 20, 2002, concert at the Apollo Theater in Harlem, New York, notes one particular aspect of Wonder's musicianship not often noted: his skill as a jazz pianist. Daniels refers to Wonder's piano work on the John Coltrane composition "Giant Steps" as "dazzling."
Darling, Cary. "Closeup." *Billboard* 91, 1 December 1979, p. 49.
 A review of Wonder's *Journey Through the Secret Life of Plants* album.
———. "Third World Is Spreading Reggae; Latest Columbia LP Features Wonder Collaborations." *Billboard* 94, 3 April 1982, pp. 34ff.
 Includes a report on Paul McCartney's *Tug of War* album.
Davis, Sharon. *Stevie Wonder: The Biography.* London: Robson, 2003.
Davis, Thulani. "Riffs: Stevie Wonder Beyond Naivite." *Village Voice* 25, 19 November 1980, p. 73.
 A review of a Wonder concert and the *Hotter Than July* album.
DiMartino, Dave. "Motown Sets Long Life for Wonder's *Characters.*" *Billboard* 99, 14 November 1987, p. 22.
 A brief report on the marketing of Wonder's *Characters* album.
Doerschuk, R. L. "Milestones: The Top 20 Keyboard Albums of the Past 20 Years." *Keyboard* 21, September 1995, pp. 61–62ff.
———. "Stevie." *Keyboard* 21, July 1995, pp. 28–32ff.
 On the heels of his comeback album, *Conversation Peace,* Wonder is profiled in this feature article.
Dowling, Claudia. "Stevie Wonder's World." *Life* 9, October 1986, p. 66ff.
 A feature-length article on Wonder, his health and exercise regimen, and his then-current work on the *Characters* album.
Dr. Gloster Weeps as He Awards Wonder Last Degree as President of Morehouse." *Jet* 72, 8 June 1987, p. 24.

A report on Morehouse College's awarding of an honorary degree to Stevie Wonder.

Dragonwagon, Crescent. *Stevie Wonder.* New York: Flash Books, 1977.
    A biography of Wonder.
Driscoll, O'Connell. "Growing Up Stevie Wonder." *Rolling Stone* no. 189, 19 January 1975, pp. 44–46ff. Reprinted in Paul Scanlon, *Reporting: The Rolling Stone Style.* New York: Anchor Press/Doubleday, 1977.
East, Kevin. "Carousel Corner." *Sensible Sound,* December 1999, p. 71.
    According to the author, the best music of the 1970s was not pop, nor so-called classic rock, but soul. Wonder's recordings of the decade, in particular, are featured and given generally high praise.
Eddy, Steve. "Nnenna Freelon's Latest CD Is a Labor of Love and a Tribute to a Hero." Knight Ridder/Tribune News Service, 20 June 2002.
    This is a report on jazz singer Nnenna Freelon's recording *Tales of Wonder.*
Edwards, Audrey, and Gary Wohl. *The Picture Life of Stevie Wonder.* New York: Avon Books, 1978.
    A young reader's biography of Wonder.
Effenberger, Don. "Song from Target Ad Gets Surprise Nod for Grammy." Knight Ridder/Tribune Business News, 14 January 2003.
    A report that India.Arie and Wonder's recording of "Christmas Song," which was used by Target stores in its commercials, has been nominated for a Grammy Award.
Eldridge, R. "Stevie Gets His Number 1." *Melody Maker* 44, 20 December 1969, p. 7.
——. "Stevie's a Big Star Now." *Melody Maker* 44, 15 March 1969, p. 6.
——. "Will Stevie Wonder Become Another Sammy Davis?" *Melody Maker* 44, 5 April 1969, p. 7.
Elsner, Constanze. *Stevie Wonder.* New York: Popular Library, 1977.
    A biography of Wonder.
Erlewine, Stephen Thomas. "*Conversation Peace.*" In *All Music Guide to Soul,* ed. Vladimir Bogdanov, John Bush, and Stephen Thomas Erlewine. Ann Arbor, Mich.: Backbeat Books, 2003, p. 766.
Escamilla, Brian. *Contemporary Musicians: Profiles of the People in Music.* Vol. 15. Detroit: Gale Research, 1997.
    Wonder's biography is included.
Ewen, David, ed. *American Songwriters: An H. W. Wilson Biographical Dictionary.* New York: H. W. Wilson, 1987.
    Wonder's biographical profile is included.
"Experts' Choices." *U.S. News & World Report* 100, 27 January 1986, p. 74.
    Wonder reveals that albums he is currently listening to include Whitney Houston's self-titled album, King Sunny Ade's *Aura,* Freddy Jackson's *Rock Me Tonight,* and Doug E. Fresh's *The Show.*
Farber, Jim. "*Nelson Mandela: 70th Birthday Tribute.*" *Rolling Stone* no. 549, 6 April 1989, p. 75.
    An unfavorable review of the video on which Stevie Wonder appears.
Farley, Christopher John. "*Conversation Peace.*" *Time* 145, 10 April 1995, p. 88.
    A generally favorable review of Wonder's *Conversation Peace,* which, although "not a slam dunk," is "another winner." Farley complains about "Sorry" and "Cold Chill" sounding artificial because of Wonder's overuse of

synthesizers, but emphasizes that the album takes on the serious issue of violence and is not just a collection of naïve commercial love songs like "I Just Called to Say I Love You."

———. "*Rent.*" *Time* 148, 26 August 1996, p. 60.

In this brief review of the recording of songs from the show *Rent,* Wonder's rendition of the song "Seasons of Love" is singled out for praise.

"Five Star Record." *Goldmine* 27, 9 February 2001, p. 77.

Wonder's *Innervisions* is mentioned as one of the top albums ever.

Fong-Torres, Ben. "The Formerly Little Stevie Wonder." *Rolling Stone* no. 133, 26 April 1973, pp. 48–50ff.

A feature article on Wonder in the wake of the unprecedented success of his self-written and self-produced *Talking Book* album, and the hit singles it spawned.

"For the First Time, Stevie Wonder's Biggest Hits from Throughout His Career Compiled on One CD: *Stevie Wonder: The Definitive Collection.*" Business Wire, 4 October 2002.

A brief report on the single compact disc greatest hits collection.

Fox-Cumming, Ray. *Stevie Wonder.* London: Mandabrook Books, 1977.

A biography of Stevie Wonder.

Frei, C. E. "Seeing with the Heart." *The Exceptional Parent,* November 1998, p. 22.

A feature article on Wonder with a focus on his blindness and his advice to the parents of children with exceptional needs.

"*Fullingness' First Finale.*" *Crawdaddy* no. 42, November 1974, pp. 71–72.

A review of the album.

"*Fulfillingness' First Finale.*" *Creem* 6, November 1974, p. 66.

A review of the album.

"*Fulfillingness' First Finale.*" *Rolling Stone* no. 170, 26 September 1974, p. 98.

A review of the album.

Fusilli, Jim. "*Conversation Peace.*" *Wall Street Journal,* 19 April 1995, p. A12.

Fusilli gives the Wonder recording a favorable review.

Gabel, Lars. "*Hotter Than July.*" *Down Beat* 48, February 1981, p. 29.

Wonder's *Hotter Than July* album receives a generally favorable review.

Gambaccini, Paul. "Stevie Wonder Returns with a Synthesized Howl." *Rolling Stone* no. 155, 28 February 1974, p. 14.

"Gear Guru Mick Parish: Front & Center with Stevie Wonder." *Keyboard* 21, July 1995, pp. 31–32ff.

Wonder's use of various synthesizers and samplers is detailed.

George, Nelson. "Stevie Wonder Led Drive for King Holiday." *Billboard* 101, 28 January 1989, p. 22.

———. "The Word from Byrd on Stevie." *Billboard* 96, 31 March 1984, pp. 48–49.

A recollection of working with Stevie Wonder from Gary Byrd, who collaborated with Wonder on *Songs in the Key of Life.*

Gersten, Russell. "Looking Back to When Stevie Was Little." *Village Voice* 23, 6 February 1978, p. 40.

A review of *Looking Back,* Wonder's 1977 greatest hits package.

———. Records: *Stevie Wonder's Greatest Hits.*" *Rolling Stone* no. 99, 6 January 1972, p. 70.

Gibbs, V. "Soul, Man." *Crawdaddy* no. 12, 28 May 1972, pp. 6–7.

Givens, Ron. "*Conversation Peace.*" *Stereo Review* 60, August 1995, pp. 78ff.
    Wonder's *Conversation Peace* album receives a grade of approximately B in
    this review.
Gleeson, M. "S. African B'casting's Ban on Stevie Wonder Draws Legislators' Fire."
    Variety 319, 15 May 1985, pp. 1ff.
    A report on South African Broadcasting's ban on Stevie Wonder's music as a
    result of his anti-apartheid activities.
Goaty, F. "Stevie Wonder." *Jazz Magazine* (France) no. 417, July–August 1992, p. 8.
Goldberg, Michael. "Stevie Wonder." *Rolling Stone* no. 512, 5 November 1987,
    pp. 153–54.
———. "The Timeless World of Wonder." *Rolling Stone* no. 471, 10 April 1986,
    pp. 38–40ff.
    A feature article on Wonder.
Gonzalez, Fernando, et al. "Reviews of Releases by Elton John, Stevie Wonder, Tanya
    Tucker, and More." Knight Ridder/Tribune News Service, 21 March 1995.
    This article includes a review of Wonder's *Conversation Peace*. Wonder's
    melodic sense is praised, although, according to the author, as a lyricist he
    "barely rises above banality." The songs "I'm New," "Edge of Eternity," and
    "Sensuous Whisper" receive praise.
Graff, Gary. "Stevie Wonder's Tuned and Ready for New Approach to Love and
    Peace." Knight-Ridder/Tribune News Service, 4 January 1995.
    A preview of Wonder's *Conversation Peace* album and a report on Wonder's
    recent activities.
Grein, Paul. "Wonder Score a Rarity in Films." *Billboard* 91, 15 December
    1979, p. 43.
    A report on Wonder's *Journey Through the Secret Life of Plants.*
Hamilton, Stephanie Renfrow. "*Musiquarium I.*" *Essence* 13, September 1982, p. 21.
    Hamilton gives Wonder's *Musiquarium I* recording a generally favorable review.
Hasegawa, Sam, and Dick Brude. *Stevie Wonder.* Mankato, Minn.: Creative Educa-
    tion, 1974.
    A biography of Wonder aimed at young readers.
Haskins, James. *The Story of Stevie Wonder.* New York: Lothrop, Lee & Shepard,
    1976; London: Panther, 1978.
    A biography of Wonder aimed at young readers. The author won the Coretta
    Scott King Award in 1977.
———, and Kathleen Benson. *The Stevie Wonder Scrapbook.* New York: Grosset &
    Dunlop, 1978.
    A biography of Wonder.
Hemming, Roy. "*The Envelope Please: Academy Award Winning Songs.*" *Stereo Review*
    60, March 1995, pp. 90ff.
    Hemming gives the compilation album, which includes Wonder's "I Just
    Called to Say I Love You," a favorable review.
Henschen, Robert. "*Hotter Than July.*" *Consumers' Research Magazine* 64, February
    1981, p. 36.
    Henschen gives the Wonder album a generally favorable review.
Herbst, Peter. *The Rolling Stone Interviews: Talking with the Legends of Rock & Roll.*
    New York: St. Martin's Press/Rolling Stone Press, 1981.
    An extensive 1974 interview with Wonder is included.

Herrington, Richard. "*In Square Circle.*" *Washington Post,* 10 September 1985, p. E1.

A favorable review of Wonder's album.

Hilburn, Robert. "Behind the Scene of a Pop Miracle." *Los Angeles Times,* 24 March 1985, p. C70.

A feature article on the song "We Are the World."

———. "*Stevie Wonder's Original Musiquarium I.*" *Los Angeles Times,* 20 October 1985, p. 58.

A favorable review of Wonder's compilation album.

———. "Stevie Wonder's Renewed Ambition." *Los Angeles Times,* 8 September 1985, p. 58.

A feature article on Wonder's return to the recording industry with his album *In Square Circle.*

Hill, George H. *Black Studies: The Arts.* Westport, Conn.: Meckler, 1985.

This book includes a chapter on Stevie Wonder.

Hiltbrand, David. "Characters." *People Weekly* 29, 11 January 1988, p. 21.

A favorable review of Wonder's *Characters* album, "perhaps his best since *Songs in the Key of Life* in 1976."

———. *Conversation Peace. Entertainment Weekly* no. 268, 31 March 1995, p. 61.

Although this brief review of *Conversation Peace* praises Wonder's voice and vocal arrangements, it finds the song selection "thin."

———. *Jungle Fever. People Weekly* 36, 15 July 1991, p. 17.

According to Hiltbrand, many film soundtracks are "sloppily hacked together to cross-promote a movie," but Wonder did not do that in the case of *Jungle Fever.* Hiltbrand praises "Fun Day," "I Go Sailing," "Each Other's Throat," while dismissing "Queen in the Black" as "relatively clumsy." Although the album may not be among Wonder's best, because of "cluttered" arrangements, it does well for a soundtrack.

Hoban, Phoebe. "The Well-Tempered Computer: Play It Again, Kurzweil." *New York* 18, 8 April 1985, p. 19.

Wonder lends his endorsement to the use of synthesizers in music in this article about Raymond Kurzweil's latest developments in digital sound synthesis.

Holden, Stephen. "*Hotter Than July.*" *Rolling Stone,* 5 February 1981, p. 54.

A generally favorable review of Wonder's album.

———. "*In Square Circle.*" *New York Times,* 15 September 1985, p. H19.

A favorable review of Wonder's album.

———. "Machines as Collaborators." *Atlantic* 253, June 1984, pp. 102ff.

A retrospective on the use of computers and synthesizers in popular music.

———. "Music from the Movie *Jungle Fever.*" *New York Times,* 30 June 1991, p. H24.

A brief, generally favorable review of Wonder's *Jungle Fever* soundtrack.

———. "The Pop Life: Wonder Back on Charts." *New York Times,* 7 November 1984, p. 26.

A brief report on Wonder's 1984 releases.

———. "Riffs: The Last Flower Child." *Village Voice* 24, 3 December 1979, p. 53.

A review of Wonder's *Journey Through the Secret Life of Plants.*

———. "Stevie Wonder." *New York Times,* 20 October 1983, Los Angeles edition, p. C14.

A favorable review of Wonder's concert at Radio City Music Hall, New York City.

———. "Stevie Wonder." *Rolling Stone,* 7 February 1980, p. 92.

A generally favorable review of Wonder's performance at the Metropolitan Opera House in New York City.

———. *"Stevie Wonder's Original Musiquarium I. Rolling Stone* no. 373, 8 July 1982, pp. 45ff.

A highly favorable review of Wonder's greatest hits package.

Holland, B., and D. DiMartino. "Stevie Wonder to Congress: I Like My DAT." *Billboard* 99, 4 July 1987, pp. 79ff.

In testimony to the U.S. Congress regarding consideration of legislation on digital audio tape, Wonder supported the technology and its availability.

Holsey, Steve. *"Journey Through the Secret Life of Plants." Sepia* 29, February 1980, p. 10.

A highly favorable review of Wonder's soundtrack album.

Hoover, Kent. "Stevie Wonder." *Washington Business Journal* 19, 29 September 2000, p. 2.

A brief report on Wonder's appearance at School Night '00, an event that raised more than $6 million for scholarships that enable Washington, D.C.–area children to attend private or parochial schools.

Horn, Martin E. *Innervisions: The Music of Stevie Wonder.* Bloomington, Ind.: 1stBooks Library, 2000.

A biography of Wonder.

"Hotter Than July." Down Beat 48, February 1981, p. 29.

A review of Wonder's album.

"Hotter Than July." High Fidelity/Musical America 31, January 1981, pp. 99–100.

A review of Wonder's album.

"Hotter Than July." Los Angeles Magazine 25, December 1980, p. 311.

A generally favorable review of Wonder's album.

"Hotter Than July." Melody Maker 55, 1 November 1980, p. 19.

A generally favorable review of Wonder's album.

"Hotter Than July." Musician, Player & Listener no. 30, February 1981, pp. 82–83.

A review of Wonder's album.

"Hotter Than July." People Weekly 14, 15 December 1980, pp. 22–23.

A generally favorable review of Wonder's album.

"Hotter Than July." Rolling Stone no. 336, *5 February 1981, p. 54.*

A review of Wonder's album.

Hughes, Timothy Stephen. "Groove and Flow: Six Analytical Essays on the Music of Stevie Wonder." PhD diss., University of Washington, 2003. Abstract in *Dissertation Abstracts International* 64, May 2004, p. 3898A.

Hunter, J. "Riffs: Mere Wonder." *Village Voice* 30, 12 February 1985, pp. 74ff.

"In Square Circle." Creem 17, February 1986, p. 25.

A review of Wonder's album.

"In Square Circle." Down Beat 53, February 1986, p. 29.

A review of Wonder's album.

"In Square Circle." High Fidelity/Musical America 35, December 1985, pp. 76–77.

A review of Wonder's album.

"In Square Circle." Melody Maker 60, 28 September 1985, p. 33.

A review of Wonder's album.

"*In Square Circle.*" *Rolling Stone* no. 459, 24 October 1985, pp. 63–64.
    A review of Wonder's album.
"*Innervisions.*" *Crawdaddy* no. 29, October 1973, pp. 67–68.
    A review of Wonder's album.
"*Innervisions.*" *Rolling Stone,* 27 August 1987, p. 101.
    A review of the compact disc reissue of the album *Innervisions,* in which the
    recording receives a grade of A.
"*Innervisions.*" *Rolling Stone* no. 144, 27 September 1973, p. 98.
    A review of Wonder's album.
"*Innervisions.*" *Stereoplay* no. 3, March 1992, p. 180.
    A review of Wonder's album.
Jacobs, Linda. *Stevie Wonder: Sunshine in the Shadow.* St. Paul, Minn.: EMC
    Corp., 1976.
    This book and audiocassette presents Wonder's biography for juvenile readers.
Jaffe, Cyrisse. Review of *The Story of Stevie Wonder,* by James Haskins. *School Library
    Journal* 26, August 1980, p. 39.
    A highly favorable review.
"James Brown Voted No. 1 Black Recording Star." *Jet* 68, 22 July 1985, p. 65.
    Although James Brown was voted the top black recording star in a newspaper
    poll, Stevie Wonder, Michael Jackson, Aretha Franklin, and Marvin Gaye also
    scored well.
Japenga, Ann. "Pop Star's Song Fuels Anti-Drunk Driving Campaign." *Los Angeles
    Times,* 14 December 1984, p. V1.
    A brief article on Wonder's contribution of a song for the cause of preventing
    drunk driving.
Jarvis, Jeff. "An All-Star Celebration Honoring Martin Luther King, Jr." *People Weekly*
    25, 20 January 1986, p. 11.
    A brief report on the television program starring Wonder, Joan Baez, Bill
    Cosby, Elizabeth Taylor, and Eddie Murphy, to celebrate the first national
    holiday to honor the slain civil rights leader.
———. "*Stevie Wonder Comes Home.*" *People Weekly* 21, 18 June 1984, p. 9.
    A highly positive review of Wonder's Showtime television concert special.
———. "Stevie Wonder's Characters." *People Weekly* 29, 2 May 1988, p. 11.
    A generally positive review of Wonder's *Characters* program on MTV.
Jennings, Nicholas. "*Conversation Peace.*" *Maclean's* 108, 17 April 1995, p. 83.
    A generally favorable review of *Conversation Peace,* although the author pro-
    nounces Wonder "sometimes guilty of adding too much saccharin to his songs."
    Jennings wishes that Wonder would balance his optimism with "a little more
    bracing realism."
Jewell, Thomas N. "*Hotter Than July.*" *Library Journal* 106, 15 February 1981,
    p. 426.
    A generally favorable review of Wonder's album *Hotter Than July.*
———. "*Journey Through the Secret Life of Plants.*" *Library Journal* 106, 15 February
    1981, p. 426.
    A decidedly lukewarm review of Wonder's soundtrack album.
———. "*The Original Musiquarium I. Library Journal* 108, 1 May 1983, p. 878.
    A favorable review of Wonder's compilation album.
Johnson, Robert E. "Stevie Wonder Returns with *Conversation Peace,* His First Album
    in Four Years." *Jet* 87, 8 May 1995, pp. 56ff.

Johnson gives Wonder's album a highly positive review, singling out the songs "Rain Your Love Down," "For Your Love," "My Love Is with You," "Take the Time Out," "Sensuous Whisper," "Edge of Eternity," and "Taboo to Love" for special mention.

———. "Stevie Wonder Talks about New Record Label, Career Changes, Being Blind, How He Tells If a Woman Is Beautiful or Ugly, His Home Paul Robeson Owned." *Jet* 64, 4 July 1983, pp. 60ff.

A feature-length profile of Wonder.

Jones, James T., IV. "Stevie's Jungle Adventure." *Down Beat* 58, September 1991, pp. 16ff.

A feature article on Wonder's compositional and musical production work for the Spike Lee film *Jungle Fever.*

Jones, Nic. "It's Not Such a Drag Being Blind." *Melody Maker* 42, 14 October 1967, p. 11.

A report on Wonder's blindness and how he deals with it.

Jones, Patricia. "*Hotter Than July.*" *Essence* 11, April 1981, p. 16.

A favorable review of Wonder's album.

"*Journey Through the Secret Life of Plants.*" *Creem* 11, February 1980, p. 52.

A review of Wonder's soundtrack album.

"*Journey Through the Secret Life of Plants.*" *Down Beat* 47, January 1980, pp. 31ff.

A generally negative review of Wonder's soundtrack album.

"*Journey Through the Secret Life of Plants.*" *High Fidelity/Musical America* 30, February 1980, p. 118.

A review of Wonder's soundtrack album.

"*Journey Through the Secret Life of Plants.*" *Melody Maker* 54, 3 November 1979, p. 27.

A review of Wonder's soundtrack album.

"*Journey Through the Secret Life of Plants.*" *People Weekly* 13, 7 January 1980, p. 13.

Favorable review of Wonder's soundtrack album.

"*Journey Through the Secret Life of Plants.*" *Rolling Stone* no. 309, 24 January 1980, pp. 62–63.

A review of Wonder's soundtrack album.

"King 'Birthday Bill' Gains Strength as Date Nears." *Jet* 59, 15 January 1981, p. 14.

Stevie Wonder's advocacy of a national holiday to honor Dr. Martin Luther King, Jr., is noted in this article on the eve of the congressional vote on the matter.

Kurtchik, B. "Stevie Wonder: *Jungle Fever* & Funk." *Musician* no. 154, August 1991, pp. 21–22.

A feature article on Wonder's *Jungle Fever* soundtrack.

Lambert, Pam. "In a Square Circle." *Wall Street Journal,* 9 October 1985, East Coast edition, p. 30.

A favorable review of Wonder's *In Square Circle* album.

Landau, Jon. "A Whiter Shade of Black." *Crawdaddy* no. 11, September–October 1967, pp. 35–40.

A report on Wonder's middle-of-the-road recordings that were aimed at a white audience.

Lane, Bill. "Stevie Wonder Tells Why Nation Needs MLK Holiday." *Sepia* 29, December 1980, pp. 39ff.

A feature article on Wonder's push to establish a national holiday honoring Dr. Martin Luther King, Jr.

"Lately." *Variety* 302, 1 April 1981, p. 72.

> Despite its modest success on the sales charts, Wonder's single "Lately" receives a favorable review.

Lewis, Randy. "Wonder Leads Energetic Benefit at the Forum." *Los Angeles Times,* 18 December 2000, p. F8.

> A favorable review of Wonder's Los Angeles performance.

Light, Alan. "Music from the Movie *Jungle Fever.*" *Rolling Stone* no. 610, 8 August 1991, pp. 83ff.

> A favorable review of Wonder's soundtrack album from the Spike Lee film.

Linden, Amy. "Stevie Wonder." *Us* no. 208, May 1995, p. 85.

> Among Wonder's revelations in this interview are that country singer Garth Brooks is among Wonder's favorite contemporary artists and that Wonder would like to record a country album himself.

Loupien, S. "Stevie Wonder." *Jazz Magazine* (France) no. 290, October 1980, p. 14.

Love, Dennis, and Stacy Brown. *Blind Faith: The Miraculous Journey of Lula Hardaway.* New York: Simon & Schuster, 2002.

> This is a controversial biography of Stevie Wonder's mother. Wonder himself objected to the material on Hardaway turning to prostitution in order to earn money for the family. Some critics have questioned the book's focus on Wonder himself at the expense of the purported subject of the book.

Lovitt, Chip. "Stevie Wonder: From Boy Wonder to Master Musician." *Co-Ed* 26, March 1981, pp. 35ff.

> A feature biographical profile on Wonder.

Mandel, Howard. "Stevie Wonder." *Down Beat* 47, March 1980, pp. 56–57.

> A generally favorable review of Wonder's performance with the National Afro-American Philharmonic Orchestra at the Auditorium Theatre in Chicago.

Marcus, Greil. "We Are the World." *Artforum International* 31, March 1993, p. 8.

> Noted rock critic Marcus gives the "We Are the World" single a lukewarm review, suggesting that the song may be little more than idle propaganda for an administration (Bill Clinton) that only "means to leave the country as it found it."

McAdams, Janine. "Stevie Wonder Tells Musical Tale of *Jungle Fever.*" *Billboard* 103, 8 June 1991, p. 30.

> This article includes several quotes from Wonder on his working relationship with *Jungle Fever* director Spike Lee.

———. "Stevie Wonder 35th Anniversary Salute: A Songbook in the Key of Life." *Billboard* 107, 13 May 1995, p. 30.

> Includes tributes to Wonder on the occasion of his 35th year in the music business.

"The *Melody Maker* Albums of the Year: *Hotter Than July.*" *Melody Maker* 55, 20 December 1980, p. 12.

> Wonder's *Hotter Than July* is numbered among the top albums of 1980.

Mewborn, Brant. "Marley Tributes Draw 20,000 to Montego Bay." *Rolling Stone,* 1 October 1981, p. 91.

> Wonder's performance is noted.

Milkowski, Bill. "*In Square Circle.*" *Down Beat* 53, February 1986, p. 29.

> Jazz critic Milkowski gives Wonder's album *In Square Circle* a highly favorable review.

Miller, Edwin. "*Hotter Than July.*" *Seventeen* 40, January 1981, p. 77.
    A generally favorable review of Wonder's album.
———. "*Stevie Wonder's Original Musiquarium.*" *Seventeen* 41, September 1982, p. 120.
    A generally favorable review of Wonder's greatest hits album.
Miller, Michael. "Musical Wonders." *Pittsburgh Business Times* 19, 14 January 2000, p. 8.
    The reviewer describes Wonder's *At the Close of a Century* collection as "a forceful reminder of Wonder's prowess," especially in light of the fact that most younger listeners remember him for "latter-day treacle like 'I Just Called to Say I Love You.'"
Milward, John. "*Conversation Peace.*" *Rolling Stone* no. 704, 23 March 1995, pp. 121ff.
    A favorable review of Wonder's *Conversation Peace* album.
Mitchell, Gail. "Add Another 2004 'Event' to a List That Includes Prince's Triumphant Return and Usher's *Confessions.*" *Billboard* 116, 5 June 2004, p. 18.
    A brief report on Wonder's upcoming album *A Time 2 Love.*
Molotsky, Irvin. "Kennedy Center Lauds 5 in the Performing Arts." *New York Times,* 15 September 1999, p. B3.
    A report on the awarding of Kennedy Center honors to Wonder, Victor Borge, Judith Jamison, Jason Robards, and Sean Connery.
"More Gold for Stevie." *Jet* 60, 9 July 1981, p. 21.
    A report on the strong sales of *Hotter Than July* that generated a gold disc for the album.
Morris, C. "*Beast* Gets 3 Oscar Song Nominations; Motown Fumes as Academy Snubs Stevie Wonder." *Billboard* 104, 7 March 1992, p. 16.
    A report on Motown Records' dismay that Wonder received no Academy Award nominations for his score for the Spike Lee film *Jungle Fever.*
Morthland, John. Liner notes to *Sounds of the Seventies: 1970.* Compact disc. Time-Life Music SOO-01, 1989.
    Included are notes on the song "The Tears of a Clown," of which Wonder was one of the writers.
Moses, Mark. "*In Square Circle.*" *High Fidelity* 35, December 1985, pp. 76–77.
    A mixed review of Wonder's album.
"*Motown Returns to the Apollo.*" *Variety* 319, 22 May 1985, p. 59.
    A highly favorable of the television program on which Stevie Wonder appeared.
"Motown 25: Yesterday, Today, Forever." *People Weekly* 19, 16 May 1983, p. 9.
    A favorable review of the television program that celebrated the 25th anniversary of Motown Records. Wonder performed.
"Moved by King's Spirit: Thousands March to Make King Day a National Holiday." *Jet* 59, 5 February 1981, pp. 36ff.
    Wonder's contributions to the movement to establish a national holiday to honor Dr. Martin Luther King, Jr., are noted in this feature article on the Washington, D.C., demonstrations.
"*Music from the Movie 'Jungle Fever.'*" *Melody Maker* 67, 15 June 1991, p. 40.
    A review of Wonder's *Jungle Fever* soundtrack album.
"*Music from the Movie 'Jungle Fever.'*" *Musician* no. 154, August 1991, p. 94.
    A review of Wonder's *Jungle Fever* soundtrack album.

"*Music from the Movie 'Jungle Fever.*'" *Rolling Stone* no. 610, 8 August 1991, pp. 83–84.

   A review of Wonder's *Jungle Fever* soundtrack album.

"*Music of My Mind.*" *Rolling Stone* no. 107, 27 April 1972, p. 8.

   A review of Wonder's *Music of My Mind* album.

"Music Publishing: The Top R&B Songwriters of the Year." *Billboard* 104, 16 May 1992, p. M6ff.

   Wonder is included in the list on the strength of his soundtrack for the Spike Lee film *Jungle Fever.*

"N.J. Governor Tomas H. Kean Kicks Off Drunk Driving Campaign with Stevie Wonder Video." PR Newswire, 23 October 1985.

   A brief report on Wonder's donation to the cause of preventing drunk driving.

Nashawaty, Chris. "Playlist." *Fortune* 141, 15 May 2000, p. 528.

   According to the author, the remastered CD release of *Innervisions* is a must-purchase item.

Nathan, David. "Freelon Honors Wonder on Latest Concord Set." *Billboard* 114, May 2002, p. 17.

   A report on jazz artist Nnenna Freelon's album *Tales of Wonder.*

———. "Stevie Wonder 35th Anniversary Salute: The *Billboard* Interview." *Billboard* 107, 13 May 1995, pp. 27ff.

   A feature-length interview with Wonder, who talks about his relationship with Motown Records, his songs and their role in society, his start in music, and the state of music in the mid-1990s.

"*Natural Wonder.*" *Popular Music and Society* 20, no. 1, 1996, pp. 203–4.

   A review of the *Natural Wonder* album.

"New Albums: *Songs in the Key of Life.*" *Melody Maker* 51, 9 October 1976, p. 33.

   A review of *Songs in the Key of Life.*

"New Record to Benefit AIDS Study." *New York Times,* 26 October 1985, p. 14.

   A report that Dionne Warwick, Stevie Wonder, Elton John, Gladys Knight, and Carol Bayer Sager will donate proceeds from the sale of the single "That's What Friends Are For" to the American Foundation for AIDS Research.

Norment, Lynn. "*Conversation Peace.*" *Ebony* 50, June 1995, p. 20.

   A brief, yet favorable review of Wonder's *Conversation Peace* album, a recording on which "Stevie demonstrates that he is still a master at his craft."

———. "Stevie Wonder Returns!" *Ebony* 59, July 2004, pp. 24–25.

   An overview of Wonder's career and report on his recent activities.

Novak, Ralph. "Dreamland Express." *People Weekly* 24, 26 August 1985, p. 26.

   A generally positive review of John Denver's album *Dreamland Express.* "If Ever," a song written by Wonder and Stephanie Andrews, is noted for the musical exchanges between guest harmonica player Wonder and saxophonist Jim Horn.

———. "*In Square Circle.*" *People Weekly* 24, 28 October 1985, pp. 27ff.

   A favorable review of Wonder's *In Square Circle* album. In response to some of the naive lyrics of "Spiritual Walkers," Novak writes that, "Wonder has such an unflagging sense of melody that the words often don't matter."

The Octopus's Garden—Misinterpreted Music Lyrics. http://www.rareexception.com/ Garden/Misinterpreted/Lyrics.php (accessed February 27, 2005).

   Contains references to Wonder's "Part Time Lover."

"100 Classic Album Covers: *Journey Through the Secret Life of Plants*." *Rolling Stone* no. 617, 14 November 1991, p. 137.

Although Wonder's late 1970s soundtrack album was less than universally acclaimed, *Rolling Stone* recognized it as one of the most memorable examples of album cover art.

Palmer, Robert. "Stevie Wonder." *New York Times*, 14 November 1980, p. 19.

A somewhat favorable review of Wonder's performance at Madison Square Garden in New York.

———. "Stevie Wonder Message of Love and Protest." *New York Times*, 7 October 1985, p. 13.

A feature article on Wonder's social activism.

———. "Stevie Wonder Takes a Long Look Back." *New York Times*, 6 June 1982, p. H25.

A report on *Stevie Wonder's Original Musiquarium I*.

Panion, Henry III. "Do You Hear What I Hear?" Keynote address, Great Lakes Chapter Meeting of the College Music Society, Western Kentucky University, Bowling Green, Kentucky, April 2, 2005.

Panion discussed his work as an orchestrator and conductor for Wonder.

Pareles, Jon. "*Characters*." *New York Times*, 22 November 1987, p. H27.

A favorable review of Wonder's *Characters* album.

———. "*In Square Circle*." *Rolling Stone*, 24 October 1985, pp. 63–64.

A favorable review of Wonder's album.

———. "Stevie Wonder." *New York Times*, 28 September 1986, Los Angeles edition, p. 74.

A favorable review of Wonder's concert at New York's Madison Square Garden.

———. "Stevie Wonder." *New York Times*, 26 January 1995, p. B1.

A favorable review of Wonder's performance at New York's Radio City Music Hall.

———. "Stevie Wonder Plays His Own Keys of Life." *New York Times*, 13 July 1984, p. 19.

An unfavorable review of Wonder's television program.

"Pop 100: 17—Stevie Wonder: 'Superstition.'" *Rolling Stone* no. 855, 7 December 2000, p. 73.

Wonder's "Superstition" is rated by *Rolling Stone* as one of the top singles ever released.

"Pop 100: 59—Stevie Wonder: 'You Are the Sunshine of My Life.'" *Rolling Stone* no. 855, 7 December 2000, p. 94.

Wonder's "You Are the Sunshine of My Life" is rated by *Rolling Stone* as one of the top singles ever released.

"Pop Albums: *Where I'm Coming From*." *Melody Maker* 46, 19 June 1971, p. 40.

A review of the Wonder album.

Powers, Ann. "A Hip-Hop Master Invokes Cultural Deities." *New York Times*, 22 January 2001, p. B1.

Stevie Wonder is acknowledged as one of the important influences on hip-hop music.

Pride, Dominic. "Bennett and Wonder among World Music Award Winners." *Billboard* 107, 13 May 1995, pp. 16–17.

A report that Princess Stephanie of Monaco presented Wonder with a special award for outstanding contribution to the pop music industry for his work to promote musical and racial harmony.

"Prince, Stevie Wonder Spice up Oscar Awards as Top Music Winners." *Jet* 68, 15 April 1985, pp. 14ff.

Wonder's Academy Award for "I Just Called to Say I Love You" is mentioned.

"Prince, Wonder Honored by Motion Picture Academy." *Billboard* 97, 6 April 1985, p. 6.

Wonder's Academy Award for "I Just Called to Say I Love You" is mentioned.

"The Prophetic Character of Black Secular Music: Stevie Wonder." *Black Sacred Music* 3, no. 2, 1989, pp. 75–84.

The prophetic, religious references in Wonder's music are explored.

Puterbaugh, Parke. "*Songs in the Key of Life.*" *Rolling Stone* no. 587, September 1990, p. S4.

A favorable review of one of *Rolling Stone*'s top 25 albums of the 1970s.

———. "Stevie Wonder (Coliseum, Greensboro, North Carolina)." *Rolling Stone*, 9 October 1986, p. 34.

Wonder's performance receives a grade of B.

"*Q* Review—Re-Releases: *At the Close of a Century.*" *Q* no. 164, May 2000, p. 123.

A favorable review of the 4-CD set.

"Ray Charles Tribute Rocks L.A." *Pro Sound News,* 1 July 2004, p. 5.

A report on the jam session honoring the late Ray Charles that Stevie Wonder led.

"Records: *Looking Back.*" *High Fidelity/Musical America* 28, March 1978, pp. 129–30.

A review of Wonder's *Looking Back* collection.

"Reissues: *Music of My Mind, Talking Book, Innervisions, Fulfillingness' First Finale.*" *Goldmine* 26, 16 June 2000, p. 128.

A report on the compact disc reissue of four of Wonder's most significant albums of the 1970s.

"Reissues: *Songs in the Key of Life, Hotter Than July.*" *Goldmine* 26, 28 July 2000, p. 95.

A report on the compact disc reissue of the two albums.

Ressner, Jeffrey. "Stevie Wonder Releases *Characters.*" *Rolling Stone,* 19 November 1987, p. 15.

A brief report on the release of the album *Characters.*

Review of *The Wonder of Stevie. Music Week,* 19 June 2004, p. 27.

Reynolds, J. R. "Stevie Wonder 35th Anniversary Salute: 'Inspiration to a Generation.'" *Billboard* 107, 13 May 1995, p. 34.

A collection of testimonials about Wonder's importance as a musical figure, particularly in the 1960s and 1970s.

Reynolds, J. R. "Uptight and More Than All Right: Back-Catalog Sales Move Three Decades of Wonder on Disc." *Billboard* 107, 13 May 1995, p. 36.

A report on compact disc reissues of Stevie Wonder material by Polygram, the then-owners of the Motown catalog.

"The Rhythm and the Blues: Wonder Speaks Out on South Africa." *Billboard* 97, 25 May 1985, p. 62.

A brief report on Wonder's anti-apartheid statements at the Academy Awards ceremony, as well as his subsequent statements on the subject.

"Rhythm & Blues Foundation Announces Details for Eleventh Annual R&B Foundation Pioneer Awards." Business Wire, 20 June 2000.

Includes information related to the Foundation's selection of Wonder to receive the Lifetime Achievement Award.

Ritz, David. "In a Gangsta-Rap World Stevie Wonder Still Believes in the Healing Power of Music." *Rolling Stone* no. 712–713, 13 July 1995, pp. 80ff.

A feature article in which Wonder discusses his belief in God and his belief that music can heal many of the wounds in individuals' personal lives and in society. He also discusses the social significance of rap music. The article revolves around Wonder's new album *Conversation Peace.*

———, and Leonard Pitts, Jr. Biographical and Program Notes for *At the Close of a Century.* 4 compact discs. Motown 012 153 992–2, 1999.

Includes valuable biographical information and information about the writing and recording of Wonder's hits.

Roberts, Roxanne. "For BET and Stevie, It's a Wonder-ful Life." *Washington Post,* 21 October 2002, p. C1.

A report on Black Entertainment Television's plans to produce a BET Walk of Fame celebration honoring Stevie Wonder, and starring, among others, Mariah Carey, India.Arie, Eric Clapton, and Louis Farrakhan.

Robins, W. "Further Fulfillingness." *Melody Maker* 49, 9 November 1974, p. 59.

A follow-up report on *Fulfillingness' First Finale,* which won the 1974 Grammy for album of the year.

"Rock Star Stevie Wonder Honoured for Work Against Apartheid." *UN Chronicle* 22, May 1985, pp. 60–61.

A report on Wonder's anti-apartheid work and the fact that he was honored for this work on May 13, 1985 (his 35th birthday) by the Special Committee Against Apartheid of the United Nations for his work.

Rockwell, John. *"Hotter Than July." New York Times,* 9 November 1980, p. A33.

A lukewarm review of Wonder's *Hotter Than July* album.

"The Rolling Stone 200: *Innervisions.*" *Rolling Stone* no. 760, 15 May 1997, p. 82.

Wonder's *Innervisions* is included among *Rolling Stone*'s top 200 albums of the rock era.

"The Rolling Stone 200: *Talking Book.*" *Rolling Stone* no. 760, 15 May 1997, p. 82.

Wonder's *Talking Book* is included among *Rolling Stone*'s top 200 albums of the rock era.

Rosenbluth, Jean. "Testimony May Cost Stevie Wonder His Academy Award." *Variety* 338, 14 March 1990, p. 48.

A report on the copyright infringement case concerning authorship of "I Just Called to Say I Love You" and how the outcome of the case could affect the Oscar Wonder received for the song.

Ruuth, Marianne. *Stevie Wonder.* Los Angeles: Holloway House, 1980.

A biography of Wonder.

Sandler, A. "Peers Sing Wonder's Praises." *Variety* 374, 1 March 1999, p. 100.

Sanford, William R., and Carl R. Green. *Stevie Wonder.* Mankato, Minn.: Crestwood House, 1986.

A biography of Wonder intended for children.

Santoro, Gene. "*Characters.*" *Down Beat* 55, March 1988, p. 29.

A favorable review of Wonder's *Characters* album.

Scheck, Frank. "Stevie Wonder." *The Christian Science Monitor* 87, 8 February 1995, p. 12.

A favorable review of Wonder's performance at Radio City Music Hall, New York City.

Schruers, Fred. "*In Square Circle.*" *Rolling Stone*, 19 December 1985, pp. 156–57.

Wonder's album *In Square Circle* receives a mediocre review from Schruers.

"The Secret Dreams of Stevie Wonder." *Ebony* 42, December 1986: 152ff.

This interview with Wonder deals with the psychological aspects of his blindness.

Segers, Frank. "Politics Put a Damper on 1982 ChicagoFest—PUSH Asks Blacks to Boycott, Wonder Backs Out." *Variety* 308, 4 August 1982, p. 57.

When Operation PUSH requested that black performers boycott the annual ChicagoFest to protest racial inequalities, Wonder pulled out of a scheduled performance.

Seifert, Catherine. "Wonder to Receive Songwriting Award." The America's Intelligence Wire, 16 April 2004.

A report that Wonder will receive the National Academy of Popular Music/ Songwriters Hall of Fame Johnny Mercer Award on June 10, 2004.

Serpick, Evan, and Rob Brunner. "Hear & Now: This Week on the Music Beat." *Entertainment Weekly* no. 684, 29 November 2002, p. 102.

Included in this report is a note that Wonder objected to passages in the book *Blind Faith* that detailed how his father forced his mother to prostitute herself to earn money for the family.

Sessions, Laura. "Stevie Wonder: Black Music's Champion." *Sepia* 30, June 1981, pp. 22ff.

Wonder's work, including his "Sir Duke," which honored Duke Ellington and other important swing-era musicians, is heralded in this article.

Shaw, Rufus. "The Next Black Leader: Who Will Be King?" *Sepia* 30, October 1981, pp. 17–18.

A discussion of the contributions of several prominent black leaders including Wonder, Muhammad Ali, Jesse Jackson, Richard Pryor, Andrew Young, and others.

"*Signed, Sealed, Delivered,* A Celebration of Music & Wonder to Open May 25 at The Showroom in the Venetian Resort-Hotel-Casino." Business Wire, 3 April 2002.

A report on the Vegas-style show, which was created and directed by Billy Porter.

Slater, Jack. "The Secret Life of Stevie Wonder." *Ebony* 35, April 1980, pp. 31ff.

A feature-length interview with and profile of Wonder.

Smith, Ethan. "*Natural Wonder.*" *Entertainment Weekly* no. 303, 1 December 1995, p. 74.

A brief, favorable review of the album *Natural Wonder.*

Smith, Giles. "Realms of Wonder." *The New Yorker* 71, 13 March 1995, pp. 78ff.

A biographical profile of Stevie Wonder to coincide with the release of *Conversation Peace.*

Songs in the Key of Life. VHS video recording. 75 minutes. Los Angeles: Rhino Home Video R3 2383, 1998.

 Also issued on DVD. This documentary includes Wonder's reminiscences about the making of the *Songs in the Key of Life* album. Berry Gordy, Jr., Quincy Jones, Herbie Hancock, and Gary Byrd also discuss the album. The musicians who performed on the album also appear in a reunion.

"*Songs in the Key of Life.*" *Crawdaddy* no. 67, December 1976, pp. 65–66.

 A review of *Songs in the Key of Life.*

"*Songs in the Key of Life.*" *Creem* 8, January 1977, p. 57.

 A review of *Songs in the Key of Life.*

"*Songs in the Key of Life.*" *Down Beat* 43, 16 December 1976, p. 24.

 A review of *Songs in the Key of Life.*

"*Songs in the Key of Life.*" *High Fidelity/Musical America* 27, February 1977, pp. 141–42.

 A review of *Songs in the Key of Life.*

"*Songs in the Key of Life.*" *Jazz Hot* no. 332, November 1976, pp. 18ff.

 A review of *Songs in the Key of Life.*

"*Songs in the Key of Life.*" *Rolling Stone* no. 228, 16 December 1976), pp. 74ff.

 A review of *Songs in the Key of Life.*

"S. Africa May End Stevie Wonder Ban." *Variety* 319, 17 July 1985, p. 46.

Stevens, Mark. "'Whiz Kid' Stevie Wonder's Latest." *Christian Science Monitor* 69, 3 January 1977, p. 22.

 A report on *Songs in the Key of Life.*

"Stevie Wonder." *Variety* 323, 9 July 1986, pp. 78–79.

 A favorable review of Wonder's concert at the Inglewood Forum in Los Angeles.

"Stevie Wonder." *Variety* 332, 31 August 1988, p. 78.

 A generally favorable review of Wonder's performance at Radio City Music Hall in New York City.

"*Stevie Wonder: The Definitive Collection.*" *Ebony* 58, January 2003, p. 32.

 A brief review of the 21-song collection, which is labeled a "must have."

"Stevie Wonder: *Jungle Fever* & Funk." *Musician* no. 154, August 1991, pp. 21–22.

 A review of Wonder's *Jungle Fever* soundtrack album.

"Stevie Wonder: Neverending Song of Peace." *Rolling Stone* no. 712–713, 13–27 July 1995, pp. 80–82ff.

 A review of Wonder's *Conversation Peace* album in the context of his social and political activism.

"Stevie Wonder and Kodak Batteries Join Forces in Concern for Cancer." PR Newswire, 3 March 1989.

 A report that Wonder is being honored with Eastman Kodak's Ultra Technologies' Humanitarian Award. Wonder's work in raising funds for the American Cancer Society is noted.

"Stevie Wonder Appears at Benefit Concert for Indians." *Jet* 70, 21 July 1986, p. 32.

 A brief report that Wonder performed at a benefit concert for Native Americans who had been evicted from land in Arizona.

"Stevie Wonder Arrested in Anti-Apartheid Protest." *Jet* 67, 4 March 1985, p. 54.

 A brief report on Wonder's arrest after protesting at the South African embassy.

"Stevie Wonder Auctions Rare Items on eBay to Benefit House Full of Toys." PR Newswire, 24 December 2003.

A report that Wonder is auctioning off harmonicas and some of his personal compact discs to benefit his House Full of Toys charity.

"*Stevie Wonder Comes Home.*" *Variety* 315, 20 June 1984, p. 52.

A lukewarm review of Wonder's television special.

"Stevie Wonder Denies Charges by Woman in $30 Mil. Palimony Suit." *Jet* 100, 22 October 2001, p. 64.

I have included this news item to show the extent to which both Wonder's professional and private lives have been documented by *Jet* magazine, a leading African American publication.

"Stevie Wonder Didn't Steal Song, Appeals Court Rules." *Jet* 82, 7 September 1992, p. 27.

A brief report on the finding of the U.S. Circuit Court of Appeals in San Francisco, California, dismissing charges against Wonder that he stole the song "I Just Called to Say I Love You" from songwriter Lloyd Chiate.

"Stevie Wonder Discusses Car Crash." *Rolling Stone* no. 144, 27 September 1973, p. 14.

"Stevie Wonder, Gil Scott-Heron (Madison Square Garden, New York)." *Variety* 301, 19 November 1980, p. 6.

A highly favorable review of Wonder and Gil Scott-Heron's concert appearance at Madison Square Garden.

"Stevie Wonder Honored at TransAfrica Forum Dinner." *Jet* 80, 8 July 1991, p. 33.

A report on Wonder receiving the Nelson Mandela Courage Award from the TransAfrica Forum.

"Stevie Wonder Not Offended By Murphy's Blind Jokes." *Jet* 67, 24 December 1984, p. 37.

A brief report on Wonder's reaction to jokes at the expense of his blindness made by comedian Eddie Murphy.

"Stevie Wonder Performance to Benefit Garment Workers." PR Newswire, 10 June 1999.

A report on Wonder's performance to raise money for Stitches Technology, a nonprofit agency that helps unemployed and underemployed workers in the apparel industry.

"Stevie Wonder Rejects White House Invitation for Keys to Motown." *Variety* 321, 25 December 1985, p. 1ff.

A report on Wonder declining an honor from the Reagan administration.

"Stevie Wonder Reveals Why He Idolizes King." *Jet* 60, 3 September 1981, p. 24.

Wonder discusses the reasons he supports a national holiday to honor Dr. Martin Luther King, Jr.

"Stevie Wonder Signs New Motown Record Contract." *Jet* 62, 26 April 1982, p. 61.

Includes details about Wonder's new contract with Motown.

"Stevie Wonder Tells Musical Tale of *Jungle Fever.*" *Billboard* 103, 8 June 1991, p. 30.

A report on Wonder's work on the soundtrack to the Spike Lee film *Jungle Fever.*

"Stevie Wonder Tells Why He Takes Risks in Fight to Destroy South Africa's Racism." *Jet* 68, 9 September 1985, pp. 14ff.

"Stevie Wonder 35th Anniversary Salute: Uptight and More Than All Right—Back-Catalog Sales Move Three Decades of Wonder on Disc." *Billboard* 107, 13 May 1995, p. 36.

A report on Motown's reissue of Wonder's material on compact disc.

"Stevie Wonder to Receive Special Award of Merit." *Jet* 61, 14 January 1982, p. 58.

A brief report on one of the many honors Wonder received in the 1980s.

"Stevie Wonder Turns Down $1 Mil. Offer for Japan Gig." *Jet* 76, 31 July 1989, p. 26.
    Describes Wonder's rejection of an offer for a potentially lucrative perfor-
    mance in Japan.
"Stevie Wonder Uses Fame in Campaign for King Holiday." *Jet* 59, 4 December
    1980, pp. 20ff.
    A feature article on Wonder's work toward the establishment of a national
    holiday to honor Dr. Martin Luther King, Jr.
"Stevie Wonder Visits Girl with Brain Tumor." *Jet* 76, 28 August 1989, p. 59.
    I have included this and several other brief reports from *Jet* to show the extent
    to which Stevie Wonder's professional and private lives have been documented
    by this leading African American publication.
"Stevie Wonder Welcomes S. African Ban on Music." *Jet* 68, 15 April 1985, p. 56.
    A report on Wonder's ongoing battle with the nation of South Africa over
    apartheid.
"Stevie Wonder, Wynonna, and Bill Maher Take the Stage at Larry King Cardiac
    Foundation Gala." PR Newswire, 22 September 2000.
    A report on performers who will be appearing at the "Evening with
    Larry King and Friends" on November 3, 2000, to raise funds for King's
    foundation, which provides funding for individuals who need, but cannot
    afford, cardiac care.
"Stevie Wonder's Award." *Variety* 254, 23 April 1969, p. 61.
    A report of President Nixon presenting Wonder with a Distinguished Service
    Award from the President's Committee on the Employment of Handicapped
    People.
"*Stevie Wonder's Original Musiquarium I.*" *Creem* 14, October 1982, p. 58.
    A review of Wonder's greatest hits collection.
"*Stevie Wonder's Original Musiquarium I.*" *Melody Maker* 57, 22 May 1982, p. 17.
    A favorable review of the compilation album.
"*Stevie Wonder's Original Musiquarium I.*" *People Weekly* 18, 5 July 1982, pp. 14ff.
    A favorable review of Wonder's greatest hits package.
"*Stevie Wonder's Original Musiquarium I.*" *Rolling Stone* no. 373, 8 July 1982, pp.
    45–46.
    A favorable review of Wonder's compilation album.
"*Stevie Wonder's Original Musiquarium I.*" *Rolling Stone,* 23 December 1982, p. 108.
    A highly favorable of Wonder's compilation album.
"*Stevie Wonder's Original Musiquarium I.*" *Variety* 307, 19 May 1982, p. 106.
    A favorable review of Wonder's compilation album.
"Stevie Wonder's Talents Highlight Black Music Month." *Jet* 60, 18 June 1981,
    pp. 60ff.
    A feature on various concerts planned to celebrate Black Music Month in the
    United States. It is interesting to note that Stevie Wonder's concert appearances
    are singled out as the month's highlight. This suggests the impact that he had in
    1981, both politically—through his successful campaign to establish a national
    holiday to honor Dr. Martin Luther King, Jr.—and musically, through his *Hotter
    Than July* album and concerts supporting the recording.
Strauss, Neil. "Stevie Wonder's Politics." *New York Times,* 25 January 1995, p. B5.
    This article concerns Wonder's integration of social and political concerns
    into his compositions.

Streiber, Art. "Oprah Talks to Stevie Wonder." *O: The Oprah Magazine* 5, May 2004, pp. 223ff.

A feature-length article on Wonder.

"Suit Says Wonder Stole Oscar-Winning Tune." *Jet* 77, 26 February 1990, p. 59.

A report on the lawsuit brought by Lloyd Chiate claiming authorship of the song "I Just Called to Say I Love You."

Sutherland, Sam. "*Hotter Than July*." *High Fidelity/Musical America* 31, January 1981, pp. 99–100.

A favorable review of Wonder's album.

———. "Motown Debuts History Special." *Billboard* 93, 31 October 1981, pp. 23ff.

Wonder's appearance in a television program on Motown records is noted.

Swenson, John. "The Boy Wonder Comes of Age." *Crawdaddy* no. 18, November 1972, pp. 26–30.

A major article about Wonder and the musical maturity he exhibited on *Talking Book*.

———. *Stevie Wonder*. New York: Perennial Library, 1986.

A biography of Wonder that includes a discography.

———. "*The Woman in Red*." *Saturday Review* 10, December 1984, p. 74.

A somewhat favorable review of Wonder's soundtrack recording for the film *The Woman in Red*.

Tabor, L. "Rock On." *International Musician* 84, November 1985, p. 6.

Wonder's recent activities are mentioned in the official magazine of the International Federation of Musicians.

"Talent in Action." *Billboard* 90, 22 April 1978, p. 65.

A brief report on Wonder's performances.

"*Talking Book*." *Rolling Stone* no. 125, 4 January 1973, pp. 61–62.

A highly favorable review of Wonder's *Talking Book* album.

"*Talking Book*." *Rolling Stone*, 27 August 1987, p. 129.

A highly favorable review of the CD reissue of Wonder's album *Talking Book*.

Taylor, Rick. *Stevie Wonder*. London and New York: Omnibus Press, 1985.

A biography of Wonder.

Tearson, Michael. "Sound Recording Review: *Hotter Than July*." *Audio* 65, April 1981, pp. 62–63.

A favorable review of Wonder's *Hotter Than July* album.

———. "*In Square Circle*." *Audio* 70, January 1986, pp. 138ff.

A generally favorable review of Wonder's *In Square Circle* album.

Terry, Wallace. "Love Is the Key." *Parade,* 28 June 1992, pp. 4–5.

Of primary importance in this article is Wonder's assertion that his blindness has caused him to concentrate on the theme of love more in his songs than other songwriters, because of love's healing power.

"That Girl." *Variety* 305, 6 January 1982, p. 63.

A favorable review of Wonder's single recording.

Theakston, Rob. "*Hotter Than July*." In *All Music Guide to Soul*, ed. Vladimir Bogdanov, John Bush, and Stephen Thomas Erlewine. Ann Arbor, Mich.: Backbeat Books, 2003, pp. 765–766.

Thomas, J. N. "Stevie Wonder." *Down Beat* 51, May 1984, p. 60.

A favorable review of Wonder's concert at the Circle Star Theater, San Francisco.

Tiven, Sally, and John Tiven. *Characters. Audio* 72, February 1988, p. 114.
    This is a brief review of Wonder's album *Characters.*
"Top Black Artists of the Year." *Billboard* 94, 25 December 1982, p. TIA12.
    Wonder is included in the list.
Torgoff, Martin. "Stevie Wonder." *Interview* 16, June 1986, pp. 43ff.
    A feature-length interview with Wonder.
"*A Tribute to Martin Luther King, Jr.: A Celebration of Life.*" *Variety* 313, 18 January
    1984, p. 70.
    A mixed review of the television program on which Wonder appeared.
Tucker, Ken. "Stevie Wonder's *Journey Through the Secret Life of Plants.*" *Rolling
    Stone* no. 309, 24 January 1980, pp. 62–63.
    A decidedly negative review of Wonder's soundtrack album.
———, et al. "The Joy of Sets." *Entertainment Weekly* no. 517, 17 December 1999,
    pp. 81ff.
    At the Close of a Century is one of the featured box sets praised in this review.
"*Tug of War.*" *People Weekly* 17, 7 June 1982, pp. 18–19.
    A mixed review of Paul McCartney's album *Tug of War,* on which Wonder
    appeared.
"25 Giants of Keyboard Music." *Keyboard* 26, January 2000, p. 32.
    Stevie Wonder is included among *Keyboard* magazine's most influential
    keyboard artists.
"22nd Annual Gala Celebrates Kennedy Center Honorees." *New York Times,*
    6 December 1999, p. A16.
    A report on Wonder and four other performers being honored by the Kennedy
    Center for the Performing Arts.
Underwood, Lee. "Stevie Wonder Grows Up." *Down Beat* no. 41, 12 September
    1974, pp. 14–15ff.
    An interview that focuses on Wonder's new creative control and his social
    concerns.
Vail, M. "Vintage Synths: The E-Mu Emulator: First Affordable Digital Sampler."
    Keyboard 19, 18 June 1994, pp. 108–111.
    Wonder's work with synthesizers is mentioned.
"The *Vibe* 100: *Innervisions.*" *Vibe* 7, December 1999–January 2000, p. 158.
    Wonder's 1973 album *Innervisions* is included in this close-of-the-millennium
    listing of the magazine's selection of the top 100 albums.
Warren, Kate. "Re-Born Stevie Wonder." *Songwriters Review* 32, Winter no. 1,
    1977, p. 7.
    A report on *Songs in the Key of Life.*
Warwick, Knight, "Wonder Song Proceeds Go to AIDS." *Jet* 69, 23 December
    1985, p. 59.
    A brief report on Wonder, Dionne Warwick, and Gladys Knight donating
    receipts from the recording of "That's What Friends Are For" to efforts for the
    prevention of AIDS.
Wells, Chris. "The Wonder Stuff." *The Guardian,* 24 February 1995, p. 2.
    Wonder discusses cover versions of his compositions and his love of the
    country of Ghana in this interview.
Wener, Ben. "Stevie Wonder Offers Songs in the Key of Healing." Knight Ridder/
    Tribune News Service, 28 September 2001.

Wener heaps praise on Wonder for his appearance on the *America: A Tribute to Heroes* telethon, especially for his emotional performance of the song "Love's in Need of Love Today."

Werner, Craig. "Stevie Wonder: Singing in the Key of Life." *Goldmine* 25, 8 October 1999), pp. 14–20ff.
A feature-length retrospective on Wonder's career and life.

Werner, Craig Hansen. *Higher Ground: Stevie Wonder, Aretha Franklin, Curtis Mayfield, and the Rise and Fall of American Soul.* New York: Crown Publishers, 2004.
A thorough analysis of Wonder's place in the history of the soul genre.

Whitburn, Joel. *Top Pop Singles, 1955–1996.* Menomonee Falls, Wisc.: Record Research, Inc., 1997.
Includes information on Wonder's pop singles.

White, A. "Berry Gordy: Gordy Speaks—The *Billboard* Interview." *Billboard* 106, 5 November 1994, pp. 63–64ff.

White, Ronald D. "Stevie Wonder Changes Tactics in Campaign for King's Birthday." *Washington Post,* 7 January 1983, p. B2.
A brief report on Wonder's ongoing campaign to establish a national holiday to honor Dr. Martin Luther King, Jr.

White, T. "*In Square Circle.*" *Musician* no. 86, December 1985, p. 98.
A review of Wonder's *In Square Circle* album.

Wild, David. "*Characters.*" *Rolling Stone* no. 518, 28 January 1988, p. 47.
A generally favorable review of Wonder's album.

Williams, Tenley. *Stevie Wonder.* Philadelphia: Chelsea House, 2002.
A biography of Wonder intended for junior and senior high school students.

Willis, Ellen. "Rock, etc.: The Importance of Stevie Wonder." *New Yorker* 50, 30 December 1974, pp. 56–57.
An analysis of the career and significance of Wonder in light of his huge commercial and critical successes of 1972–1974.

Wilson, Beth P., and James Calvin. *Stevie Wonder.* New York: Putnam, 1979.
A biography of Stevie Wonder for young readers.

Woldu, Gail Hilson. "Contextualizing Rap." In *American Popular Music: New Approaches to the Twentieth Century,* ed. Rachel Rubin and Jeffry Melnick. Amherst: University of Massachusetts Press, 2001, pp. 173–91.
Deals with the place of rap in the continuum of African American cultural expression.

"*The Woman in Red.*" *Melody Maker* 59, 22 September 1984, p. 28.
A review of Wonder's soundtrack.

"*The Woman in Red.*" *Musician* no. 75, January 1985, p. 81.
A review of Wonder's soundtrack album.

"*The Woman in Red.*" *People Weekly* 23, 25 February 25, 1985, p. 23.
According to this unfavorable review of the soundtrack of *The Woman in Red,* "Wonder will not be remembered in history for the saccharine 'I Just Called to Say I Love You' or for 'Don't Drive Drunk,' which resembles a jingle more than a song."

"*The Woman in Red.*" *Saturday Review* 10, November–December 1984, p. 74.
A review of Wonder's soundtrack.

"Wonder Arrested." *Jet* 67, 4 March 1985, p. 41.
A report on Wonder's arrest for demonstrating against apartheid in front of the South African embassy.

"Wonder Asks $1.5-mil in Truck Crash Suit." *Variety* 284, 18 August 1976, p. 66.
  A report on Wonder's civil suit against the driver who caused his near-fatal 1973 automobile accident.
"Wonder Called Plagiarist." *Billboard* 97, 26 October 1985, p. 6.
  A brief report on charges that Wonder stole the song "I Just Called to Say I Love You" from songwriter Lloyd Chiate.
"Wonder Cleared in Recent Song Plagiarism Lawsuit." *Jet* 77, 12 March 1990, p. 61.
  A brief report on dismissal of charges against Stevie Wonder that he stole the song "I Just Called to Say I Love You" from songwriter Lloyd Chiate.
"Wonder Copyright Suit to Continue." *Variety* 329, 18 November 1987, p. 91.
  A report on the continuing lawsuit against Wonder over charges that he stole the song "I Just Called to Say I Love You" from songwriter Lloyd Chiate.
"Wonder Gives Recording Gear to Ellington School." *Jet* 84, 25 October 1993, p. 24.
  A brief report on Wonder's donation of sound recording equipment to the Duke Ellington School of the Arts in Washington, D.C.
"Wonder Has Fan Mail Transcribed to Braille." *Jet* 58, 20 March 1980, p. 62.
  A report that Wonder has his fan letters transcribed into Braille so that he can read them.
"Wonder Honored at U.N." *Jet* 68, 27 May 1985, p. 13.
  This article deals with Wonder being honored for his work against apartheid by the United Nations Special Committee Against Apartheid.
"Wonder Look-a-like Causes Double Take." *Jet* 60, 6 August 1981, p. 22.
  A brief report on Stevie Wonder impersonator Alturo Shelton.
"Wonder, McCartney Soon Making Album Together." *Jet* 61, 24 September 1981, p. 60.
  A brief report on Paul McCartney's album *Tug of War,* which eventually included two contributions by Wonder.
"Wonder Offers Song of Caution to Drunken Drivers." *Jet* 68, 17 June 1985, p. 30.
  A brief report on Wonder's song "Don't Drive Drunk" which he has offered for public service use.
"Wonder Plagiarism Suit Bounced after One Plaintiff Splits, But…" *Variety* 324, 27 August 1986, p. 95.
  A report on the ongoing lawsuit over the authorship of "I Just Called to Say I Love You."
"Wonder Re-Signs with Motown for Multi-Million $$." *Variety* 306, 14 April 1982, pp. 79ff.
  A report on Wonder's latest contract extension with Motown Records.
"Wonder Tells Why He Has Stuck with Motown." *Jet* 70, 1 September 1986, p. 60.
"Wonder Wins." *Hollywood Reporter,* 22 March 2002, p. 3.
  This is a brief report on the 6th U.S. Circuit Court of Appeals ruling that Stevie Wonder did not violate a copyright with his recordings of the song "For Your Love." Songwriter Derrick Coles had claimed that he owned the copyright for the song.
"Wonder's Oscar Speech Riles S. African Radio." *Variety* 318, 3 April 1985, p. 70.
  A brief report on South African Broadcasting's decision to ban Wonder's work after he spoke out against apartheid at the Academy Awards ceremony.
Wonder's Records Back on S. African Radio." *Variety* 320, 2 October 1985, p. 143.

After receiving international pressure, South African radio lifted the ban it placed on Stevie Wonder's work after he spoke out in spring 1985 against apartheid.

"Wonderful World." *Stereoplay* no. 7, July 1995, pp. 128–30.
A review of Wonder's *Conversation Peace* album.

Wynn, Ron. "*In Square Circle.*" In *All Music Guide to Soul,* ed. Vladimir Bogdanov, John Bush, and Stephen Thomas Erlewine. Ann Arbor, Mich.: Backbeat Books, 2003, p. 766.

"The Year in Records 1985: *In Square Circle.*" *Rolling Stone* no. 463–464, 19 December 1985–2 January 1986, pp. 156ff.
The Wonder album is included in the magazine's wrap-up of the albums of 1985.

Zak, Albin J., III. "'Edition-ing' Rock." *American Music* 23, Spring 2005, pp. 95–107.
This article includes discussion on the importance of arrangements and orchestration in popular recordings.

Zappa, Frank, with Peter Occhiogrosso. *The Real Frank Zappa Book.* New York: Poseidon Press, 1989.
Zappa discusses the importance of arrangement and orchestration in compositions of the rock era. The importance of Stevie Wonder has placed on arrangement and orchestration reflects Zappa's statements about the extent to which these features define a composition.

Zimmerman, K. "Films Supply Sounds of Summer." *Variety* 343, 13 May 1991, pp. 126ff.
The author includes discussion of Wonder's music for the Spike Lee film *Jungle Fever.*

Index

About the Author

JAMES E. PERONE is Associate Professor of Music at Mount Union College, Ohio. He is the author of nearly a dozen books, including *Woodstock: An Encyclopedia of the Music and Art Fair* (2005), *Music of the Counterculture Era* (2004), and *Songs of the Vietnam Conflict* (2001). He currently serves as the series editor for the Praeger Singer-Songwriter Collection series.